Watching Television Come of Age

Focus on American History Series

Center for American History, University of Texas at Austin

Edited by Don Carleton

The New York Times Reviews

by **Jack Gould**

Watching Television Come of Age

LEWIS L. GOULD, EDITOR

University of Texas Press, Austin

Printed in the United States of America
First edition, 2002

♾ The paper used in this book meets the minimum requirements of ANSI/NISO Z39.48-1992 (R1997) (Permanence of Paper).

Library of Congress Cataloging-in-Publication Data

Gould, Jack, 1914–1993.
Watching television come of age : the New York times reviews / by Jack Gould ; Lewis L. Gould, editor.—1st ed.
p. cm. — (Focus on American history series)
Includes index.
ISBN 0-292-72844-1 (cloth : alk. paper) —
ISBN 0-292-72846-8 (pbk. : alk. paper)
1. Television broadcasting—United States—History.
2. Television programs—United States—Reviews.
I. Gould, Lewis L. II. Title. III. Series.
PN1992.3.U5 G68 2002
791.45′0973′09045—dc21 2002001064

To the memory of Richard F. Shepard

Contents

Preface and Acknowledgments xiii
Introduction: Portrait of a Television Critic 1

Chapter One: The Golden Age of Television Drama 33

34 Television Debut: Theatre Guild Makes Video Bow on NBC with Production of "John Ferguson," November 16, 1947
36 Matter of Form: Television Must Develop Own Techniques If It Is To Have Artistic Vitality, October 31, 1948
39 "Julius Caesar": Worthington Miner's Version in Modern Dress Proves Spectacular Television, March 13, 1949
41 A Plea for Live Video: Switch to Film for TV Was a Major Mistake, December 7, 1952
43 NBC Playhouse Offers Valid and Moving Hour with Production of Paddy Chayefsky's "Marty," May 27, 1953
45 "Patterns" Is Hailed as Notable Triumph, January 17, 1955
46 TV's Psychodrama: How to Keep 'Em Down on the Couch after They've Written for TV, August 7, 1955
48 Cheese, Mustard Ad Also Stars on Kraft Theatre, December 1, 1955
49 "Requiem for a Heavyweight": Rod Serling's Drama Scores a Knockout, October 12, 1956
50 Study of Alcoholism: Piper Laurie and Cliff Robertson Are Impressive in "Days of Wine and Roses," October 3, 1958

Chapter Two: The Shadow of a Blacklist 53

54 Case of Jean Muir: Principles of Fair Play Yield to Pressure, September 3, 1950
57 Again, "Red Channels": The Civil Liberties Union Revives an Issue, April 13, 1952

59 The Case of Lucille Ball: Treatment of the Star Should Be Standard in Industry, September 20, 1953

62 Fifth Amendment: Danger Seen in Union Plan to Punish Members Claiming the Privilege, July 31, 1955

65 Report on Blacklisting: Fund for the Republic Study Dealing with Radio-TV Is Found Deserving of Commendation and Censure, July 1, 1956

68 What a Blacklist Means: A Review of John Henry Faulk's "Fear on Trial," November 22, 1964

70 Blacklisting's Effect: Censored Tape of Jean Muir's Remarks on '50s Travails Shown on ABC, January 15, 1965

71 Jack Gould to John Pope, October 13, 1971

73 Jack Gould to John Pope, October 31, 1971

Chapter Three: The Rise and Fall of Edward R. Murrow 75

77 Edward R. Murrow's News Review "See It Now" Demonstrates Journalistic Power of Video, November 19, 1951

78 Murrow's "This Is Korea" Film over CBS Captures Poignancy and Frustration of Life in Battle, December 29, 1952

80 Celebrity Time: Murrow Puts Cameras into Their Homes in "Person to Person," October 7, 1953

82 Video Journalism: Treatment of Radulovich Case History by "See It Now" Is Fine Reporting, October 25, 1953

84 Murrow vs. McCarthy: "See It Now" on CBS Examines Senator and His Methods, March 11, 1954

86 "See It Now" Finale: Program Unexpectedly Ends Run of Seven Distinguished Years on CBS, July 8, 1958

88 "Harvest of Shame": Exploitation of U.S. Migratory Workers Is Documented on "CBS Reports," November 25, 1960

89 Murrow Departs: Commentator Leaving Broadcast Post for Challenging Federal Job, February 5, 1961

Chapter Four: The Influence of a Critic 95

96 Kaufman Incident: "This Is Show Business" Dismisses Panelist for Pre-Christmas Quip, January 4, 1953
98 On Faith Healing: Preacher's Timely TV Miracles Raise Questions of Stations' Standards, February 18, 1956
101 Disgrace of the Networks: Chains Ignore Session at United Nations, October 31, 1956
103 More on U.N.: Networks Make Limited Progress in Their Coverage of World's Realities, November 2, 1956
104 TV Can Be Good, Too: "The Play of the Week" Is a Case in Point, November 22, 1959
107 Madison Avenue Case Study: "The Play of the Week" Faces Doom Jan. 30, December 29, 1959
109 "The Play of the Week": Demise of Drama Series Has Economic Moral, June 11, 1961
112 Lively Panel Show: Betty Furness Is Spry Hostess on WNTA, August 2, 1961
113 Jack Gould to Louis Loeb, October 19, 1961

Chapter Five: A Critic's Likes and Dislikes 115

116 Comment on "Today": NBC's Early Morning Show Needs Some Work, January 20, 1952
119 The Nixon Telecast: Personal Story Brings High Drama to TV, September 28, 1952
121 Sweeping and Imaginative in Conception, "Omnibus" of Ford Foundation Makes Video Debut, November 10, 1952
122 Why Millions Love Lucy, March 1, 1953
125 Delightful "Peter Pan": Marriage of Media Is Noted in Inspired Video Offering, March 13, 1955
127 Johnny Carson: CBS Offers Answer to That Man Gobel, July 8, 1955
128 New Phenomenon: Elvis Presley Rises to Fame as Vocalist Who Is Virtuoso of Hootchy-Kootchy, June 6, 1956

129 Witty Commentator: Brinkley Enlivens NBC Convention Coverage, August 17, 1956
131 Elvis Presley: Lack of Responsibility Is Shown by TV in Exploiting Teenagers, September 16, 1956
133 Tribute to "Omnibus": Expected Loss of Program Brings Call for Similar Experimental Shows, July 30, 1958
135 Forthright Radio News Program: Smith's Analysis of Alabama Violence Shows Real Role of Commentator, May 28, 1961

Chapter Six: The Quiz Show Scandals 139

140 Man in the Street: The Public Often Can Outshine TV Stars, August 14, 1955
142 Quizzes Mostly Talk: "$64,000 Question" and "Big Surprise" Use Less than Half Their Times on Queries, September 26, 1956
143 Under Suspicion: Investigation of Quiz Shows Shakes Viewer's Faith in TV's Integrity, September 7, 1958
147 A Plague on TV's House: Rigged Quiz Shows Viewed as Symptom of the Age, with Many Guilty Parties, October 12, 1959
149 Journalists' Junkets: Quiz Show Headlines Raise Question of How Clear Is Conscience of Press, October 27, 1959
151 The Quiz Scandal: Legal and Moral Issues of Van Doren Affair Said to Need Resolution, November 4, 1959
153 Formula for TV: Quiz Scandal Shows a Need for New Rules, November 8, 1959
155 Assessing Effects of Life under the Table: Influence of "Payola" on Culture Weighed, November 20, 1959

Chapter Seven: Children and Television 161

162 Kukla and Ollie: Burr Tillstrom's Puppets Have a Spirit and Personality Unique in Video, March 27, 1948

164 Hail Howdy Doody! He Triumphs over Mr. X, Survives Mr. Y and Always Delights the Youngsters, November 14, 1948
166 Video and Children: Parents and Broadcasters Have Separate Roles, January 8, 1950
169 A Boy's Question: School Youngster Raises an Issue for Video, April 29, 1951
172 Pinky Lee Show Turns Children's Hour into a Conspiracy against Parents, November 8, 1954
174 Peril in Small Pills: Pushing of Vitamins by "Ding Dong School" Indicates Deficiency in Commercials, December 23, 1955
175 Juvenile Audiences Suffering from Chains' Delinquency in Planning, December 2, 1956
178 Parent-Teacher Organization Issues Its First Appraisal of Programs, September 13, 1959

Chapter Eight: Tracking the Impact of Television 181

181 The Paradoxical State of Television, March 30, 1947
186 Family Life, 1948 A.T. (After Television), August 1, 1948
190 TV Daddy and Video Mama: A Dirge, May 14, 1950
194 What TV Is—and What It Might Be, June 10, 1951
201 TV at the Crossroads: A Critic's Survey, March 9, 1952
209 Europe's TV Picture—and Ours, August 23, 1953

Chapter Nine: Television and Its Critic 217

218 TV Tube Bites TV Critic, January 3, 1954
221 Television Today: A Critic's Appraisal, April 8, 1956
227 Tuning in on Dixie: Mocking Birds Sing, but Who Listens? Everyone's Inside Looking at TV! April 15, 1956
230 Where TV Critics Strike Out: Some Sweeping Charges about Their Manifold Deficiencies, May 19, 1957

233 A Critical Reply: An Answer to Objections Raised in the TV Industry to the Role of Critics, May 26, 1957

237 Critic Dissects the Anatomy of a Flop, Ruminates about His Role in "Open End," January 27, 1959

Index 239

Preface and Acknowledgments

When my father, John Ludlow "Jack" Gould, died in May 1993, many of his friends and former colleagues urged me to write a book about his life and career. The question was what form such a volume should take. Never a systematic record-keeper, Dad retained only fragmentary papers about his years at *The New York Times.* He kept documents about the response to his attacks on the networks for their non-coverage of the United Nations during the Suez controversy in 1956. He also saved some letters relating to his efforts to save *The Play of the Week* in 1959 and 1960. Otherwise, information was sporadic, with some years relatively complete and others with almost nothing. To protect sources and because he did not consider his work to have much historical interest, he routinely discarded letters and memoranda.

As a result, a formal biography seemed impractical. While I found further materials relating to his work in the papers of Turner Catledge at Mississippi State University and in the archives of *The New York Times,* even these discoveries did not flesh out the story in sufficient detail to justify a biographical treatment. I thought the Federal Bureau of Investigation might have a file on him, and it did. However, the file only documented cross-references to him from the files of other individuals. I concluded that while my father had an interesting and complex private life, it would be better to concentrate on what made him important, his television criticism.

My task was facilitated when *The New York Times* generously made available to me all of his byline clippings from its "morgue" when the paper discontinued that institution by 1997. But the riches I reaped from the *Times'* generosity also presented me with the dilemma of selecting seventy or so columns from the thousands that he produced during his thirty-five years there.

In choosing which columns to include in this book, I tried to pick out topics and issues that had become historically important or in which Jack Gould as television critic showed special interest. The "Golden Age" of television drama seemed a natural first choice, and "blacklisting" in television and the career of Edward R. Murrow were also topics with which Dad was identified. I then pulled together some of the columns on various controversies and causes in which he was involved and organized a chapter about the programs, entertainers, and personalities that he covered and reviewed. The final three that round out his major interests are the quiz show scandals, children's programming, and the general state of television during the 1950s. I also present a few articles that represent my father's approach to his work.

I concentrated on the years 1947–1961 as the period of his greatest influence. After 1963 the changing role of critics at his newspaper and his mounting disillusionment with television made his writing more labored and less inspired than it had been during the previous decade. His own recollections focused on the 1950s, and certainly in our conversations over the years it was clear that he took most pride in what he had achieved in that decade. My hope is that this book will rekindle interest in Jack Gould as a critic and lead to analytic treatment of his role in the early years of television. I believe his prescience and clear insights shined into particularly the commercial forces that were shaping television early on and continue to determine who gains access to the public mind, as he phrased it, and for what purposes.

My father's columns and papers are now held at the Center for American History at the University of Texas at Austin. In the present volume, his articles appear as originally published, with no substantive changes. Since his editors sometimes were inconsistent in spelling a word such as "programming," I have reconciled these discrepancies. In a very few places where one word was clearly meant and the *Times* printed another, that change has been made for clarity.

I owe thanks to many individuals and institutions for assistance with this project. My first and greatest debt is to Susan Dryfoos of *The New York Times* History Project, who made it possible for me to receive copies of the archival material on my father and his byline stories. She saved me much valuable time in assembling this volume. I also benefited from the encouragement and kind assistance of the late Richard F. Shepard, a former colleague of my father, who smoothed the way for me, read early portions of the book, and was always patient and encouraging in responding to my questions. I am sorry that Dick could not live to see this book become a reality, and I hope his wife, Trudy, will enjoy the final product. Herbert Mitgang also provided support and helpful advice with his reading of the biographical introduction. Mitchel Levitas of *The New York Times* gave valuable advice and timely help.

Among friends and former associates of my father, I received wise counsel, reminiscences, and research materials from the late Franklin

Heller, the late Robert Saudek, Lisa Hamel, the late Fred Friendly, Sol Jacobson, Henry Senber, Holly Shulman, the late Allan Sloane, Dr. Frank Stanton, Mary Sullivan, and Leonard Miall. Mattie Sink at Mississippi State University was indispensable in facilitating my long-distance work with the Turner Catledge Papers. Archivists at the Loomis-Chaffee School and the Kent School kindly furnished me documents about my father's years as a student.

I am grateful to *The New York Times* for permission to reprint these columns, to Mississippi State University for allowing me to print one of my father's memos, and to John Pope for the use of the two letters from my father in his possession.

For help with acquiring photocopies and specific documents relating to my father's career, I owe thanks to Angela Burnett, Thomas Clarkin, R. Scott Harris, Byron Hulsey, Clarence G. Lasby, Nancy Beck Young, and especially Mark E. Young. My brothers, Richard Gould and Robert Gould, found family papers after my parents died that add to the book, and they shared as well their memories of life in the 1950s. Alison Brooks and Renee Zuckerbrot supported the effort at key points in bringing the project to publication. James L. Baughman and Don Carleton provided thoughtful criticism on the final draft of the manuscript. During the eight years that it took to bring this project to completion, Karen Gould encouraged me and patiently listened to me relive my early years.

Lewis L. Gould
Austin, Texas

Watching Television Come of Age

Introduction

Portrait of a Television Critic

When my father informed the management of *The New York Times* of his need to retire from the newspaper in February 1972 because of poor health, his editor, A. M. Rosenthal, summed up Jack Gould's thirty-five years of service as a reporter and television critic: "There are not many men of whom it can be said that they created a place in the newspaper business that will always be identified with their name, but by God, you are one of them."[1] Since the advent of television during the late 1940s, my father had covered and commented on the medium that changed the nature of American society. He came to the post of television critic from a background as a working reporter and from an improbable family heritage in the American aristocracy.

In his private conversation, Dad always regarded himself as a journalist who became a television critic by force of circumstances. He was never happier than when he was on the telephones at home chasing an exclusive or canvassing his many sources inside television from the *Times* office where his disorderly desk, laden with cigarette stubs, testified to his obsession with his story. Yet he also felt a larger responsibility as a critic because of the platform that the *Times* afforded him, and he harbored aspirations for television to be a medium of communication and education.

My father was an awkwardly dressed man with a perpetual cigarette, a distracted manner, and a shy demeanor. In his prime as a critic during the 1950s, he was, said one of his coworkers, "a guy who always sneaked off on vacation because he hated maudlin displays such as people saying: 'Have a nice vacation, Jack.' "[2] His unassuming character deflected queries about his ancestry in the New York City upper crust and his knowledge of the foibles of the well-to-do. On his father's side, he traced his lineage back to the Revolutionary War. He would have been eligible for membership in the Society of the Cincinnati, except that he thought patriotic organizations pretentious and absurd. Judge James Gould of the Litchfield (Connecticut) Law School and a founder of American legal education was another notable ancestor. My father's mother was the youngest of the eleven children of banker Harvey Fisk; his firm, Fisk and Hatch, had helped Jay Cooke finance the Union military effort in the Civil War. Dad's favorite relation was his aunt Susan Ludlow Warren. For many years, "Aunt Susie" was the reputed mistress of J. P. Morgan Sr.[3]

My father, John Ludlow Gould, was born on February 5, 1914, in New York City. His middle name reflected his connections with the Ludlow family of New York. His parents, John Warren Dubois Gould and Evelyn Louisa Fisk, were married in 1910 and had a daughter, Evelyn, (known in the family as "Fitter") in 1911. My grandfather graduated from New York University and was a civil engineer. He served in the Interior Department during the presidency of Theodore Roosevelt and had worked on irrigation projects in the West. By the time my father was born, John Warren Gould had become a specialist in reorganizing bankrupt companies. My grandmother, Evelyn Fisk Gould, attended Bryn Mawr for several years but did not finish college. She had taken courses in colonial American history with the young Charles McLean Andrews, who became famous for his historical work on the American Revolution. In the early 1960s, when I was reading Andrews for my orals at Yale University, she would fondly recall "the handsome Professor Andrews" of her youth.[4]

My father grew up in comfortable circumstances, though some of the family money had been lost in the crooked investment schemes of my great-uncle Pliny Fisk, an unscrupulous Wall Street financier who persuaded his sisters to back one of his many losing ventures. During World War I, John W. D. Gould served with Herbert Hoover in the U.S. Food Administration, an experience that reinforced the staunchly Republican tradition of the Gould family.[5]

As a boy, my father attended the prestigious Allen-Stevenson School in New York City, where the sons of the elite readied themselves for prep school. He also took part in the drilling rituals of the Knickerbocker Greys, a Manhattan equivalent of the Boy Scouts for upper-crust lads. When my father reached the age of ten, his parents began looking for the right prep school in New England. They visited the Kent School on September 19, 1924, and it was agreed that "young John" would go there. The next day my grandfather died suddenly of a heart seizure at the age of forty-three.[6]

In later life, my grandfather's death and his contribution to his son's upbringing rarely were discussed. A certain degree of scientific aptitude may have passed from father to son, since Dad already was fascinated with radio. He owned a shortwave set and sometimes listened to broadcasts from London.[7]

His father's death left Dad with his mother and sister in what had suddenly become tight circumstances. There was not much money, and neither of the two women was adept at practical matters. Dad seems to have been a lonely, self-sufficient boy who spent time with himself and his radio. He entered Kent School in the fall of 1927. Because of his family's situation, he was a partial scholarship student. The school labeled him "an average American youth. If he did not contribute anything to the school, we would not expect him to cause any trouble." He remained at Kent only until the late winter of 1928, when my grandmother withdrew him during an influenza epidemic. Since my aunt had chronic health problems, my grandmother did not want to risk further illness to her only son.[8]

In 1928 my father enrolled at the Loomis Institute in Connecticut, where he spent the next three years. He never adapted to the structured, elitist atmosphere of the place, and his grades were mediocre. With a friend he edited the *Loomis Post*, an early example of an underground newspaper. Two issues have survived that feature news stories from the school and even a gossip column called "High Spots." Dad pulled the column in the second issue because he did not "wish to make some people laugh by slamming or offending others." A few months later he received faculty discipline for being at an off-campus restaurant at midnight.[9]

At various points in his Loomis stay, Dad ran away and was found in seedy hotels in New York City. Not long before he died he told my brother Richard that a faculty member at one of the schools he attended had molested him sexually. In the wake of the episode, he fled the school. This third-hand story is impossible to verify, but there was always a cloud over his memories of Loomis. He often said ruefully to me that he had been "thrown out of the best prep schools on the East Coast." Although tolerant of gays in his professional life, he reacted with intense anger when a homosexual in Connecticut approached me during my teen years.[10]

His Loomis career came to a definitive end in the spring of 1932. He returned to New York without graduating. He received a high school diploma from the Brown School of Tutoring in the summer of 1932. He was then admitted to New York University but either decided not to attend or did not have the $250 tuition in the depths of the Great Depression. He said much later, "There was a backlash—maybe I was part of it—against higher education."[11]

My father's lack of a college education was a sore spot with him for the rest of his life. In his early years as a critic he sometimes felt the absence of a collegiate preparation in the liberal arts and occasionally called on more educated friends, such as television producer and literary agent Franklin Heller, for assistance in reviewing plays and nightclubs. Yet he distrusted academics as pompous and impractical, and he found it ironic that I became a professional historian. Those in television who labeled him as an intellectual when he was alive and scholars who now call him a "highbrow columnist" are far off the mark.[12]

Sometime in late 1932, Dad wangled a job as a copy boy at the New York *Herald Tribune* for a salary of $12 a week, which was soon reduced as an economy measure to $10.80. Still, in the depths of the Depression, to have any job at all was a privilege. His boss was city editor Stanley Walker, a wiry, cynical Texan who was already a famous figure in the Manhattan newspaper world. Walker had been in the job four years, and under his tutelage the *Trib* was known as "the best journalism school of all." After a few months, Walker spotted my father's talent and allowed him to try his hand at brief stories from the day rewrite basket. Longer assignments followed, and by the spring of 1933 Dad was promoted to the staff, "something unheard of at the Times or Daily News," he recalled in 1980. Walker used his young reporter and another staffer, Sanderson "Sandy" Vanderbilt, to bamboozle unwary and boring visitors about his "aristocratic" employees. "Mr. Gould," Walker would intone, "will you please go over and ask Mr. Vanderbilt to come here."[13]

Thin, redheaded, and tireless, my father reveled in the daily work of the newspaper game. Later in life he remembered combing the city for the family with the largest number of children after the *Times* had a feature on the same subject. "I spent about three days in Harlem visiting police houses, fire houses, and welfare groups. I found two bigger families. Alas, the fathers were almost as numerous as the children." On the job, Dad learned how to write under the watchful eye of Lessing L. "Engel" Engelking, the night city editor. Once Engel had him "rewrite the lead on a story fifteen times until he had what he wanted." When the two men met later that evening at Bleeck's, the watering hole for newspapermen, Engel "with a beaming smile came over to me and said: 'I owe you a drink.' It was a happy newspaper and Stanley in major measure made it so."[14]

Dad developed a specialty in the city's theater district at a time when the Federal Theater Project of the New Deal was a hot story. He cultivated sources inside the office of Hallie Flanagan, the project director, and achieved a series of exclusives that frustrated the theater staff of *The New York Times*. "Someone at the Times," he reminisced, "called Hallie Flanagan . . . to protest and threaten to keep the project out of the Times Sunday drama section." The informant, he said, "promptly gave me another story to use the following Sunday. The Times saw red."[15]

By late 1937 the *Times* and its theater reporter Sam Zolotow had had enough. He learned from my father that the Tribune would not give him a raise despite his frequent exclusives on Federal Theater Project stories. Zolotow told my father he had asked Brooks Atkinson, the *Times* theater critic, "to get you off my back by hiring you. He did."[16]

My father went to work at *The New York Times* on October 4, 1937, at a salary of $50 per week, with the title of reporter city staff—drama. He noticed the difference between working for the *Times* and the *Tribune* almost at once. "As a Herald Trib reporter I often had to wait and wait for some crumbs. As a Times reporter I was ushered in almost immediately." His first byline story appeared on October 14, 1937, in the "News and Gossip of the Night Clubs" column. He commented that the Benny Goodman and Tommy Dorsey bands were proving "that swing can be effectively dished up without making an incision in the ear drums of the paying jitterbugs."[17]

Joining the *Times* enabled Dad to make another professional change. His byline at the *Tribune* had been John L. Gould, a formal title that he disliked. At the *Times* he was able to start fresh as "Jack" Gould, even though the newspaper preferred the use of correct first names.

He was the third-string theater critic behind Atkinson and Lewis Nichols. The assignment fell to him of covering a new show that the International Ladies Garment Workers Union presented, *Pins and Needles*. His rave review was one of his first appearances as a critic of the live drama that he championed in his television days. Nightclub acts occupied most of his time, and he learned early about the underside of show business. He recalled evenings "spent with Capone thugs in Dinty

Moore's while the FBI sits hours in my home trying to learn where they are." He also listened to the nightclubbing sons of President Franklin D. Roosevelt and heard them "drop hints of White House doings, a boon to our national desk."[18]

In his travels around the entertainment world, my father often stopped at the Theater Bar run by Louie Bergen on 45th Street. At this hangout for the younger crowd, he met my mother, Carmen Lewis, then a production assistant for theatrical producers Howard Lindsay and Russell Crouse and in time Dwight Deere Wiman. Just when and how they met was always a little hazy, but on one late-night occasion during my teens, my mother argued with him about some disputed point. He leaned forward and said to me: "Lew, let this be a lesson to you. Don't marry a woman you pick up in a bar!"

Born on July 1, 1911, in Bay City, Texas, my mother had graduated from Rice University in 1932. She had flown airplanes and remembered riding in the rumble seat of a Ford with Roy Hofheinz, future developer of the Houston Astrodome. She left Houston in 1935 to try her luck on Broadway. She obtained her Actor's Equity card, but her real passion and talent was for a backstage role. By 1938 she and my father were living together.[19]

My mother's family had deep and controversial ties to Texas politics. Her attorney father, Richard R. Lewis, ran for mayor of Houston in 1938 and finished a distant third. Her maternal grandfather, Robert L. Autrey, owned the Southern Select Brewing Company in Galveston and had been a leader in the liquor industry's efforts to stave off prohibition in the state. In 1917 Autrey took $156,000 as a personal loan to then-governor James E. Ferguson, an act that helped to produce Ferguson's impeachment and removal from office when the governor refused to disclose its origin. Autrey was also the silent financial backer of the Maceo family that ran dice games ("galloping dominoes" in our family) and other aspects of organized crime in Galveston during the 1930s.[20]

Their upbringings differed, but from the time they met, my parents shared one common trait that prevailed the rest of their lives: smoking. Their tastes ran to unfiltered Chesterfields and Camels, and each of them ran through three or four packs daily. Ashtrays were everywhere, but the ashes and butts spilled out into the rest of their living space. The smell and the residue of the habit permeated their lives and mine. Neither of my brothers smokes, nor do I.

My parents became officially engaged in the summer of 1938, but their marriage had to wait until her father finished his mayoral race. Having a daughter married to a "Yankee" would not have been a political asset in Houston in the late 1930s. And my father had to make a trip to Europe with his mother. It was not his first such voyage across the Atlantic. He told me later that he had been to Germany and had once been so close to Adolf Hitler he could have spit on him. That moment probably came in 1936. In September 1938 the liner *Georgic* took him to London during the Munich crisis. He recounted to my mother in one of his daily letters to her, "This town all has the war jitters." He stopped by an exhibition of radio and television that he called "pretty damned good too," though it seemed expensive by American standards.[21]

After he returned from England, they endured another separation while my mother went out of town with the show *Knickerbocker Holiday*. Dad reported to her about his interview with Clare Boothe Luce. She was, he wrote, "a real bitch," and he "would rather have talked to a tombstone." In the interview that appeared in the *Times*, he called Luce "The Terror of Park Avenue" who had a "charming and keen personality."[22]

My parents were married on November 25, 1938, in New York City's St. Bartholomew's Episcopal Church, a stately structure designed in part by McKim Mead and White at Park Avenue and 50th Street. I was born on September 21, 1939, and my brothers Richard (1942) and Robert (1946) followed during the years our family lived in New York. We lived in a brownstone house on MacDougall Street in Greenwich Village reportedly occupied years before by Louisa May Alcott. My mother had wisely invested several hundred dollars in a show in which she worked. When *Arsenic and Old Lace* became a long-running smash hit, the extra income she received helped put the three of us boys through college.

During the early 1940s, my father became embroiled in the prolonged battle between the American Society of Composers, Artists, and Publishers (ASCAP) and Broadcast Music International (BMI) for control of the copyrights and performance rights to the nation's popular songs. From that subject he moved to an even more controversial topic, the American Federation of Musicians (AFM) and its fiery president, James C. Petrillo.[23]

Anxious to enhance the income of the federation's members and suspicious of changing technology, Petrillo instituted a series of recording bans and other devices to pressure record companies for greater royalties for working musicians. These tactics kept Petrillo on the front pages throughout World War II. Petrillo was wary of most reporters who covered him. Dad became the notable exception. Fearful of germs because one of his sons had died of an infection, Petrillo appreciated that my father understood and respected his concerns about hygiene. The union leader came to trust and confide in my father. As a result, the *Times* broke numerous exclusives about the AFM and its president. In 1947 Dad was subpoenaed to testify in federal court about whether Petrillo had declared in public that he would disobey the Lea Law that Congress had enacted to control his activities. My father's coverage of Petrillo facilitated his transfer to the radio department of the *Times* in the early years of the war.[24]

Although Dad was draft age during World War II, he was classified as 4-F because of tuberculosis in one eye and chronic stomach ulcers. Then as later, his diet was a mixture of coffee, cigarettes, and sandwiches, and his health fluctuated between fair and poor. He and my mother rode around New York City on his motorcycle in what must have then seemed a Bohemian lifestyle. They often sent me at the age of two or three across the street to bring them back cigarettes from the neighborhood store. Occasionally, I would receive a lemon ice as a reward.

My father's dedication to his job continued long after he left the city room of the *Times*. In his third floor study, he installed his radio equipment and spent countless hours monitoring shortwave broadcasts. On July 25, 1943 he heard Samuel Grafton, a commentator broadcasting on the Voice of America for the Office of War Information (OWI), analyze the surrender of Fascist Italy. Grafton called Italian monarch Victor Emmanuel, who was replacing Benito Mussolini, "the moronic little king." Recognizing that the OWI was taking a stand that differed from the policy of the Roosevelt administration, Dad called his editors and filed a story that as it played out led to a shakeup in the OWI. Two weeks after the story ran, my father's salary went from $80 a week to $92.[25]

In September 1944 his life took a sudden turn. The radio critic of the *Times*, John K. Hutchens, announced "that he could not take another year of listening to Jack Benny." Hutchens moved on to the book review and left Dad handling the radio department. After a few weeks in limbo, my father asked managing editor Edwin L. James whether he was "going to run the damn thing or did he have someone else to put in?" Dad was named editor and critic that same day. On Sunday, September 10, 1944, he became radio news editor at a salary of $100 a week.[26]

Within a month, Dad's readers got a preview of television that was to come after the war ended. In October 1944 he reviewed a presentation of *The Boys from Boise*, a musical comedy that he deemed "a valuable and important step toward television's own self-sufficiency." Yet for the next two years radio remained preeminent. Dad covered the successful attempt of the U.S. Army in January 1946 to bounce a radio signal off the moon, a forerunner of space developments that followed during the 1950s.[27]

By 1946 my mother and father had concluded, as their family grew to three sons, that the house on MacDougall Street was no longer big enough. With overcrowding of schools in Manhattan on the horizon, they made the move to suburbia that so many others would make during the next decade. They bought a house in Stamford, Connecticut, on five acres of land that had furnished topsoil for the Merritt Parkway during the late 1930s. The torn-up terrain enabled them to acquire the land for a modest price of $19,000, and they moved there in 1947. Backing up on the Mianus River, the place had a huge pond that iced up enough in the winter for skating. Along the pond's steep banks, blackberries and blueberries grew wild in abundance. It was a great home for three young boys.

For my mother, the move to Connecticut was not something that served her interests. From an active theater career, she became a housewife isolated in the "back country" of Stamford with young offspring to transport to schools, appointments, and recreation. She later said that she had been "trapped in a men's locker room for twenty-five years." Although she was active in a local dramatic group called the Playmakers, it was not Broadway, and she experienced many of the frustrations and the sense of lost opportunities that Betty Friedan would examine in *The Feminine Mystique*.

My father set up his reviewing office in the rear part of the house, and from there he followed the new programs that early television produced. Not content with just reviewing, he spent four or five days at the office chasing stories, interviewing television insiders, and working his confidential sources. Most weekdays he took the Merritt Parkway into New York and reached Times Square by a circuitous route that combined speed and complexity. On other occasions, he became a commuter on the New York, New Haven, and Hartford railroad. While others rested on weekends, he went into New York on Saturday mornings for breakfasts with Frank Stanton of the Columbia Broadcasting System, a personal relationship that often resulted in exclusive stories.

Within five years, as the baby boom exploded in the Stamford school system and double sessions loomed for children there, my parents moved once again to neighboring Old Greenwich. They purchased a three-story house on Long Island Sound that had served as the residence for servants on an adjoining estate. The twelve-room house had enough room for three boys and ample space for my father to work.

There Dad adopted the routine as a critic that he followed for the rest of his career. He believed that it was essential to watch programs as they occurred at home, just as other viewers were doing. On the third floor of his new residence, he had a rambling office overlooking the Sound, and he furnished the room with three television sets, his radio receivers, a comfortable bed, and his well-worn typewriter. On many evenings he wrote under a tight deadline of 11:15 or 11:20 P.M. when his copy had to be at the desk in New York. That meant for a program ending at 11, he had less than a half-hour to prepare a 300- to 750-word review.

We could watch the program with him but could not say anything while the show was in progress. Once it came time to write, we all left the room and the typewriter began its rhythmic chatter. When all went well, he would have the review ready and be dictating to the copy desk in New York around 11:15. He took some notes as he watched, used background material sent to him in advance, and no doubt wrote parts of the reviews in his head. Some nights the words came slowly and the tension was thick in the room. Years of practice and routine usually produced a quality appraisal in the available time.

The other primary responsibility was his regular column for the Sunday *Times*. That became known to all of us as the dreaded "Sunday piece," a longer essay that either reviewed at greater length some show of the preceding week or explored a larger issue facing the medium. Because of the Sunday paper's deadlines, this assignment had to be done by Tuesday. Thus my father often had only a hectic two-day period at the beginning of the week to produce his Sunday remarks. In these extended discussions of television and its future, Dad had a kind of personal editorial page on which he could offer prescriptions for ways to improve video. He did not write a sermon each week lest he become dull and strident. When an issue such as blacklisting of alleged Communists arose or the quiz shows scandals occurred, he used his pulpit effectively.

On occasion, Dad also wrote articles for *The New York Times Magazine* and its prickly editor, Lester Markel. In that forum he took up even larger issues about television than those he addressed on Sunday.

Faced with the potential college expenses for three sons, in the 1950s he wrote a children's book, *All About Radio and Television*, which explained the technicalities of electronics in simple and clear language. The "fox-hole" radio he taught us to build was a key feature of the text. The book sold several hundred thousand copies and was translated into numerous languages.[28]

As a critic of television, my father followed a general philosophy of his role over the course of his career. He never spent much time reading what his colleagues in the critical craft said about their profession. Instead, he hammered out principles and guidelines for himself as television evolved. From the outset, he never exaggerated his own influence over the medium and its performers. "Most criticism," he wrote in 1972, "is useless and wasteful in a mass medium distributed for free." He knew that he might assist a good show with a favorable review, and his endorsement might affect someone's career, as happened with newsmen David Brinkley and Howard K. Smith. But he also understood that he could not guide public taste or change the verdict of the ratings for shows he liked but viewers did not.[29]

My father recognized that his influence as a critic rested on his connection with *The New York Times*. Particularly during the 1940s and early 1950s, New York City was the center of television production and Hollywood remained, in the words of John Gunther in 1947, "a suburb of the Bronx." Television executives read the *Times* and the New York *Herald Tribune* daily as they commuted to work. As a result, Dad and his main competitor, John Crosby of the *Tribune*, had a significant influence on what the leaders of television thought and did. As an industry journal put it in 1954, "Even though the network brass are aware that their Nielsens are not likely to fluctuate a bit because of a critic's opinion, they wait breathlessly for The Word from the men who write the reviews."[30]

My father had an unparalleled platform from which to offer his opinions about television. Yet that opportunity could vanish quickly if he were not judicious, balanced, and objective. The *Times* management gave him a good deal of latitude for his evaluations, but his work received constant scrutiny from editors and the newspaper's publisher.[31]

When he evaluated an individual show, my father began from the assumption that "a medium which daily pre-empts the attention of millions of adults and children surely cannot be ignored." To judge how well television performed, he believed that it must be evaluated "in light of contemporary life as a whole, just as the theater, movies, and books are." He was sensitive to his detractors' claim that he lacked the intellectual and artistic competence to judge well everything that video offered. As he summarized it, this indictment contended that "the cultural conceit of the television critic is unparalleled in its fundamental arrogance." He then asked, "Is there any difference between a critic who judges all kinds of programs and a network executive who thinks he can select all kinds of programs?"[32]

When he watched an individual program, my father sought first "to understand what the program is trying to accomplish, then I try to analyze whether it has succeeded in its aim." He resisted the argument of some television insiders that he should apply less stringent standards to programming that sought to elevate the medium's cultural aspirations. If a show such as *Omnibus* or an operatic presentation fell short of excellence, he believed it was his responsibility to say so, even though he had hoped that the program would be an artistic success.[33]

Dad's aesthetic preferences grew out of his experience covering nightclubs and theaters in the 1930s. He favored the spontaneity of live television over film and later videotape. His musical tastes ran to the Broadway shows and swing-era sounds of his reporting days. As a result, he admired the witty lyrics of Lorenz "Larry" Hart over the sentimentality of Oscar Hammerstein II. Family lore had it that he predicted after seeing a performance of *Oklahoma* in 1943 that it would flop. Yet he also watched with rapt attention the classical performances of Arturo Toscanini and Leonard Bernstein. He had no patience with modern jazz or with rock and roll. His most famous and oft-quoted judgment in the popular music field occurred in 1956 when he wrote that Elvis Presley had "no discernible singing ability."[34]

While my father's critics in the television industry charged that he came at programs from an elitist and high-brow perspective, he watched and enjoyed regular programming of Westerns, situation comedies, and game shows. In the 1950s, when he relaxed after his reviewing chores of the day were done, he laughed at programs such as Jerry Lester's *Broadway Open House* with its ribald humor and burlesque-era sketches. But when it came time to evaluate a program, he struck a different pose. "I haven't got any preference for program types," he said in 1958. "I judge programs one by one."[35]

Although criticism was his major responsibility, Dad never stopped covering the news that television generated as well. Over the years he cultivated an impressive assortment of inside sources in the industry, many of whom called him at home with leaks and grievances that formed the basis for front-page stories. He guarded the confidentiality of his sources and never discussed what they said with us. He did not keep his correspondence systematically, out of concern for his sources. Some clues emerge from the fragments that are left. Frank Stanton told him much at their breakfasts, while NBC executive Joe Derby and ABC's James Hagerty shared exclusive stories with him in their time.[36]

In his notes for a book about television that never got written, my father was candid about the major executives he knew. William S. Paley of CBS was "the master of indecision," while Frank Stanton was "the best Washington witness TV has had but a lonely man who works Saturdays." Leonard Goldenson of ABC was "a movie exhibitor lost in a bewildering world." David Sarnoff of NBC was "the master plumber with only minor interest in the quality of the water." Once Sarnoff got "away from his press agents and lawyers," he was "an engaging rough neck." Dad once told me that when Sarnoff was explaining the appearance of a new satellite that NBC planned to launch, he said, "Jack, think of a cunt upside down."[37]

Over the years my father had a fascinating critical and personal relationship with Edward R. Murrow. They shared an addiction to nicotine and a passionate concern for the future of television as a positive cultural and political force in American society. When Murrow attacked Senator Joseph R. McCarthy on *See It Now* on March 9, 1954, Dad made sure that my brothers and I assembled to see the dissection of the Wisconsin lawmaker. Yet he also warned in his columns that the editorializing in Murrow's program could be dangerous in other hands. We heard much at home about the difference between the "Good Murrow" who spoke out for civil liberties and the "Bad Murrow" who pandered to popular taste in his interview program *Person to Person*. Dad's verdict in 1972 was that "the man who did more than any other for the documentary form enjoyed the very economic benefits from the operating principles he deplored." When CBS and Murrow had a falling out at the end of the 1950s, my father became the vehicle for the public disclosures that Frank Stanton used to embarrass and humiliate his network rival.[38]

After his retirement, my father recalled one instance in the political realm when his intervention as a critic made a significant difference. It came in late October 1956 when the networks failed to cover the televised deliberations of the United Nations Security Council at the height of the Suez crisis. With the threat of war in the air and the presidential election just days away, he took to his typewriter to denounce "The Disgrace of the Networks." It was television's "darkest day" in his judgment, and his impassioned column produced both greater network attention to the UN and a flood of mail praising him for his stand. There was talk of a Pulitzer Prize, but that never happened.[39]

Another column, earlier in 1956, drew a rather comical response. In it, he criticized the faith-healing tactics of evangelist Oral Roberts, who, as my father put it some years later, "always managed miraculous recoveries just before closing commercials." Irritated by the attack, Roberts urged his followers to write the *Times.* More than four thousand letters flooded in, forcing Arthur Hays Sulzberger to weave his way through the piled-up mailbags. Roberts also instructed his flock to pray for my father's salvation and for my father to see the error of his ways. A lapsed Episcopalian who recommended to us that we slip into the back of any church when we felt religious and pray on our own, Dad thought that Roberts's concern for his soul was an ironic touch in light of the evangelist's hard-sell tactics as a television pitchman.[40]

My father kept his own political opinions out of his columns and reporting. He had long since abandoned the Republican allegiance of his youth, as I discovered when I enthusiastically told him at the age of thirteen in 1952 what a great candidate Dwight D. Eisenhower was. "We're Democrats in this house," he said as he sat me down for a long lecture on the social justice tradition of Franklin D. Roosevelt and the Democratic Party. His liberalism owed a good deal to his experiences with the Federal Theater in the 1930s and his skepticism about big business as he saw it in television.

A sense of honesty and fair play shaped his reaction to the blacklisting of alleged Communists in television during the 1950s. He was an early critic of the booklet "Red Channels" and the way in which this list indicted performers for purported Communist ties without a fair hearing. When the actress Jean Muir was blacklisted in 1950, he was her most persistent defender. Although he knew some Communists, he never regarded those in entertainment as a threat to the nation. The publishers of "Red Channels" he deemed opportunists who ran a kind of protection racket of exchanging "clearances" of Communists for money from the networks.[41]

Something of a closet idealist behind his skepticism about politicians and network executives, my father cherished hopes that television might prove a means of cultural and educational enlightenment for the United States. He welcomed every evidence of such programming during the 1940s and 1950s. As time passed, however, he saw the medium becoming more devoted to profits and predictability and less concerned with creativity and positive change. His fascination with television waned. As he asked in 1958, "How much interest can be generated about a medium which is losing excitement through a repetition of forms?" He hoped that the Kennedy years might restore some sense of optimism and progress to television. Newton Minow, the chairman of the Federal Communications Commission under Kennedy, acknowledged that my father's columns helped shape his thinking about what Minow called "the vast wasteland" of television. Yet during the last decade of his work as a critic, Dad felt a growing sense of frustration and disenchantment about television. "I have been glued to the tube for twenty years," he would say to explain his malaise.[42]

A constant problem for my father throughout his career was his uncertain health. Never careful about his diet, increasingly he subsisted on coffee, cigarettes, drinks in the evening, and nervous energy. Sometimes he simply drank too much, as did my mother. Finally, Dad's system rebelled with intense duodenal ulcers that plagued him until a portion of his stomach was removed in the late 1950s. By the time he was fifty he began to have symptoms of the circulatory problems that affected him for the rest of his life. He joked about his condition and rarely complained in public, but at home it was evident that the pressures of his profession were consuming him.

My father loved working for *The New York Times* and gave the newspaper his deep personal loyalty. Yet the internal demands of his job added to the strain on his health and morale. The radio and television columns had their place at the back of the daily paper, interspersed with advertisements and notices about shipping news and other drab matters. Dad's columns and reviews competed for space in an obscure section of the paper, so readers had to make a special effort to find his criticism every day.

In addition, there was the never-ending problem of the television and radio schedule itself. Although *TV Guide* was gaining popularity with its weekly listings of programs, many readers in New York City still looked to their daily newspaper to find out what was on television each evening. My father spent endless hours balancing the limited space for program listings with demands from Arthur Hays Sulzberger for more news about reruns, color programming, and future shows. For movies, a previous review from the *Times* film critic was reduced to a phrase or two, and when viewers protested what the digested opinion said, Dad was the man responsible. Memo after memo flowed from management asking him for an improved, clearer, more readable schedule within a constricted space and for expanding network offerings. He never settled the problem to his or anyone else's permanent satisfaction.[43]

Although my father got most of the public attention as the television critic of the *Times*, he did not run a one-man operation. In the 1940s and 1950s he received invaluable help from Val Adams and John P. Shanley. Lisa Hamel worked as his efficient secretary in the mid-1950s. His closest personal relationship was with Richard F. "Dick" Shepard, who joined the radio-television department in 1955 and spent eight years there. A kind, thoughtful man, Shepard added an incisive wit and wry style to the columns of the department, and he provided my father with a sounding board for his frustrations and reservations about the direction of television.

My father's tenure as a critic fell into three distinct phases. From 1947 to 1954, when the medium was evolving its modern form, he approached his critical work with eager expectation for what the television set might offer him. In 1951 the newspaper, under his overall guidance, produced an extensive and insightful appraisal of what television was doing to and for American society. My father drove himself hard during these years, and his health suffered as he grappled with a small staff and expanding responsibilities. In 1953 a taxing visit to Europe to look at foreign television, combined with worsening stomach problems, led him to consider changes in his job. The looming prospect of college expenses for my brothers and me was also on his mind.

So when CBS president Frank Stanton offered him a job in 1954 at the network with the undefined role of "information adviser," which would involve forecasting the future direction of the industry and a higher salary, he took it. He told friends, "It was a hard decision to make, but the new job is an exciting and interesting one." He resigned from the *Times* in the summer of 1954 and discovered almost at once that he had nothing real to do at CBS. Stanton had simply silenced him as a critic. My parents realized that he had made a dire professional mistake, and the job at the *Times* would soon be filled with his successor.[44]

One evening after work he ran into Turner Catledge, the *Times* managing editor, at the Algonquin Hotel bar. Over a drink he mentioned his unhappiness with CBS. Meanwhile, the newspaper had not been able to find anyone as my father's successor, and Catledge asked him whether he would simply like to have his old job back. Catledge himself had once left the *Times* for another paper and then returned. He told Dad, "You can't describe this kind of experience. You must live through it to know what the Times means." Relieved and happy, my father agreed. The *Times* called the six weeks at CBS a personal leave of absence, and by September 1954 the ill-fated experiment was history. As my father wrote to his publisher, "After the strange and rich sauces of Madison Avenue, there is nothing quite like home cooking."[45]

During the second major phase of his critical career, from the mid-1950s through the early 1960s, Dad enjoyed the peak of his influence. In 1956 the Oral Roberts controversy attracted wide attention. The Suez Canal debate at the end of the year illustrated his clout with the industry and the public. For his stinging assault on the inept performance of the networks, he received a Pulitzer Prize nomination from fellow critic Gilbert Seldes and then was the recipient of the George Foster Peabody Radio and Television Award in March 1957.[46]

During the quiz show scandals of the late 1950s, Dad chastised his fellow reporters for their arrogance about the misfortunes of the video industry. After clearing his intentions with the management of the *Times*, he wrote a column about the time-honored practice of "the junket," in which reporters had their expenses paid to cover some event of interest to the corporation that picked up the tab. At the end of the piece he also mentioned " 'the Christmas loot,' the practice of showering holiday presents upon the high and low in journalism."[47]

This column had the most direct impact on my brothers and me of all the writing that my father did. For many years we had marveled at the arrival of the cases of grapefruit, oranges, and liquor that came magically to our house in Old Greenwich. One year there were suspenders with little cigarette packages or Stork Club ties. We couldn't have the liquor just yet, but we all enjoyed the fruit and other goodies. Then in 1957 and 1958 Dad began to refuse to accept the majority of the gifts before he wrote his 1959 exposé. Although John Crosby said that Dad "had fouled his own nest," my father's column did change the culture of taking gifts at the *Times* for a few years. Thereafter he refused to accept even the smallest gift from a broadcaster or publicist.[48]

Two months after the junket column, he once again wrote a review that touched a nerve with his readers and illustrated his influence. He warned that *The Play of the Week* on New York's Channel 13, WNTA-TV, would end by January 30, 1960, because of a lack of advertising support for the drama series. Dad asked, "Is a season of perhaps twenty-six plays with fine casts worth a 3-cent postcard to WNTA-TV, 10 Columbus Circle, to demonstrate that there is a sizable audience for grown-up television? The viewer must help too." WNTA received twenty-eight thousand letters; others were sent to my father, some with monetary contributions, which he returned. Standard Oil of New Jersey came forward in January 1960 to sponsor the program. Michael Dann, a CBS executive, wrote to Dad, "It isn't often that a critic saves a show, and we are all grateful." The triumph proved only a temporary one. In mid-1961 Channel 13 became a noncommercial educational station, and *The Play of the Week* series ended.[49]

During these productive years, my father's colleagues profiled him for the house publication, *Times Talk*, in an article that captured well his devotion to his work and his absentminded approach to everyday matters. He took home the overcoats of his coworkers, often forgot his keys, and came to the office dressed with mismatched socks and bedraggled suits. As he pursued an exclusive story he would say, "The roof is falling in," amid his round of phone calls and industry contacts. His reluctance to go on vacation was also legendary at the *Times* and at home. Several times he filed copy about stories that he had encountered while traveling. During the mid-1950s he spent a hectic and tiring day working as a television repairman in Stamford, Connecticut, and then wrote a piece for *The New York Times Magazine* about his adventures.[50]

Shy and reserved on the job, he indulged in lengthy conversations when he came home in the evening. He would plop down the four or five evening newspapers he brought with him, sit on the living room couch (where his pockets left a small wealth of change amid the cushions), and recount the day's events. After the column was written in the evening, he would prepare a fried egg sandwich, open a bottle of Michelob, and talk into the night about television and affairs at the *Times*. A lifetime in the newspaper business left him with few illusions about humanity and its foibles, but he retained a vein of idealism that produced high expectations for himself and his family.

Because he worked for *The New York Times*, he set forth certain ground rules for the family. As my mother often told us, our father was "a minor celebrity," and we must always behave as though whatever we did might appear on the front page of the *Greenwich Time* or a New York tabloid. We were warned that any display of the anti-Semitism that pervaded southern Connecticut during the postwar years was both wrong and inappropriate because of the Sulzberger family and the *Times*. That meant that my younger brothers had to forgo the swimming club that was a half-mile from our house because, as Dad put it, "they don't take Jews." My parents were not free of the racial and ethnic prejudices of that time and place, but they did their best not to pass on these biases to their sons.

Sometimes the subjects of Dad's criticism reacted with anger and written rebuttals to what he had said about their performances. My father believed that, since he had had his say in the *Times*, his detractors had a right to make their case as well. He often told me that he reviewed the performance of those who appeared on television and tried to separate his comments from personal attacks on those about whom he wrote. That may not always have been true of the New York personalities "Jinx" Falkenburg and "Tex" McCrary, with whom he seemed to have a running testiness, but for the most part Dad avoided the personalism and cheap shots in his journalism that would pervade the profession in the 1990s.

The targets of my father's criticisms did not always take a detached view of what he had said about them. In 1961 outspoken atheist Joseph Lewis filed a libel suit against Dad for his review of Lewis's appearance on the Betty Furness talk show. One of the guests was a man without arms and legs, and Lewis said that the man's condition raised questions about whether a compassionate God existed. Dad observed that "in casting aspersions on the efficacy of prayer and challenging God's presence because there are blind, mute and crippled among us, Mr. Lewis struck a note bordering on the sadistic." Lewis's legal action never went beyond the preliminary stages and eventually was dropped.[51]

The final phase of my father's career as a critic began in the spring of 1962 when Turner Catledge overhauled the cultural/critical departments of the *Times*, known to other reporters as "Culture Gulch." For decades the critics had run their departments and reported to the city desk. Now they were placed under the supervision of a cultural news editor, Joseph Herzberg, who had been installed to coordinate their activities. In my father's mind, these changes reduced his autonomy within the paper and reflected management's lessening confidence in his performance as a critic. Further shaking his faith in the *Times* was the prolonged and bitter newspaper strike of 1962–1963. That walkout, with the erosion of morale that followed it, convinced Dad that the paper he had known and loved was changing in new and sometimes unpalatable ways.[52]

An event that symbolized these problems came in the autumn of 1963 when he reviewed Lester Markel's television program *News in Perspective*, which featured *Times* reporters commenting on the issues of the day. The program was in conception a forerunner of the format of journalistic talking heads that would become popular in the 1980s. A brainchild of the talented and abrasive Markel, "it was a personal undertaking from start to finish. The dramatis personae happened to have been recruited from the Times staff," said Ivan Veit, one of my father's colleagues. When he saw the show, Dad knew he was in trouble. In his review he wrote, "The New York Times has everything to learn about doing news on television" because the program was "over-organized" and "a long discussion of disconnected fragments."[53]

When the review came in to the night editor, he called Turner Catledge at home because of the potential reaction from Markel. "Jack Gould has written a terrible review about Mr. Markel's debut on Channel 13," Catledge was told. To which Catledge replied, "Well, why are you calling me?" The night editor replied, "Well, I didn't want to take the responsibility for running it." Before Catledge slammed down the phone he asked, "How would you like to take the responsibility for not running it?" And the column appeared. The fiery Markel took his displeasure to the columns of *Time* and *Newsweek* and sent my father a long and carping memo as well. Eventually the two men patched up their dispute, though the scars lingered. Ivan Veit told my father that he had "ordered a Congressional Medal of Honor for you with two oak leaf clusters."[54]

In the summer of 1966, my father obtained an exclusive interview with President Lyndon Johnson about television issues. Dad was unimpressed with the president and later told me that it was an odd sensation to sit in the Oval Office and have its occupant lie to you. The incident gained some historical significance because the White House aide who arranged the event was former NBC president Robert Kintner. He had been brought out of retirement to help manage the inner workings of the Johnson White House. An insecure alcoholic, Kintner looked for ways to underscore his influence. To hype the importance of the interview, Kintner submitted a memo to Johnson reporting that my father had visited Kintner's office after his meeting with the president and said,

"Why doesn't the President appear on television the same way he talked to me—the President is so gracious, affable and well informed." These words have appeared in several accounts of Johnson and the media.[55]

When the quotation came to my attention in the mid-1980s, I asked my father what he remembered about the incident. He said that he left the White House immediately after the interview and did not see Kintner nor say what had been reported in the memorandum. The episode impressed me as a cautionary tale about relying on archival materials without double-checking the sources used.

By the middle of the 1960s my father's personal interest in television was waning. During a spring trip to Europe in 1966 he told my mother that he was concerned about his "attitude toward TV as a whole. I think I've just about had it, U.S., U.K., or whatever. I've run out of things to say and find myself repeating over and over." Talks within the management of the *Times* about using guest television critics added to my father's apprehension. He suffered a nasty fall during the European trip that underlined the uncertain state of his health.[56]

Throughout the rest of the decade Dad remained an active critic, but his physical condition continued to give him problems. The exact nature of his ailment never came into clear focus. He experienced intense headaches, fatigue, and some depression. A lifetime of smoking and heavy drinking wore down his resources. In 1971 he again said to me, "I'm really written out on looking at the screen after twenty years." That year he relinquished his duties as a critic and devoted his energies to reporting about the television industry. In a final burst of productivity, he filed story after story about the medium's problems, including one about the Nixon Administration's plans to loosen regulation of broadcasting.[57]

His last major exclusive came in January 1972. He received a leaked copy of the conclusions of the forthcoming report from the Surgeon General on the impact of televised violence. Throughout his career my father had written at length about the failures of broadcasters to address the needs of younger viewers. He had praised such programs as *Ding Dong School* and *Captain Kangaroo* and assailed the lapses in taste of such performers as Pinky Lee. In the case of the Surgeon General's report, he conveyed the information that a direct link between children and violence had not been identified. The resulting *Times* headline and his story diluted the impact of the report's other findings and set off a controversy among scholars of the issue that continues to the present.[58]

By this time, however, my father had decided that it was time to retire.

Tensions with his colleagues were growing, and he knew the quality of his professional performance was suffering. There are some hints that he was eased out. In any case, on January 25, 1972, he asked Abe Rosenthal to "quietly set in motion the procedures for my withdrawal from the *Times*." He told another executive at the newspaper, "My health isn't bad, simply erratic. I always prided myself on doing a day's work for a day's pay and when that didn't pan out I thought it wisest to call it quits."[59]

When the announcement of the retirement came on February 15, 1972, the Sunday editor asked Fred Friendly, formerly of CBS News, to write a tribute. In 1969, Friendly had nominated my father for a Pulitzer Prize for his criticism. In the retirement piece, Friendly referred to Dad as "the conscience of the industry" and reviewed his contributions to the medium. Near the end, however, he speculated on my father's motives for retiring. He called him "a complex man, and the New York Times is now a complicated newspaper. As he would have put it, there is more here than meets the eye."[60]

The oblique suggestion that my father's decision owed as much to reservations about the *Times* management as to his health had some basis in fact. In his private letters, Dad alluded to "the chaos at the Times." Yet he would never have made such complaints in public and what Friendly wrote mortified him. As he told Abe Rosenthal, "If I had any bitching to do it would have been with you and not outsiders. I detest public scenes involving myself."[61]

Dad wrote a follow-up letter to the *Times* rebutting Friendly's claim: "After 26 years of staring at the tube on a daily basis the initiative was entirely mine." He added that "Fred's retirement from CBS News was fraught with emotion and bitterness; at the Times warm friends handle such matters differently." Fred Friendly told me in a telephone interview in 1993 that five or so years after these events he received a letter from my father. Dad apologized for the line about CBS News, which he said had been added at the insistence of Abe Rosenthal.[62]

After my father's retirement, he received letters from those he had covered and those with whom he had worked, summing up what he had meant to television and its early development. His coworker Richard F. Shepard predicted "that in three or four generations no one will remember him clearly." Julian Goodman, the president of NBC, told him, "You have always gone about your work with diligent intelligence, and you have been a real force in the development of television." Reuven

Frank of NBC News wrote, "You will be missed by the television business, the newspaper business, and, primarily, by the public whose interest you served far better than a lot of flamboyant and self-serving types we both could name." Finally, William S. Paley observed, "You were a good influence on the industry and you worked for the best interests of the public, especially the more discriminating part of it."[63]

My father and mother lived in Old Greenwich for two years and then moved to Berkeley, California, where they remained until their deaths in the early 1990s. My father talked about doing a book of reminiscences, but nothing came of it other than a five-page outline. He wrote a few pieces about television and its prospects during the 1970s until his lack of stamina and energy made even such work no longer possible. He corresponded with Lester Markel, and the two old adversaries discussed collaborating. That too went nowhere. Authors writing about television regularly interviewed him, and he responded in the same conscientious manner that had marked all of his reporting. My mother died on March 1, 1991. My father's death came two years later on May 24, 1993, of complications arising from a gall bladder infection.

Although my father's criticism and reporting on television frequently have been cited in histories of the medium, assessments of his impact have been spotty. Some academic evaluations of his criticism appeared during his working career. A doctoral dissertation in 1980 analyzed his published work in a generally favorable manner, but most of the recent verdicts of newer scholars in television studies have been mixed at best.[64]

The most frequently recurring indictment has to do with Dad's preference in the 1950s for live drama over filmed programming. His position, argue detractors such as Professor William Boddy, missed the change in entertainment technology during the decade and, worse yet, reflected an elitist, East Coast point of view in his judgment of good and bad shows. My father has become, to this line of thinking, an apologist for an elusive and to some modern analysts a nonexistent "Golden Age of Television" in the 1950s.

My father was not a sentimental man or one given to careless nostalgia. He knew that not all live television drama was priceless or enduring. What he cherished was the sense of possibility and excitement that live television conveyed. He deplored "the crucial loss of novelty in the medium. With his knowledge of the technical side of television, he knew why "efficiency prevailed and heart was lost." Yet his contemporary critics too readily accept the formulaic sterility of much prime-time television and tolerate that flawed product as the best the industry can do.[65]

That his derisive comments regarding Elvis Presley have become his most quoted words would have amused my father. His judgments on Elvis prompted one scholar to say that he "led the charge to immobilize Presley," quite a feat for two newspaper reviews. To be sure, Dad missed Presley's emergence as a national cultural phenomenon. But the tawdry arc of Presley's career indicates my father's aesthetic assessment was not as far-fetched as historical second-guessing makes it appear.[66]

My father always had his own critics during his time and in the years that have followed. The director Arthur Penn said of his reviews, "I don't think we paid much attention to him." Reuven Frank's memoirs assail Dad as someone whose "judgments were old-maidish, his writing tortured, and his tastes unsophisticated, but his power was palpable." In a recent biography of Gilbert Seldes, Michael Kammen joins his subject in relegating Dad merely among "the professional critics of television."[67]

Other comments about my father's work and influence are more positive. David Bianculli, a contemporary critic, calls him "one of the first and best TV critics to serve on an influential newspaper." Sylvester "Pat" Weaver, the NBC executive who created the *Today Show*, said that Dad "had a strong sense of fair play." When my father died, Phil Rosenthal of the Los Angeles *Daily News* inquired, "Where would the television business be today if not for the formative influence" that Jack Gould exerted?[68]

The appropriate answer to Rosenthal's question is my father's own work as a critic. Some of the best and more representative of his columns from 1947 to 1963 follow in this book. They would not have been the ones he would have chosen, but then he probably would have laughed wryly at the idea of the project as a whole. Yet he was proud of what he had written as a reporter and critic. I believe his work deserves to be more accessible than what the microfilmed editions of *The New York Times* now provide to researchers interested in his work and its impact on television. In these columns, readers will find those qualities that made Jack Gould such a positive force in the early years of television—integrity, idealism, and an intolerance for the second-rate. Abe Rosenthal had it right in 1972. My father had created a special place for himself in the history of American television and journalism during the twenty-five years of evaluating how a new medium reshaped the nation's culture.

Notes

1. A. M. Rosenthal to Jack Gould, January 26, 1972, *New York Times* archives (NYTA).

2. Richard Shepard, "Jack Gould, Always Retiring, Retires Voluntarily," *Times Talk*, March 1972, Jack Gould Papers (JLG Papers), Center for American History, University of Texas.

3. Harvey Edward Fisk, "Record of the Fisk Family, Forebears of Harvey Edward Fisk and Mary Lee (Scudder) Fisk from 1642 to 1942," courtesy of Gerrish Thurber, JLG Papers.

4. Obituary notice, John Warren Dubois Gould, *American Society of Civil Engineers*, JLG Papers. My grandmother discussed her college experiences with me in the 1960s.

5. Gerrish Thurber to Lewis L. Gould, February 27, 1996, confirmed the crimes of Pliny Fisk that had been discussed in our family for many years. My grandfather's service in the Food Administration is detailed in the Hoover Institution on War, Revolution, and Peace, which kindly furnished copies of letters and memoranda now in the JLG Papers.

6. The JLG Papers contain certificates of achievement at the Allen-Stevenson School and a flyer from the Knickerbocker Greys. The circumstances of the choice of Kent School and his father's sudden death are discussed in Evelyn Fisk Gould to Father Frederick Still, January 4, 1925, Kent School archives, Kent, Connecticut.

7. My father's youthful radio listening habits are mentioned in "Most Influential Fellow," *Newsweek*, May 9, 1966.

8. Entrance record, John Ludlow Gould, and Evelyn Fisk Gould to Father Still, March 19, 1928, Kent School archives.

9. *Loomis Post*, January 14 and 21, 1931, JLG Papers. For his disciplinary problems, Marillyn D. Loomis to Lewis L. Gould, February 8, 1994. My father's grades, with three B's and the rest C's and D's, are recorded in the archives of the Loomis Chafee School.

10. My brother informed me of Dad's recollection of the molestation in a 1993 interview, and relatives often spoke of his tendency to run away from school in the early 1930s.

11. Frederic L. Brown to Evelyn Fisk Gould, July 6, 1932; Theodore A. Distler to John L. Gould, September 19, 1932 (an admissions letter from New York University); and Jack Gould to Lewis L. Gould, September 12, 1975, JLG Papers.

12. Mary Ann Watson, *The Expanding Vision: American Television in the Kennedy Years* (New York: Oxford University Press, 1990), 28.

13. Jack Gould to Anita Brewer, February 28, 1980, JLG Papers. I am indebted to Anita Brewer Howard of Austin, Texas, for a copy of his letter and other materials relating to my father's years with the New York *Herald Tribune.* The quotations from my father are taken from this letter. Walker's anecdote is from Stanley Walker, *Home to Texas* (New York: Harper and Brothers, 1956), 29–30. Walker's 1934 book, *City Editor,* was reprinted by the Johns Hopkins University Press in 2000 and gives a good sense of Walker's leadership style. For a penetrating assessment of Walker's impact on the *Tribune* see Richard Kluger, *The Paper: The Life and Death of the New York Herald Tribune* (New York: Random House, 1986), 239–245.

14. Gould to Brewer, February 28, 1980, JLG Papers.

15. Gould to Brewer, May 21, 1980, JLG Papers. John L. Gould, "Federal Theater Speaks Through Its Director," New York *Herald Tribune,* July 5, 1936, copy in Jack Gould file, New York *Herald Tribune* "morgue," Center for American History, University of Texas.

16. Sam Zolotow to Jack Gould, February 16, 1972. Said Brooks Atkinson to Jack Gould, July 28, 1954, "You were committing almost daily nuisance by scooping us in the Tribune," JLG Papers.

17. Gould to Brewer, February 28, 1980, JLG Papers; "News and Gossip of the Night Clubs," *New York Times* (NYT) October 17, 1937. All of my father's byline stories are now part of the JLG Papers, courtesy of the generosity and kindness of *The New York Times.* Unless otherwise indicated, all *New York Times* stories quoted were written by my father.

18. The two quotations are taken from a five-page autobiographical memorandum that Dad prepared in the autumn of 1972 for a memoir about television that was never written, hereinafter called "Gould memo." Since he was writing from memory thirty-five years after the event, his reference to "Capone thugs" probably was a generic comment about organized crime figures in New York rather than a direct reference to the Chicago mobster.

19. Carmen Lewis Gould, autobiographical notes, JLG Papers.

20. Lewis L. Gould, *Progressives and Prohibitionists: Texas Democrats in the Wilson Era* (Austin: University of Texas Press, 1973), 202, 246; Jack Gould to Lewis L. Gould, July 8, 1973, JLG Papers.

21. Jack Gould to Carmen Lewis, September 1938, JLG Papers.

22. Jack Gould to Carmen Lewis, October 1938, JLG Papers; "The Terror of Park Avenue," *NYT*, November 6, 1938.

23. "Radio Music Dispute Raises Complex Issues," *NYT*, February 9, 1941; "Effects of ASCAP-Radio Dispute on Programs," *NYT*, January 12, 1941.

24. "Permanent Ban on Records Is Now Ordered by Petrillo," *NYT*, July 2, 1943; "Petrillo for New Law," *NYT*, August 15, 1943; "Portrait of the Unpredictable Petrillo," *New York Times Magazine*, December 28, 1947; Otto Kerner to Jack Gould, December 16, 1947, JLG Papers, ordering him to appear for the trial; "3 Newspapermen Heard at Petrillo Trial," New York *Herald Tribune*, January 1, 1948. Lewis L. Gould, "James Caesar Petrillo," in Kenneth T. Jackson et al., *Scribner Encyclopedia of American Lives*, vol. 1, *1981–1985* (New York: Charles Scribner's Sons, 1998), 637–639.

25. Leonard Miall, "The O.W.I. and the Fascist King," Leonard Miall Diaries, courtesy of Mr. Miall, who worked for the British Broadcasting Company during World War II. Holly Cowan Shulman, *The Voice of America: Propaganda and Democracy, 1941–1945* (Madison: University of Wisconsin Press, 1990), 100–101.

26. Gould memo; Louis Salbach, "Jack Gould: Social Critic of the Television Medium" (Ph.D. diss., University of Michigan, 1980), 14, copy in JLG Papers. My father's salary and job status are given in H. H. W. to Arthur Hays Sulzberger, May 10, 1946, NYTA.

27. "The Boys from Boise," *NYT*, October 8, 1944; "Contact with Moon Achieved by Radar in Test by the Army," *NYT*, January 25, 1946; "Moon Is Late for Demonstration of How It Is Reached by Radar," *NYT*, January 28, 1946. Meyer Berger, *The Story of the New York Times, 1851–1951* (New York: Simon and Schuster, 1951), 279.

28. Jack Gould, *All About Radio and Television* (New York: Random House, 1953); "Television: Boon or Bane," *Public Opinion Quarterly* 10 (fall 1946): 314–320. For an example of his work for *The New York Times Magazine*, see "The Paradoxical State of Television," March 30, 1947, in chapter 8 of this volume.

29. Gould memo.

30. James L. Baughman, "Take Me Away from Manhattan: New York City and American Mass Culture, 1930–1990," in Martin Shefter, ed., *Capital of the American Century: The National and International Influence of New York City* (New York: Russell Sage Foundation, 1993), 117–143; "Group Profile: The Critics," *Television Magazine* 11 (December 1954): 44.

31. Arthur Hays Sulzberger to Jack Gould, April 23, 1953, June 8, 1953, March 30,

1954; Gould to Sulzberger, March 30, 1954; Sulzberger to Turner Catledge, January 4, 1956, NYTA.

32. "A Critical Reply: An Answer to Objections Raised in the TV Industry to the Role of Critics," *NYT,* May 26, 1957 (first two quotations); "Where TV Critics Strike Out," *NYT,* May 19, 1957 (third quotation); Leon Morse, "Inside Jack Gould," *Television* 15 (November 1958): 94.

33. Morse, "Inside Jack Gould," 51.

34. "TV: New Phenomenon—Elvis Presley Rises to Fame as Vocalist Who Is Virtuoso of Hootchy-Kootchy," *NYT,* June 6, 1956.

35. Morse, "Inside Jack Gould," 94.

36. Joseph Derby to Jack Gould, April 13, 1971, and March 6, 1972. One of the few times he alluded to one of his sources, though not by name, was in Jack Gould to Carmen Gould, March 1966, JLG Papers.

37. Gould memo, except for the last Sarnoff quotation, which was conveyed to me in conversation during the 1960s.

38. "TV and McCarthy," *NYT,* March 14, 1954; Gould memo (quotation); A. M. Sperber, *Murrow: His Life and Times* (New York: Freundlich Books, 1986), 574–577.

39. Morse, "Inside Jack Gould," 50. "Disgrace of the Networks," *NYT,* October 31, 1956.

40. Gould memo. "On Faith Healing: Preacher's Timely TV Miracles Raise Questions About Station's Standards," *NYT,* February 18, 1956.

41. For my father's comments on blacklisting see the columns reproduced in chapter 2 of this volume. William L. Shirer, *20th Century Journey,* vol. 3, *A Native's Return, 1945–1988* (Boston: Little Brown and Co., 1990), 171; Shirer credits Dad with "guts" and says "he never ceased attacking *Red Channels* and exposing the hollowness and greed of those who caved in to it." The file titled "Subject: John Ludlow Gould, File Number Cross References," which the Federal Bureau of Investigation furnished me in response to a Freedom of Information Act request, contains a memo to J. Edgar Hoover dated September 28, 1954, from a blacked-out author; it notes that Dad had "criticized the security policy of CBS." Cartha DeLoach to "Mr. Mohr," February 15, 1965, has some critical remarks about my father's reaction to the series about the FBI that was on television at that time. See FBI File Number 94-8-51-464. The file of cross-references and related copies has been deposited with the JLG Papers.

42. Morse, "Inside Jack Gould," 50. His comments about his growing weariness

with television were common during the 1960s. See also Donald McDonald, "An Interview with Jack Gould, Television Critic of The New York Times" (Center for the Study of Democratic Institutions of the Fund for the Republic, 1961), copy in JLG Papers. For similar reactions to the predictability of television during the late 1950s see James L. Baughman, *Television's Guardians: The FCC and the Politics of Programming 1958–1967* (Knoxville: University of Tennessee Press, 1985), 20–30; James L. Baughman, *The Republic of Mass Culture: Journalism, Filmmaking, and Broadcasting in America since 1941* (Baltimore: Johns Hopkins University Press, 1992), 92–98; and Erik Barnouw, *Tube of Plenty: The Evolution of American Television*, 2nd rev. ed. (New York: Oxford University Press, 1990), 212–213, 236–237.

43. Glenn C. Altschuler and David I. Grossvogel, *Changing Channels: America in TV Guide* (Urbana: University of Illinois Press, 1992), 5–7, 30; the authors document *TV Guide*'s success by the end of the 1950s. For examples of the continuing dialogue about the television schedule see Arthur Hays Sulzberger to Turner Catledge, November 11, 1959, and Gould to Sulzberger, November 12, 1959, Turner Catledge Papers, Mitchell Memorial Library, Mississippi State University, Starkville, Mississippi, hereinafter called Catledge Papers.

44. Jack Gould comment in Mortimer Kroll to Jack Gould, July 15, 1954, and Turner Catledge to Gould, August 18, 1954, JLG Papers; Gould to Catledge, August 23, 1954, Catledge Papers.

45. Catledge told a friend that "even though I was trying to bring about his return, I didn't have the slightest idea it would work." Catledge to Sol Taishoff, October 1, 1954, Catledge Papers. Gould to Catledge, April 27, 1968, Catledge Papers, mentions the "Hotel Algonquin seance which retrieved me from the clutches of Stanton, et al." Gould to Sulzberger, September 28, 1954, JLG Papers.

46. Gilbert Seldes to Barry Bingham, January 1957, JLG Papers; John E. Drewry to Jack Gould, March 25, 1957, Catledge Papers.

47. "TV: Journalists' Junkets," *NYT*, October 27, 1959.

48. *New York Herald Tribune*, November 2, 1959; Richard F. Shepard, *The Paper's Papers: A Reporter's Journey through the Archives of the New York Times* (New York: Random House, 1996), 315–317.

49. "TV: Madison Avenue Case Study," *NYT*, December 29, 1959; "Significant Step," *NYT*, January 14, 1960; Michael Dann to Gould, January 14, 1960, JLG Papers.

50. *Times Talk*, November 1962; *NYT*, May 25, 1993 (Gould obituary). "TV Tube Bites TV Critic," *New York Times Magazine*, January 3, 1954.

51. "TV: Lively Panel Show," *NYT*, August 2, 1961; Gould to Louis Loeb, November 20, 1961, Turner Catledge Papers; Lord Day and Lord to Joseph Lewis, October 19, 1961, JLG Papers.

52. Turner Catledge, *My Life and the Times* (New York: Harper and Row, 1971), 237–248, deals with the changes in the paper's cultural coverage but does not mention my father or his situation. See also Gay Talese, *The Kingdom and the Power* (New York and Cleveland: World Publishing Co., 1969), 415.

53. "TV: News in Perspective," *NYT*, October 2, 1963; Ivan Veit to Gould, October 2, 1963, JLG Papers.

54. The anecdote about Catledge's reaction to my father's review is in the Eileen Shanahan interview, June 5, 1993, Washington Press Club Foundation, online at npc.press.org/wpforal/shan8.htm. Veit to Gould, October 2, 1963; Markel to Gould, October 4, 1963; Gould to Markel, October 5, 1963; Gould to Lewis L. Gould, October 10, 1963, JLG Papers; "Cactus Jack," *Time* 82 (October 11, 1963): 58.

55. The Johnson episode is recounted in Kathleen J. Turner, *Lyndon Johnson's Dual War: Vietnam and the Press* (Chicago: University of Chicago Press, 1985), 161.

56. Jack Gould to Carmen Gould, February 1966, JLG Papers.

57. Jack Gould to Lewis L. Gould, January 30, 1971, JLG Papers. "White House Aide Urges Major Changes for TV," *NYT*, October 7, 1971.

58. Newton Minow and Craig L. Lamay, *Abandoned in the Wasteland: Children, Television and the First Amendment* (New York: Hill and Wang, 1995), 29–30; this view is critical of my father's performance in this episode. The leaked copy of the conclusions from the Surgeon General's Report is in the JLG Papers. "TV Violence Held Unharmful to Youth," *NYT*, January 11, 1972.

59. Gould to A. M. Rosenthal, January 25, 1972; Gould to Clifton Daniel, February 17, 1972, NYTA.

60. "Gould Retires from the Times after 25 Years in Radio-TV Post," *NYT*, February 15, 1972; Fred Friendly, "Dear Jack Gould: They Say You've Retired," *NYT*, February 17, 1972. For an article that my father wrote after his retirement see "What public TV can be: 1. Britain's BBC," *Columbia Journalism Review*, July/August 1972, reprinted in *Vesper Exchange* 12 (September 1972): 1–5.

61. Gould to Lewis L. Gould, February 3, 1972, JLG Papers; Gould to A. M. Rosenthal, February 28, 1972, NYTA.

62. Gould to radio and television editor, February 28, 1972, NYTA; Fred Friendly interview, May 25, 1994.

63. Shepard, "Jack Gould, always retiring"; Julian Goodman to Jack Gould, February 15, 1972; Reuven Frank to Gould, February 16, 1972; William S. Paley to Gould, February 19, 1972, JLG Papers. See also Don Russell, "Former TV critic and set repairman," *Stamford (Conn.) Advocate*, May 28, 1993.

64. For evaluations of my father's work during his lifetime see "Big Men on the Papers," *Newsweek*, April 15, 1957, 104, 107; "Measuring the Giant," *Time*, November 9, 1959, 77; Maurice E. Shelby Jr., "Patterns in Thirty Years of Broadcast Criticism," *Journal of Broadcasting* 9 (winter 1966–1967): 27; and J. B. McGrath and Margaret Nance, "Television Reviewing: A Search for Criteria," *Journal of Broadcasting* 9 (winter, 1966–1967): 57–61. The most critical contemporary assessment of my father's work is by Patrick M. McGrady Jr. in "Television Critics in a Free Society," Papers of the Fund for the Republic, Seely G. Mudd Manuscript Library, Princeton University.

65. Gould memo. See, for example, William Boddy, *Fifties Television: The Industry and Its Critics* (Urbana and Chicago: University of Illinois Press, 1990), 8, 80–81, 85.

66. Karal Ann Marling, *As Seen on TV: The Visual Culture of Everyday Life in the 1950s* (Cambridge, Mass.: Harvard University Press, 1994), 169, 176, 180.

67. Gorham Kindem, *The Live Television Generation of Hollywood Film Directors: Interviews with Seven Directors* (Jefferson, N.C.: McFarland and Co., 1994), 174; Reuven Frank, *Out of Thin Air: The Brief Wonderful Life of Network News* (New York: Simon and Schuster, 1991), 78; Michael Kammen, *The Lively Arts: Gilbert Seldes and the Transformation of Cultural Criticism in the United States* (New York: Oxford University Press, 1996), 276.

68. David Bianculli, *Teleliteracy: Taking Television Seriously* (New York: Simon and Schuster, 1992), 59; Pat Weaver, with Thomas M. Coffey, *The Best Seat in the House: The Golden Years of Radio and Television* (New York: Alfred A. Knopf, 1994), 236; Phil Rosenthal, "Just Keep Those Questions Coming," *Los Angeles Daily News*, May 26, 1993. Another favorable appraisal of my father appears in R. D. Heldenfels, *Television's Greatest Year: 1954* (New York: Continuum Books, 1994), 10.

Chapter One

The Golden Age of Television Drama

The "Golden Age of Television" in the early 1950s was the heyday of live drama productions that originated from New York City and featured the plays of such writers as Rod Serling, J. P. Miller, and Paddy Chayefsky. My father reviewed the work of these dramatists as their plays appeared. A positive review often signaled whether an aspiring writer would succeed in the new medium. This first chapter of his columns represents some of his more important and enduring comments about television drama. It begins with Theatre Guild's production of *John Ferguson* in November 1947 and shows his reservations about the trends in television drama at the end of the 1950s. Here I include Dad's notices of the most famous plays of the period; in chapter 4 on his influence as a critic I include his intervention on behalf of *The Play of the Week.*

My father's criticism addressed the qualities that made for good television drama. He encouraged producers such as Worthington Miner and Fred Coe in their attempts to mold television into an effective way of presenting plays for a mass audience. The most controversial issue, and the one about which academic critics have been most scathing, was his preference for live drama over film and later videotape. In his mind, the spontaneity and excitement of live drama led to rewards for the viewer that no filmed or taped version of the show could provide. Yet he knew that technology and economics worked against his position. By the end of the 1950s he saw that the brief day of live drama had passed. His columns and reviews recapture some of the passion and excitement of that formative period of television's history.

Television Debut: Theatre Guild Makes Video Bow on NBC with Production of "John Ferguson"

November 16, 1947

The Theatre Guild, venerable doyen of the Broadway stage, ventured out in the strange, new world of television last Sunday night, and promptly fell on its art.

In its hour before the cameras at NBC, it offered a pretentious truncation of St. John Ervine's "John Ferguson," which left no emotion or electron unused. The result was more than a little as if "The Perils of Pauline" had been wired for sound and Stanislavsky.

The Guild's proprietors, Lawrence Langner and Theresa Helburn, allowed sentiment to get the best of them. Their choice of "John Ferguson" was dictated by the fact that it was their first Rialto success in 1919, a fact, incidentally, of which the television audience was reminded in a ten-minute Guild commercial before the curtain went up in Radio City. But television-wise it would be hard to find a more inept vehicle.

In the 28-year-old "John Ferguson" Mr. Ervine emerges as the daddy of the soap-opera writers. In three acts he works in the mortgaged homestead, the cowardly clerk who would lift the lien in exchange for the daughter's hand, the villain-mortgagor who ravishes the girl, the brother who avenges her honor and, of course, the lovable old father who says it is all God's will. There is enough to keep NBC and CBS going in the daytime for years.

Under the appalling direction of Denis Johnston, the Guild company, too, did not let a trick get by. There was breast-beating, grieving, crying, shrieking, foot-stomping, hand-waving, sneering, leering, sympathizing, feuding, fighting and fussing. Marconi sure wrought something last Sunday night.

Most of the Guild's difficulties stemmed from obvious unfamiliarity with the television medium. Instead of boldly capitalizing on the unique capabilities of the video camera, the Guild staff seemingly merely stood out on the apron of the stage and went to work as if holding a Brownie. The consequence was that the audience saw little more than a succession of slides. The Guild would do well to abandon the notion of many showfolk that television is just waiting for the blessings of stage techniques; many of the techniques simply will not work in video.

Basically, the Guild and Mr. Johnston got off on the wrong foot by what they did to Mr. Ervine's original script. In presuming to cut it in half, they settled for the straight narrative, leaving the element of characterization on whatever is the equivalent of the cutting room floor in the television business. The effect was to squeeze together one emotional peak right after the other until the whole was only an unrelieved succession of hysterical outbursts. It was an invitation to scenery chewing.

Without any restraining hand on the part of Mr. Johnston, the cast accepted the invitation. Led by Thomas Mitchell in the title role, the players to a man had a fine and frenzied time, unaware that the television camera magnifies a thousandfold even the slightest inclination to overplay. Apparently Mr. Mitchell despaired of the evening at the outset, never seeming even to get headed in the direction of a characterization of Ferguson and quickly settling for a caricature. For the first half of the program, Joyce Redman, who is of the English stage, held herself in check as the daughter, but finally succumbed to the undisciplined mood that prevailed.

Oddly enough, however, it was in the production end that the Guild seemed most ill at ease. In particular, there was practically no use of background music to give fluidity and emphasis to the major moods of the drama per se, the melodic scraps being confined to such unimportant sequences as the opening and closing list of credits. Admittedly, the Petrillo ban on "live" music in television imposes a handicap in this regard, but skillful employment of records and transcriptions would have been immeasurably helpful. The unrelieved tedium of mechanically reproduced voices, particularly when those voices are projecting deep brogues, made for an unnecessarily static quality. The extreme contrasts in the microphone levels for actors holding different stage positions also was most disconcerting.

In his employment of the cameras, Mr. Johnston held to an excessively conservative approach—favoring for the most part routine full-length views. His staging of the scene wherein the brother murders the villain was straight out of nickelodeon tintype and a long way from the effective television attained by the NBC, CBS and DuMont house staffs in staging similar episodes in the past. That the shotgun used in the murder should go off in dead silence and without a trace of smoke was inexcusably careless production. In 1947, too, it hardly seems unreasonable to ask that a view of a barking dog also be accompanied by a few audible barks.

All in all, the Theatre Guild's debut was most disappointing if only because so much hope had been raised by it. But in the long run last Sunday's performance may have served the eminently useful purpose of demonstrating with particular vividness that television is neither the stage nor the motion picture but a medium distinctive in its own right about which a great deal still has to be learned. Nobody in television, not even the Theatre Guild, is ready yet to ride no hands.

Matter of Form: Television Must Develop Own Techniques If It Is To Have Artistic Vitality

October 31, 1948

In the recent Town Meeting discussion of television's future, Rouben Mamoulian, the Hollywood and Broadway director, advanced the thesis that television could not be considered a new art form. Rather, Mr. Mamoulian held, television was merely a new medium of communication which drew its techniques from already well-established arts.

Superficially, Mr. Mamoulian may have a point. As has been noted practically since the first image appeared on a cathode tube, television combines the close-up of the motion picture, the spontaneity of the living stage and the instantaneousness of radio.

But it is difficult to go along with Mr. Mamoulian's apparent implication that because these older elements are present in video it necessarily follows that television is not new as an artistic form. Actually, it is in the fusion of these three elements, in the creation of a distinctive trinity of staging techniques, that television is wholly apart and unique. Conversely, it is the insistence of Mr. Mamoulian and others who think of television in terms of the older forms that offers a major handicap for video at the moment.

Television's claim as a new art form rests essentially on a factor which is not noticeable—and should not be noticeable—on the professional video production, but is most apparent in the case of the inept venture. This factor is the almost magical elimination of the proscenium arch, the structural arc in the theatre which traditionally has marked the dividing line between the "live" player and the audience.

The camera lifts the television viewer out of the usual orchestra or balcony seat and takes him directly into the group upon the stage. Unlike the "canned" Hollywood film, however, this is done without sacrifice of the qualities of spontaneity and sustained performance, which are the heart of true theatre.

What television has done, in short, is to introduce the elements of intimacy and immediacy to a degree scarcely imaginable before the advent of home theatre. For the writer, the actor and, most importantly, the director, this entails a whole new concept of compact craftsmanship, wasteful motion or wasteful thinking standing out like the proverbial sore thumb.

Television's craftsmen must work not in terms of an audience of hundreds or thousands at a given moment but in terms of the three or four persons who make up the average family group. Literally, video is the first form where both the artist and the audience fulfill their respective functions on a face-to-face basis, separated only by the width of the viewer's living room.

To suggest that this does not involve a distinctive and new form of theatre is palpably poppycock. The intensity of the television eye in grasping detail speeds up enormously the viewer's absorption, putting an unprecedented premium on the importance of personality and natural behavior before the camera. A gesture which on stage might go unnoticed or on the screen might be corrected can be of fatal consequence on television, as more than one radio and film personality already has learned when working without the protection of the unseeing microphone or unlimited "retakes."

But probably the chief difference between television and the other visual theatrical forms lies in the role of the director. In both the theatre and the films his work is finished before the curtain goes up. But in television he is the integral and unifying factor in the actual performance which the public sees.

Upon the director's choice of one of the several scenes simultaneously being picked up by different cameras depends the finished product projected on the home screen. For the first time, in short, the director, too, must always be "on stage" with all the uncertainties and responsibilities which it entails.

The most spectacular demonstration of television's unique artistic capabilities undoubtedly was Toscanini's initial telecasts, when the viewer could watch the extraordinary mobility of the maestro's face as he brought the NBC ensemble to full crescendo. And no matter what Hollywood may like to think to the contrary, an essential part of the audience's excitement over his performance was to witness it as it happened, not later.

More recently the Actors Equity-Philco Television Playhouse has demonstrated the extraordinary fluidity of movement and the fresh perspective which can be gained by not being subservient to the physical framework of the theatre. By bridging the gulf which the footlights represent, the television adaptations of "Dinner at Eight" and "Counsellor-at-Law" in particular made a participant rather than a spectator of the viewer at home, at the same time achieving that elusive extra dimension which made for depth and substance.

Ironically it was the Equity-Philco production of last Sunday, a video version of "Angel in the Wings," which vividly illustrated the pitfalls of being aware of the proscenium arch. The viewer at home was put out with the studio audience, and what happened on stage was merely photographed.

As a consequence there was almost wholly lost the wonderful pantomime artistry of Mr. Hartman, whereas in detailed closeup it would have made a rare visual treat. Similarly, by employing only conventional front-on views, the closing comedy dance by the Hartmans was seriously circumscribed in terms of movement and the subtleties of the routine all but obscured.

The consequences of lack of originality in television production are even more vividly borne out in the plethora of cases where recourse is taken to photographing what are little more than night club floor shows or radio programs. Practically without exception the results are awkward and stilted affairs, strange fish in even stranger waters.

However plausible Mr. Mamoulian's reasoning may sound in theory, it does not square with the practicalities which have become evident to those who have looked with some thoroughness at television. Video's future does not lie in supine acceptance of the belief that it is destined to be merely a transmission belt for Hollywood or Broadway. Its moments of greatness come when it projects old things in a new form.

"Julius Caesar": Worthington Miner's Version in Modern Dress Proves Spectacular Television

March 13, 1949

Let there be no quibbling this morning. Worthington Miner's production of "Julius Caesar" in modern dress, presented last Sunday evening over CBS, as part of the "Studio One" series was the most exciting television yet seen on the home screen—a magnificently bold, imaginative and independent achievement that stands as an event of the season.

What Mr. Miner did for sixty minutes was truly to "think with his eyes." With inspired disregard for the supposed limitations of video, he imbued the Shakespearean tragedy with a visual power and vitality that lifted television to the status of a glorious art.

Inevitably the production invited comparison with the memorable Orson Welles modernization of "Julius Caesar" in 1937 and, superficially, there were similarities. In each case the text was edited to a swiftly moving documentary on revolution that none the less retained its substance as a social document and theatre classic. On both occasions, too, Caesar and Antony and their followers wore uniforms and gave fascist salutes, the others in the cast being in street clothes.

But the existence of the Welles precedent cannot detract from Mr. Miner's triumph in television. In his production he went to the heart of video's needs, which is to make a picture and not take one. He fused movement, word and lighting into a creative imagery that vividly thrust his audience into the midst of the turmoil in Rome. Not until it was over did the viewer remember he was at home.

Scene after scene in the telecast was breath-taking in effect. The use of depth of field to overcome the camera's awkwardness in encompassing a wide stage was superbly illustrated in the staging of Brutus' oration over the body of Caesar. On the left hand side of the screen only the head of Brutus was visible as he spoke in the distance, the foreground being filled by the shoulders and backs of the crowd arranged in graduated perspective. On the right hand of the screen there was a pillar against which Antony stood in close-up, a cigarette hanging from his mouth as he smiled derisively and waited his turn to alter the course of events. The contrast in composition was overwhelming in its dramatic impact and visual artistry.

Mr. Miner achieved his climactic peaks, however, by the most sparing and simple employment of cameras. When finally Antony aroused the crowd to seek revenge on Brutus and the other conspirators, the action was not lost in the usual yells or the large panorama. Instead, Mr. Miner picked up the movement of the legs and feet of the crowd as it rushed off. The effect was virtually a ballet on mob hysteria.

Again, in his inventive final curtain, Mr. Miner offered a visual editorial on the irony inherent in the implementation of idealism by violence. First, the camera picked up Antony speaking of the "noblest Roman of them all." Then the viewer saw Antony's foot, rolling the body of Brutus into the street.

The intimacy of television was almost terrifyingly realized in the instance of Cassius. After he had planted the seed of revolution in Brutus, Cassius was shown in contemplative thought. His lips did not move, but his voice, recorded in advance, told that Brutus' "honorable metal may be wrought." At the same time, the camera relentlessly advanced from a full-figure view into a final close-up that showed only the scheming eyes of the master conspirator. If this technique of penetrating the mind is a familiar one in the films, it is a new experience when it comes in the stillness of one's own living room.

Much of the visual tempo was due to Mr. Miner's brilliant concept of setting, executed most skillfully by Richard Rychtarik. The center "stage" was bound by colonnades with seven separate archways, each separately lighted, which afforded astonishing variety in perspective. There was no conventional thinking in terms of the theatre's proscenium arch and walls; the emphasis was on movement in which the audience participated. "Julius Caesar" had the fluidity of the films and the actuality of the stage, which made it pure television.

Great credit must go to George Stoetzel for his lighting, which marked an epochal departure from television's prevalent tendency to work only in extremes of black and white. Using hardly a fraction of the candlepower which so often washes out an image, he achieved a symphony in delicate shadings that always implemented Mr. Miner's purpose and sustained the mood of tragic inevitability.

The cast rose to the occasion to equal degree. Philip Bourneuf's Antony was singularly outstanding. Possessed of a voice of rich timbre, he made Shakespeare seem present-day language and never once was guilty of overplaying, exercising a masterful restraint so that Antony would be remembered in terms of intelligence rather than emotion. As

Brutus, Robert Keith brought a knowing sensitiveness to his interpretation of the confused idealist. John O'Shaughnessy's Cassius was excellent in its discipline and naturalness and the Julius Caesar of William Post Jr. was becomingly straightforward. Vaughn Taylor's brief scene as Casca was of the highest order.

Cumulatively, in short, "Julius Caesar" provided a new insight into what television can be: the perfect integration of a host of older arts into a new form which stands on its own. It had the elusive quality of kaleidoscopic oneness, with its appeal being rooted in the unorthodox use of the orthodox tools of stage craft.

For the viewers who missed the original presentation and for the television industry as a whole, CBS has a very real obligation to present a repeat performance of "Julius Caesar."

A Plea for Live Video: Switch to Film for TV Was a Major Mistake

December 7, 1952

The decision of television to put many of its programs on film has turned out to be the colossal boner of the year. On every count—technically and qualitatively—the films cannot compare with "live" shows and they are only hurting video, not helping it.

From the standpoint of the viewer, which after all should be the determining criterion, the films are like having a cinder in the eye; you can still see but not without irritation. The much vaunted "improvement" in the reproduction of film on TV simply has not come about and the standard of the medium as a whole has been compromised.

To deal with technical matters first, the pictures on film, with very few exceptions, are just plain bad as compared with "live" TV. Almost invariably there is a grainy overcast on the home screen and the faces and figures lose all of the sense of added dimension that is felt with the "live" show. The lighting also is diffuse and fuzzy, never sharp and vivid as on "live" video.

The sound tracks on even the latest films especially made for TV are incredibly inferior. On "live" TV voices sound like voices and musical instruments sound like musical instruments, thanks to the high fidelity of frequency modulation. But the sound tracks come into the home sounding just what they are: second-rate recordings of speech and music that reach the ear with a tinny and artificial quality.

In short, both the visual and aural aspects of films lack that intangible sense of depth and trueness which the wizardry of science did impart to "live" TV. This season's trend to films simply does not make sense; it represents a step backward from the most up-to-date and satisfactory way of transmitting pictures through the air.

But where the TV films are most unsatisfactory is in terms of content. The proponents of motion pictures for video have argued that film would permit a larger panorama, an escape from the limiting confines of the studio. And further, they have argued, films would preserve all the magic of the true performance, yet eliminate all the fluffed lines, forgotten cues or other unpredictable mishaps.

Both arguments do have a genuine merit when the motion picture is treated as a creative art in its own right and permitted to do those things which no other medium can. The superb production by Henry Salomon, Jr., of "Victory at Sea" is one illustration; so was Richard de Rochemont's production of the homeward trip of the Abraham Lincoln funeral train, recently seen on "Omnibus."

Neither of the arguments, however, apply to the dog-eared films which Hollywood is turning out for television, the pedestrian little half-hour quickies that are cluttering up the facilities of even the best of networks.

The vast majority of TV films produced in Hollywood have precious little more "panorama" than the "live" shows produced here in New York. The plays or comedies on film take place in one or two sets and, except for westerns, the outdoor scenes are dragged in by their heels and seldom are of vital importance to the advancement of the narrative.

As for the alleged guarantee of perfection to be found in the use of films, that, too, is balderdash in the case of television, at least in the grade B jobs turned out thus far for the home screen.

The perfection is artificial and achieved only at the price of the reality and spontaneity that are part and parcel of the "live" performance, whether it takes place on television or on stage. There simply is no substitute for the intangible excitement and sense of anticipation that is inherent in the performance which takes place at the moment one is watching.

The supporters of Hollywood films for TV are raising a false cry—and sponsors are being seriously misled—if they think the uncertainties in a "live" show are to be avoided: they are what makes true television. No human being is always letter perfect and no viewer expects everyone on television to be. The unforeseen occurrence or the occasional mishap on stage are the best possible testaments of television's power to transmit actuality. Take away the actuality of television and there is lost the heart of TV. To regard television merely as a variation on the neighborhood motion picture house is to misunderstand the medium.

Anyone working in the creative side of television can vouch for the fact that there is a real yet subtly different state of mind in working for "live" television as opposed to films. The same difference has existed between the stage and the screen.

What makes the difference—players, musicians, stage hands and wardrobe mistresses feel it and so does an audience—is the witching hour of the theatre: the first night. The knowledge that there is a fateful moment of reckoning is both the exciting challenge and the exacting discipline to be found in genuine theatre.

The lasting magic of television is that it employs a mechanical means to achieve an unmechanical end. Producers and sponsors of films may not be aware of that fact, but viewers are. Perhaps it is time that viewers made themselves heard: bring television back alive.

NBC Playhouse Offers Valid and Moving Hour with Production of Paddy Chayefsky's "Marty"

May 27, 1953

Dramas that undertake to study of the lives of "little people" more often than not are tedious stuff, but the Television Playhouse, seen on Sunday evening over NBC, avoided most of the pitfalls and offered a theatrically valid and moving hour in its production of "Marty," an original play by Paddy Chayefsky.

Mr. Chayefsky's play was uneven and rather redundant in construction; apparently he didn't have quite enough to say for sixty minutes. But thanks to one of the better productions of the season and the casting of Rod Steiger and Nancy Marchand for the principal roles, "Marty" on the whole had an austere and tender artistry and caught the poetic element that can exist in even the most unglamorous and drab individuals.

Marty in effect was the masculine wallflower, the only child in a large

Italian family who had not married. He was a butcher by trade and in his middle thirties. He had none of the social graces and was tormented by a loneliness made more acute because everyone asked him when he was going to find a girl. His Saturday nights were haunted by the familiar refrain of those whose youth is passing and have yet to find a lasting companionship: "What'll we do tonight?"

Almost in desperation, Marty went to a cheap dance hall and there found a girl whom the sharp beau brummels of the neighborhood classified as "a real dog," a gangling awkward outcast. The halting and hesitant discovery by Marty and the girl that they have a rapport was the substance of Mr. Chayefsky's love story.

In much of his dialogue Mr. Chayefsky caught the touching pathos of his two principal characters. At moments he also painted in with a delicate and sensitive brush the plight of Marty's mother, who wants her son to be happy but dreads the day when her job of cooking and keeping house for others will be over.

Where Mr. Chayefsky faltered slightly was in overly sharp transitions and a tendency to telegraph in advance his climactic scenes. But if these shortcomings of craftsmanship weakened a little the cumulative power of "Marty" they were of minor moment in comparison to Mr. Chayefsky's disciplined appreciation of reality in everyday life. There seems scant doubt that more fine plays should be coming from his typewriter.

The role of Marty was Mr. Steiger's first starring assignment since his memorable bit as the radar operator in the Kraft Theatre's production of "My Brother's Keeper." While at times sounding uncannily like Wally Cox in "Mr. Peepers," he brought a controlled spontaneity to the part that was unusually effective. To imbue life and credibility into an intentionally flat character is never easy, but Mr. Steiger did it.

As the girl, Miss Marchand came very close to stealing the show. The qualities of numb pain and pathetic relief that she imparted to the girl represented acting of a very high order indeed.

Delbert Mann's direction has the sparing simplicity of a documentary and in the excellent dance hall scene had many fine touches, particularly the "shot" of the chic couple dancing by after a moving interlude with the unpreposing [sic] Marty and the girl.

"Patterns" Is Hailed as Notable Triumph

January 17, 1955

Nothing in months has excited the television industry as much as the Kraft Television Theatre's production of "Patterns," an original play by Rod Serling. The enthusiasm is justified. In writing, acting and direction, "Patterns" will stand as one of the high points in the TV medium's evolution.

"Patterns" is a play with one point of view toward the fiercely competitive world of big business and is bound to be compared with the current motion picture "Executive Suite." By comparison, "Executive Suite" might be "Babes in Toyland" without a score. For sheer power of narrative, forcefulness of characterization and brilliant climax, Mr. Serling's work is a creative triumph that can stand on its own.

In one of those inspired moments that make the theatre the wonder that it is, "Patterns" was an evening that belonged to the many, not only to Mr. Serling. The performances of Everett Sloan, Ed Begley and Richard Kiley were truly superb. The production and direction of Fielder Cook constituted a fluid use of video's artistic tools that underscored how little the TV artistic horizons really have been explored.

"Patterns" was seen from 9 to 10 P.M. Wednesday over the National Broadcasting Company's network; a repeat performance at an early date should be mandatory.

In his play Mr. Serling deals with the world that is the executive floor of Ramsey & Co. Ramsey, head of the firm, who is played by Mr. Sloane, is dedicated to the growth and expansion of the company's business; it is his way of life. His chief aide has been an executive named Andy, portrayed by Mr. Begley, whose perspective is influenced by human values. Brought into the company by Ramsey is an ambitious yet sensitive young executive named Staples, played by Mr. Kiley, whose destiny it is to supplant Andy.

The compelling strength of "Patterns" is in the determination of Ramsey to force Andy out of the firm not by firing him but by creating a succession of situations that will lead Andy to resign. It is the lot of Staples, anxious to hold his job, to go along with this strategy, distasteful though it is. At a conference Andy succumbs to a heart attack.

In the climactic confrontation Staples is ready to quit and be the heroic martyr but instead is challenged by Ramsey. In a gripping, ironic passage, Ramsey emerges as a fascinating if almost frightening disciple of competition for its own sake. He defies Staples to get his job and be a corporate conscience, but in any case demands that Staples help make the business grow. Staples accepts the arrangement. It is Mrs. Staples who senses the long-range implications; now her husband, too, always will be working late at the office.

In the role of Ramsey, Mr. Sloane was extraordinary. He made a part that easily might have been only a stereotyped "menace" a figure of dimension and almost of stature. His interpretation of the closing confrontation speech was acting of rare insight and depth. As Andy, Mr. Begley abjured the maudlin, yet caught the tragedy of the executive who is the victim of personality and policy conflict. Mr. Kiley was fine as Staples.

The supporting company was of the same high order, especially Joanna Roos as the secretary to both Andy and Staples.

Mr. Cook's direction was the work of a man who thinks with his eyes as well as his mind. His montages, especially several of his shots of the deserted executive floor, represented use of the camera to say something, not merely as an instrument of photography. Mr. Cook, shockingly denied screen credit under the Kraft Theatre's archaic rules, is a TV craftsman.

TV's Psychodrama: How to Keep 'Em Down on the Couch after They've Written for TV

August 7, 1955

A great deal of television drama is sick. Too many original dramas presented at choice evening hours are nothing more than dreary true confessions wired for sight and sound. The soap opera that once was heard in fifteen-minute stretches is now being offered in sixty-minute doses, and some eager beavers are suggesting that it's theatre. It isn't.

There's been much talk about how television is giving birth to an exciting new crop of writers. Well, there may be a few but not many more. Take a long look at the general run of TV drama and there's no disguising the truth. The TV medium is spawning a bunch of psychoneurotics who have found it more profitable to work off their frustrations on a typewriter than on a couch.

From the looks of the home screen a viewer has every reason to conclude that his set is being serviced by Oedipus. The writing boys, most of them, are frightened away by the demands of the stage. Heaven forbid that they should occasionally come up with a little entertainment. Let's face it, there's only one dominant theme on TV: life is hell.

The prescription for the prevalent TV drama of today follows a carefully set course.

First, there is the leading character. He must always be The Little Person in a Little Job in a Little Office who lives in a Little Home with a Little Wife and Little Children. He lives in a Little Neighborhood where there are Little Minds. For the dramatist, life in the Little World leaves the delightful illusion of a big grasp of life; you also don't have to write but very little.

Next, the writer maps out the construction of his work. In the first act he explains that the Little Person never was anything; in the second act, that he isn't anything, and, in the third, that he never will be anything. Progression on a treadmill is basic to the contemporary video art.

Now comes the time for the TV dramatist to show what sets him apart from the rest of mankind. Never, never must he leave the slightest doubt that he truly understands, that he has an absolute and uncompromising faith. As a TV writer he verily believes in mankind's highest aspiration: failure.

If the hero is tempted by a prospect of happiness, drag the poor slob back into his misery. If he has a chance for a promotion, let his wife ask, "John, should we?"

The concomitant of the hero's failure, of course, is the TV dramatist's most sturdy crutch: loneliness. A hero's lonely when he's in a crowd and when he's by himself. He's lonely, his girl is lonely, his friends are lonely. Everybody's lonely, including the television viewer.

From the dramatist's standpoint there is a very special advantage in using the lonely failure as the central figure. It follows logically that he also should be inarticulate. Thus there is no need for a dramatist to sweat out a scene that involves some reasoning, some resolution of a dilemma, some conflict or, as an extreme measure, some interesting dialogue.

With the inarticulate lonely failure the dramatist can forego playwriting and just let the director do his job. When a touch of tension, suspense or climax might be required, all that is necessary in a TV drama is to use a close-up. The quivering lips! The hurt eyes! The trembling throat! In the electronic age, the writer does not have to see into his character; the image orthicon attends to that.

What in the world has gone wrong with so much of TV drama? A few years ago it wasn't ashamed to recognize that every three months or so there might be justification to use a happy ending. Or that conceivably some stimulating and alive characters might be shown in a play. Or that there was a place for dialogue that had something to say wittily and tellingly. Or that a wisp of gaiety or a successful hero occasionally might not be amiss in a brief hour upon a stage.

Whatever the answer, TV's neuropsychological kick is getting to be a big bore. There always will be some starkly realistic drama, to be sure, and there always should be. But the TV producers and writers have gone overboard with their introversion business and it's getting to the point where amateur psychiatry threatens to supplant professional playwriting.

If nothing else, the video dramatist should recognize that he is not the only hot-shot in comprehending neurotic behavior. The viewer is no slouch either. You sure can't look at TV these days and not experience deep suffering and acute depression.

Cheese, Mustard Ad Also Stars on Kraft Theatre

December 1, 1955

The Kraft Television Theatre presented three thoroughly appetizing specialties last night, and no doubt viewers differed in their preferences.

Via the facilities of Channel 4 between 9 and 10 o'clock, there was offered initially a two-minute spectacular in which the tomatoes and macaroni and cheese were outstanding.

The second installment featured cheese slices arranged like the spokes of a wagon wheel.

For the finale there was deluxe mustard dressing.

The play? No.

"Requiem for a Heavyweight": Rod Serling's Drama Scores a Knockout

October 12, 1956

"Requiem for a Heavyweight" by Rod Serling, presented last night on "Playhouse 90," was a play of overwhelming force and tenderness. It was an artistic triumph that featured a performance of indescribable poignancy by Jack Palance in the part of the inarticulate has-been of the prize ring.

Mr. Serling wrote a searing, inspired indictment of the worst side of the prize-fight game, the greedy mortals who live off the flesh and blood of helpless youths who want to be champions. His play depicted the utter brutality and inhumanity of a so-called sport that can leave men in the wreckage of their own punch-drunk double talk.

The essential figure of "Requiem for a Heavyweight" was a fighter who fought once too often and was told by a physician that he could not continue. But his avaricious manager, having taken the boy's health, now covets his spirit; he wants to use him as a clown in a wrestling match.

Only a compassionate second arranges for the towering man to take a train home to Tennessee; the fighter then has visions of making some use of his life after all. But on the train he shows a little boy how to box, and in the process he starts refighting his own past matches.

The climax may have been a little obscure. It could have been interpreted that in helping the youth the fighter had found himself. Or that for some pugilists there never is an escape from the ring. Either way, Mr. Serling's play had immense power and poetry, and is certain to win many a prize.

Mr. Palance contributed a brilliant interpretation of the fighter. He projected the man's incoherence and bewilderment with a superb regard for details. To the huge and scar-ridden boxer he imparted a glowing and tragic humanness.

Ed Wynn, in his debut in a straight drama, was very good as the second who put the man's pride before the purse. His son, Keenan Wynn, playing the ruthless manager, was not quite so successful; he seemed neither smooth nor mean enough to be entirely convincing. Maxie

Rosenbloom had several very good scenes as the reigning monarch of the babbling hangers-on in a saloon patronized by former fighters.

Mr. Serling and Mr. Palance contributed a notable evening of theatre last night on Channel 2.

Study of Alcoholism: Piper Laurie and Cliff Robertson Are Impressive in "Days of Wine and Roses"

October 3, 1958

A searching and frightening study of the tragedy of alcoholism was contributed last night by J. P. Miller to "The Days of Wine and Roses" on "Playhouse 90." It was a brilliant and compelling work (Channel 2).

Piper Laurie and Cliff Robertson, portraying the attractive young couple who were ultimately driven apart by the bottle, added two memorable portraits as the victims of what began as social drinking and ended as a disease. Both portrayals should be remembered when annual awards are distributed in the spring.

Mr. Miller wrote a play of ascending power that carried its two principal figures steadily down the road of degradation, yet left a closing moral. For the alcoholic who will help himself, there is redemption; for the weak, only continuing despair.

In the "Days of Wine and Roses" Kristen and Joe Clay are New Yorkers—she a secretary and he a public relations man—who come from not altogether happy families. Both had their seeds of insecurity when they met and in alcohol and each other they found a prop for their morale.

With remarkable attention for detail and magnificent characterization, Mr. Miller showed the couple as alcohol slowly proved their master. They lied to each other and to the world, they fled from reality and they began the slow descent to personal chaos.

It was the man, with the aid of Alcoholics Anonymous, who gradually found the path back to respectability. But his wife could not come to face the world as it was and she still sought refuge in the haze. Mr. Miller's dialogue was especially fine, natural, vivid and understated.

Miss Laurie's performance was enough to make the flesh crawl, yet it also always elicited deep sympathy. Her interpretation of the young wife just a shade this side of delirium tremens—the flighty dancing around the room, her weakness of character and moments of anxiety and her charm when she was sober—was a superlative accomplishment. Miss Laurie is moving into the forefront of our most gifted young actresses.

Mr. Robertson achieved first-rate contrast between the sober man fighting to hold on and the hopeless drunk whose only courage came from the bottle. His scene in the greenhouse, where he tried to find the bottle that he had hidden in the flower pot, was particularly good. The difficult final scene when the young man had to send his wife away because he knew she could not yet walk the hard road beside him, had a heart rending impact in Mr. Robertson's delicate delineation.

In the supporting company were Charles Bickford as the girl's father and Malcolm Atterbury, who portrayed the helpful representative of Alcoholics Anonymous.

John Frankenheimer's direction was magnificent. His every touch implemented the emotional suspense, but he never let the proceedings get out of hand or merely become sensational.

This was a production by Fred Coe, who should feel very proud this morning.

Chapter Two

The Shadow of a Blacklist

The blacklisting of alleged Communists on American television during the 1950s is a less-known aspect of the McCarthy era. It represented an assault on the industry both from anti-Communist pressure groups and from fast-buck artists who sold "clearances" for performers accused of Communist ties. My father covered the hunt for reputed subversives in broadcasting from the moment it began in August 1950 with the dismissal of actress Jean Muir from the cast of "The Aldrich Family." General Foods dropped Muir because she became controversial when right-wing groups attacked her political connections of the late 1930s and her liberal allegiances in Hollywood and New York.

My father broke the story and followed the sad tale of Muir's descent into ideological and artistic obscurity. Throughout the decade that followed, he spoke out about the impact of "Red Channels," the so-called bible of anti-Communists, and the effect of Aware, Inc., the anti-Communist organization that portrayed itself as dedicated to ridding television of subversive influences in television productions, on the question of which actors got parts in television productions. He regarded Aware as simply a shakedown scheme to sell approvals of repentant Communists to the major networks. My father held no regard for Communism, and his columns often echoed the cold war consensus of the times. But when it came to a "Red purge" he displayed public outrage that people's lives and careers could be ended on the basis of unsubstantiated charges and public pressure. His reporting revealed the commercial and mercenary motives that lay behind much of the blacklisting campaign.

In these columns my father emerges as champion of civil liberties in the time of McCarthyism. His connection with *The New York Times* insulated him from some of the threats that came to those who questioned the wisdom of a mindless quest for Communists everywhere. Nonetheless, the archives of the *Times* and the materials about him in the FBI files reveal that many on the right labeled him an apologist for Moscow. As his columns on blacklisting make clear, his stance was rooted in traditional precepts of fair play and respect for individuals rights. His views appear in clearest perspective in his responses to John Pope, a University of Texas at Austin graduate student working on what would become in 1972 his master's thesis, "Trial without Jury: A Study of Blacklisting in Broadcasting."

Case of Jean Muir: Principles of Fair Play Yield to Pressure

September 3, 1950

The case of Jean Muir constitutes one of the more disheartening chapters in broadcasting's history. The precipitous ouster of the actress from the cast of "The Aldrich Family" has set off a chain of events which has had consequences of the utmost seriousness.

The sponsors and advertisers have put the future of the medium in the hands of a "kangaroo court" largely of their own devising. There now is under way in both radio and TV a "Red purge" which could lead anywhere. The minimum American standards of fair play have been thrust aside in timid appeasement of a handful of pressure groups. Incredible as it may seem, the sale of groceries has been regarded as more important than the due process of law.

Before taking up the details of the Muir incident it should be made clear that fundamentally the case has not involved the question of whether an actor's political sympathies should be a consideration in his employment. Important as that issue is—and undoubtedly it will come to the fore in the immediate days ahead—the controversy over Miss Muir has rested on a far simpler issue. She was presumed guilty without being given an opportunity to prove her innocence.

The Muir case first "broke" last Sunday night on the screen of NBC television. "The Aldrich Family" was scheduled to have its premiere at 7:30 and Miss Muir had been announced for the role of Mother Aldrich, formerly played by Lois Wilson. Without explanation the premiere was canceled.

Inquiry quickly disclosed that a number of anti-Communist groups had protested the appearance of Miss Muir. In all, the protests consisted of approximately fifteen or twenty telephone calls and a dozen or so letters. Included among those protesting was Mrs. Hester McCullough of Greenwich, Conn., who had been the defendant in the libel suit brought against her by Paul Draper, dancer, and Larry Adler, harmonica virtuoso. The suit ended in a hung jury.

Others were Rabbi Benjamin Schultz, coordinator of the Joint Committee Against Communism; Stephen C. Chess, Queens County Commander of the Catholic War Veterans, and Alfred Kohlberg, chairman of the American Jewish League Against Communism.

The protests were based on the fact that Miss Muir's name was included in a booklet called "Red Channels." This is a privately compiled and privately printed publication which purports to list the affiliations of some 150 artists with allegedly left-wing groups and Communist fronts. Much of its incriminating data is based on press clippings, letterheads and the files of the House Committee on Un-American Activities. It is published from the offices of American Business Consultants, 55 West Forty-second Street, and is edited by Theodore Kirkpatrick, a former agent for the Federal Bureau of Investigation.

"Red Channels" identifies Miss Muir as having been associated at one time or another with nine different organizations, either as a supporter or official.

A telephone call to Miss Muir only an hour or so after the cancellation of "The Aldrich Family" revealed that she had received no explanation for the move. The program's sponsor, the General Foods Corporation; its advertising agency, Young & Rubicam, and the National Broadcasting Company all declined to explain.

On Monday morning Miss Muir categorically denied that she was or ever had been a Communist or Communist sympathizer. She specifically denied that she ever had supported or belonged to seven of the organizations listed in "Red Channels." She acknowledged that she had belonged to two groups several years ago but had resigned when she suspected they were Communist fronts.

The General Foods Corporation, however, did not voluntarily invite Miss Muir and her husband, Henry Jaffe, who is counsel to the American Federation of Radio Artists, to present their side of the case. Only after Mr. Jaffe persisted most of the day did he finally receive—at the end of the afternoon—an audience with the corporation's representatives.

Then the actress was confronted with a fait accompli. The General Foods Corporation issued a statement explaining that because of the anti-Communist protests Miss Muir had become "a controversial personality." If she appeared on the program, the company said, she might antagonize prospective customers. The purpose of the firm's advertising, the statement added, was to attract as many customers as it could.

The corporation emphasized, however, that it was not passing judgment on the merits of the protests which it had received from Mrs. McCullough and others. It paid Miss Muir for the full amount of her contract, which had covered eighteen weeks.

The effect of the General Foods decision, of course, was very much to pass judgment on the merits of the protest. By dismissing Miss Muir the corporation did exactly what the protestors asked it to do. To take refuge behind the curtain of "controversiality" is to beg the issue.

By acting as it did, General Foods, with its enormous prestige and influence, put a policing power behind the allegations contained in "Red Channels." It lent the weight of reliability to charges which still remain to be substantiated and corroborated and admittedly were compiled by private parties with strong political feelings. Without having her day in court, Miss Muir has paid all the penalties—loss of job, earning power and reputation—which go with conviction.

If this policy is extended—and unfortunately it already has been to considerable degree—radio and TV no longer can call their soul and conscience their own. They will live under the shadow of a blacklist. The pressure groups, with their own personal standards of what constitutes a Communist sympathizer, will be the dictators of the airwaves. Then the legitimate and much-needed fight against the introduction of totalitarian methods in this country will have been lost on a major front. The Muir incident has helped the Communist cause, not ours.

Clearly, it is time that both the sponsors and the broadcasters took their courage and their faith in democracy in hand and recognized, no matter how reluctant they may be to do so, that they have been caught up in one of the major issues of our times. The Muir case is not just a radio and advertising matter. Rather it is a national question of whether common sense and ordinary standards of fair play are to prevail in this country.

The overwhelming majority of both executives and employees in radio and advertising belong to what might be loosely called the "political middle." With the rest of us, they abhor communism and rightism with equal vigor. It is time that this "political middle," which in a very real sense is America, began to assert itself. By our silence we are running the risk of being crushed between the two extremes. It is time that we made our influence felt because the Muir incident and its ramifications suggest that the hour may be much later than many of us had thought.

Again, "Red Channels": The Civil Liberties Union Revives an Issue

April 13, 1952

The controversy over "Red Channels" refuses to die. The incredible mischief wrought by the publishers of "Counterattack" in issuing their private list of persons whom they deemed sympathetic to communism or Communist fronts continues to be a matter of concern far transcending the broadcasting industry itself. This is as it should be.

The latest developments have come from the American Civil Liberties Union. First, there was the long-awaited publication last week of "The Judges and the Judged," an exhaustive study of the blacklisting of actors, writers and directors in radio and television, which was made for the union by Merle Miller (Doubleday & Company).

Secondly, there was the simultaneous action of the Civil Liberties Union in filing a formal complaint with the Federal Communications Commission against four television networks and two independent stations. The networks and stations were cited for allegedly either barring employment to individuals variously accused of being pro-Red or denying access to the microphone to persons out-spokenly anti-Communist.

"The Judges and the Judged," which is reviewed at length in today's Book Review of the Times, is an eminently comprehensive summary of the "Red Channels" case since that Sunday evening in August 1950 when Jean Muir suddenly learned that she had been ousted from the cast of "The Aldrich Family" because she had become "controversial."

Important as is the publication of "The Judges and the Judged," the concurrent step of the American Civil Liberties Union in filing a complaint with the FCC is perhaps of even more immediate interest. For this move represents the first tangible attempt to go a point beyond where the book ends—to do something concrete about the tacit blacklisting born of the eagerness of sponsors and networks to "stay out of trouble."

Whether the appeal to the FCC will amount to anything is highly problematical. The commission thus far has shown an inclination to sidestep the "Red Channels" matter, but the Civil Liberties Union has injected a new factor by naming names and making allegations against specific licensees of broadcasting stations.

Stripped of legal phraseology, the Civil Liberties Union in its complaint asks the commission to deprive a broadcasting station of its license if the outlet practices blacklisting itself or permits anyone using its facilities, such as an advertising agency, to do so. To guard against that contingency it would require a broadcaster to take an oath guaranteeing not to discriminate against any person on the basis of that person's political associations or beliefs.

Certainly the union's move is a novel one for broadcasting and in itself fraught with controversy. To go to the core of the situation, the union's position would mean that a broadcaster could not deny employment to a known and avowed Communist, assuming that the Communist was otherwise qualified for a job as an actor or writer, etc.

Since membership in the Communist party per se is not illegal, the position is tenable. But certainly the fur would fly if a Communist were to make a test case of the matter with the result that a broadcaster found himself directed by an agency of the Federal Government to provide employment to a Red. Under such circumstances what would be the broadcaster's civil liberties in the matter of employment? Oh, to be a lawyer!

In asking the FCC to make "a general investigation" of the consequences of blacklisting, the Civil Liberties Union manifestly assumes that such an investigation would not go beyond the blacklisting phase itself. Yet the whole history of the "Red Channels" case shows that this is not likely to be the case.

Sooner or later specific personalities are drawn into any inquiry or even discussion of "Red Channels" and there arises the question of separating the innocent dupes of the Communists from the practicing sympathizers. The idea of the FCC entertaining the slightest notion of adjudicating such matters is not very appealing from the standpoint of protecting civil liberties.

A further irony is that the complaint of the Civil Liberties Union employs some of the techniques for which "Red Channels" has been properly condemned. Thus, the American Broadcasting Company is cited because "it may have" kept two anti-Communist spokesmen off a program, but no mention is made of the fact that the same network has presented as vigorously anti-Communist documentary programs as any outlet in the country. The DuMont network is challenged on the failure to continue the employment of Hazel Scott, but is not given credit for running the Charlie Chaplin films which were dropped from WPIX, another station cited in the complaint.

In short, just as "Red Channels" gave a distorted picture of some individuals because of inadequate and incomplete investigation, the Civil Liberties Union in its complaint tends to over-simplify its indictment. For the immediate legal purposes of filing a complaint this procedure admittedly may be routine; in the court of public opinion, where the "Red Channels" issue is being fought out just as much, it is unfortunate.

Whatever the merits of its complaint to the FCC, the American Civil Liberties Union, by moving on several fronts at once, is performing a valuable service in keeping attention riveted on the problem of "Red Channels." In this connection, the filing of the complaint should stand as a warning to the broadcasters and the advertising agencies.

Both the broadcasters and the agencies long have expressed abhorrence of excessive Government control or any impingement on their own freedom. Yet to have the FCC in effect sit as arbiter of their employment practices would be their greatest setback in years.

By taking refuge behind the credo of controversiality as a means of avoiding the issue of civil liberties involved in the publication and use of "Red Channels" the agencies and networks have callously and cynically toyed with the basic freedoms of others. For having failed to defend their neighbor's freedom, their own now is threatened. It was always thus.

The Case of Lucille Ball: Treatment of the Star Should Be Standard in the Industry

September 20, 1953

Lucille Ball is an extremely fortunate woman. Apparently her career in "I Love Lucy" is not to be affected seriously by her acknowledgement that in 1936 she had registered to vote as a Communist. Her sponsor is standing by her; the Columbia Broadcasting System has announced that her television show will continue and many of her fans have written to make known their support.

This is as it should be, of course. Miss Ball said that she registered as a prospective Red voter only to humor her ailing grandfather, whom she described as "a Socialist." She insisted that she never had been a Communist.

Significantly enough, Representative Donald L. Jackson, Republican of California and member of the House Committee on Un-American Activities, revealed that the committee had known of Miss Ball's registration for over a year and had not thought it fair to divulge it. The committee was satisfied that the actress was not now and had not been a clear and present danger to the country and that there was no need to jeopardize her career for what essentially is an emotional act of seventeen years ago.

But in 1953 in the United States it is not always enough to satisfy a duly constituted Congressional body of one's loyalty. Self-appointed sleuths who reserve to themselves the right to judge a fellow citizen's patriotism pointed the finger at Miss Ball. And such is their persistence that the star's agony may not yet be over. One can never tell.

For the moment, however, Miss Ball has received all the breaks. Every effort was made to obtain her version of events before the damaging innuendo was spread from coast to coast. Once this was known, relative calmness and reason prevailed.

But in the radio and television industry last week one question was widely heard: what if the person involved had been plain Lizzie Glutz, an unknown actress with no hold on the affections of the millions of viewers and not the star of video's top-ranking comedy series in which there was an investment of millions of dollars? And the answer was unanimous: Lizzie Glutz never would have been heard from again. She would have been finished in radio and TV, a woman bearing the fatal brand of "controversial."

Consider some of the facts of record in Miss Ball's case. She registered to vote as a Communist and, according to an investigator for the House committee, voted in a primary in 1936. She did not vote in the general election. She was named to the California State Central Committee of the Communist party, but this was done, she explained, without her knowledge or consent. There had been testimony that Communist meetings had been held at her home, but it was noted that she had not been present.

Miss Ball was quoted as testifying in part: "How we got to signing a few things, or going among some people that thought differently, that has happened to us all out here in the last ten or twelve years, and it is unfortunate."

In broadcasting there are actors, writers and directors whose degree of involvement in Red causes might easily be construed as no greater than Miss Ball's and perhaps less. They, too, "got to signing a few things or going among some people" that, in retrospect, they wish they hadn't. If Miss Ball was a dupe for her grandpa, others were dupes for a friend or a good-sounding cause.

Unlike the comparatively clean-cut manner in which Miss Ball's case was handled, with everyone leaning over backward to presume her innocence before thinking of any question of her guilt, few in broadcasting have been accorded such fair and equitable treatment.

Too often the mere act of accusation has been enough to leave a permanent cloud over an artist's career. The whim of a grocery man who writes letters or self-appointed experts on a fellow citizen's thinking and loyalty have been sufficient to brand an individual "controversial" and, for all practical purposes, unemployable.

Blacklists still exist today and their use is often a consummate mystery. On the same network an actor may be "cleared" for one show and not for another. A gifted actress who had the honor of playing the lead on the opening of an important new series—with no adverse mail, incidentally—cannot be cleared for the part of a walk-on on another chain. Is she a loyal artist in one studio and a dangerous traitor in another?

Writers may not be permitted credits but their work will be accepted sub rosa. One individual reportedly had to engage an attorney at substantial cost to make clear his loyalty; his name had been put in a network file of unemployables through error. Another individual futilely has sought a hearing. But the network in question stands by its indictment, its decision and its sentence, which is no work.

In Miss Ball's case there were rumors, an investigation, an explanation and a clearance. But for lesser fry in broadcasting the procedure often works quite differently. The telephone merely stops ringing. To avoid even a chance of controversy or difficulty the sponsor or a network may just ignore the challenged individual. And the employer is, of course, perfectly within his rights to hire whom he wants. Such is the viciousness of the blacklist once it takes hold; it is a weapon to which there is no practical counter-strategy.

But the main contention of the users of blacklists has been that it is only smart business to avoid "controversy" lest it offend a possible customer for a sponsor's product. Under this unconscionable credo it makes no difference whether the individual is guilty or innocent, whether he has an explanation or not. The mere fact that he is involved at all often means his undoing.

Once the apprehension of sponsors over "controversiality" became known, pressure groups and self-appointed guardians of national security had a literal field day. They threatened boycotts of advertised wares and sponsors quaked in their boots.

In this respect, Miss Ball's experience is enlightening. For once the accusation and rebuttal became known simultaneously and the public had an opportunity to judge an act for itself. Did millions of viewers as one man swear to forego Philip Morris cigarettes because seventeen years ago Miss Ball registered as a Communist voter? To the contrary, after hearing all the facts, they deluged her with wires of support.

No doubt, this may have been largely emotional reaction and further evidence that everyone does love Lucy. But one still cannot help but wonder if the fear of boycotts is not largely in the minds of those who subscribe to the use of blacklists and private loyalty files of dubious reliability.

Miss Ball is indeed a lucky girl. That she is may be the true lesson to be drawn from the whole incident. The courteous and fair treatment which she was accorded should not be unique but rather should become standard for cases of this kind.

Broadcasting should study Miss Ball's case to see whether perhaps it does not provide a formula for handling its loyalty problem with far more maturity and equity than previously have been displayed. The procedure that is available to the biggest star should also be available to the bit player in similar trouble.

Fifth Amendment: Danger Seen in Union Plan to Punish Members Claiming the Privilege

July 31, 1955

The American Federation of Television and Radio Artists has under consideration a critically important proposal designed to combat Communist influences in broadcasting. Unfortunately, there has been little or no discussion of the measure, yet it merits the most searching and careful study before its adoption.

The proposal, upon which performers must vote by 5 P.M. on Aug. 8, is concerned with an actor who refuses to tell a Congressional committee whether he is or was a member of the Communist party.

Under the terms of the suggested resolution a performer pleading the Fifth Amendment may be subject to charges of conduct prejudicial to the union's welfare. The accused may be investigated and the charges heard by the union's board. In its discretion, the union may fine, censure, suspend or expel the accused, subject to such appeals as are provided in the federation's constitution.

The resolution and the vote assume a special urgency because the House Committee on Un-American Activities is scheduled to open hearings in New York on Aug. 15. The committee already has subpoenaed a number of television and radio performers.

A word on the background of the resolution is pertinent. It is an outgrowth of an existing rule on the West Coast branch of the AFTRA that makes it mandatory for the local union there to take action against a member pleading the Fifth Amendment. Three actors in California are under indefinite suspension as a result.

The new resolution was advanced and adopted by the union's national executive board immediately after the membership voted condemnation of Aware, Inc., a private anti-Communist group, on the basis of the methods it has used. Frank Nelson, AFTRA president, noted that the proposed resolution, if approved by the membership, would show all Government agencies the desire of the union and its members "to cooperate in the drive to keep Communists out of the union's field."

It is unfortunate that the proposed resolution should be linked to the Aware fight. The measure should be examined unemotionally for itself.

In considering the resolution there must be a distinction made between holding union office and holding union membership.

Where officers and candidates for office are concerned, a union has an obligation to give pause if they plead the Fifth Amendment. While no inference of guilt can be legally attached to a performer invoking his privilege, his act does leave unresolved the question of his involvement.

When such an actor is running for or holds a policy-making position—a sensitive post, in short—the union would seem to have every right to make inquiry as to whether or not there are other factors bearing on his fitness for office. If the individual does not display candor toward those whose trust he solicits this of itself could be justifiable grounds for denying him eligibility to hold a responsible assignment. When there is no legal jeopardy involved an individual aspiring to leadership can be asked properly to resolve a situation that he left up in the air when there was a threat of self-incrimination.

When the terms of the resolution are applied to union membership, however, a different set of circumstances comes into play. The AFTRA has a union shop with the networks and major stations; this means that an individual actor must be in good standing if he is to work.

In short, if AFTRA prefers and then sustains charges against a member pleading the Fifth Amendment, this means that an actor could be deprived of a livelihood because he chose to invoke a privilege guaranteed him under the Bill of Rights.

This is an extreme sanction and, in this corner's opinion, represents an abuse of the federation's power of the union shop. Under the resolution AFTRA could economically disfranchise a citizen who had not broken the law but had merely sought the protection of the law.

It is one thing for an employer to reach his own decision as to an individual's employability; the Constitution does not offer an individual pleading the Fifth Amendment protection from the social and economic consequences of his act.

But it is quite another for a union to remove officially a person's elementary right to work on the basis of its own judgment as to the propriety or wisdom of that person's perfectly legal behavior. How such a stipulation squares with the Taft-Hartley Law, with its provisions for safeguarding individual workers, certainly should be studied.

In the resolution the AFTRA board comes uncomfortably close to equating a plea of the Fifth Amendment with an admission of guilt. If the proposal means what it says, an actor is subject to accusations before an inquiry, not afterward. To assume in advance that an individual has no valid reasons for invoking a Constitutional privilege hardly inspires confidence in the board's fundamental understanding of a principle that goes back to the Magna Carta of 1215.

In this connection it should be noted that the AFTRA resolution runs counter to the position of many large and strongly anti-Communist unions which have constitutional bans on a Red being a member, but concede the legal right of a member to plead the Fifth Amendment.

The AFTRA national executive board unquestionably was sincerely motivated and this corner believes, in a strong position in urging cooperation with the House Committee. But it does seem altogether possible to be intelligently anti-Communist without going to hasty extremes on which many attorneys of a conservative leaning have serious reservations.

In any case, it is regrettable that AFTRA elected to ask its members to vote on such a difficult and complex proposal without any discussions of its possible good or bad features, or without mailing its members statements by responsible attorneys reflecting different viewpoints.

Whatever may be the honest differences of opinion on dealing in a democratic society with the problems posed by communism, on one count there always should be agreement. Adequate information is a prerequisite to a sound decision.

Report on Blacklisting: Fund for the Republic Study Dealing with Radio-TV Is Found Deserving of Commendation and Censure

July 1, 1956

The report on blacklisting in radio and television, issued last week by the Fund for the Republic, has revived the complex controversy over civil liberties and communism in matters of employment in broadcasting. The document so far has drawn commendation and censure; both are deserved.

The report was prepared by John Cogley, former executive editor of The Commonweal, and is part of a broader study of blacklisting; a separate report on the Hollywood motion-picture industry was issued simultaneously. Copies of the report sell for $1.25 each and may be obtained at the fund's office, 60 East Forty-second Street.

The study of the radio-TV phase is recommended reading. The book runs to 287 pages and covers a great deal of ground. It is not, frankly, easy reading. The material is very poorly organized and tends to ramble. The amateurish editorial organization has hurt the volume's clarity and, accordingly, limited its broad educational usefulness. But for those willing to wade through the many chapters there is information and opinion of pertinency and value.

Mr. Cogley details the private groups and individuals who set themselves up as authorities on communism—the publishers of "Red Channels," Aware, Inc., Vincent Hartnett and Laurence Johnson, et al. He enumerates the private "security officers," lawyers, "public relations counselors" and other executives who were or are engaged in providing "clearances" for some artists and exile for others.

Mr. Cogley goes into the cases of mistaken identification or false evidence that have had cruel consequences for the individual concerned.

Instances of giant corporations virtually panicking in the face of a handful of organized complaints or threatened boycotts similarly are related. Indeed, the best parts of the book are those explaining how the business world was practically cowed into submission by a carefully generated hysteria.

In a foreword to the book, Paul G. Hoffman, board chairman of the Fund for the Republic, asserts that Mr. Cogley has brought in no indictments. Most readers will probably disagree.

It is Mr. Cogley's chief conclusion that blacklisting of personnel is now thoroughly "institutionalized" and a basic way of life in broadcasting. Under the guise of avoiding controversy, some sponsors, agencies and networks are sitting in private judgment on fellow citizens and presuming to decide whether they are Communists, former Communists, sympathizers, dupes or innocents.

In so doing, the American business interests that constitute the radio-TV industry are assuming the burdens of government, Mr. Cogley maintains. If they assume those burdens, he says, then they must accept the companion responsibility of dispensing justice.

"They cannot have it both ways," Mr. Cogley continues. "They cannot argue on the one hand that economic considerations come before all else, and on the other, speaking glowingly of the contribution 'business statesmanship' is making to a business-oriented democratic society."

If this isn't an indictment, surely it is very close to one. The conclusion is neither novel nor difficult to reach. All the questionable lists and private investigations in television obviously would not exist without their endorsement and use by sponsors and advertising agencies of influence.

Unfortunately, the study does not adequately reflect the climate of public opinion that existed at the start of blacklisting nor does it make sufficiently clear that the practice was part of the larger problem of coping with communism within the framework of a democracy.

A reader might also wish for a deeper probing of the complex factors that lie beneath the mechanics of blacklisting. Mr. Cogley tiptoes around the very basic question of whether or not political matters should enter into a judgment of an artist's qualifications for a job.

Is there a distinction to be drawn, for instance, between a playwright endeavoring to advance Communist ideas and a performer merely playing a part in a play already approved by a sponsor? Even liberal groups have suggested that there is. In such a case, when is a sponsor blacklisting and when isn't he? There are a host of such thorny yet genuine issues that need examination.

The major importance and contribution of Mr. Cogley's is in showing how the many interests in radio and TV did not recognize the enormous gravity and complexity of the industry's whole problem. Instead they abdicated their responsibility and citizenship to outsiders, many of them emotional zealots who acted as prosecutors, judges and parole officers. Television became engulfed in a labyrinth of intrigue, suspicion, opportunism and fear. Standards of patriotism were a dime a dozen.

But Mr. Cogley's report is not without a number of faults. Primarily, the Fund for the Republic was at a disadvantage in sponsoring such a study. Its feelings on blacklisting were common knowledge before Mr. Cogley began his study. As a consequence, many doors in the industry were closed to Mr. Cogley's researchers and reporters. The industry may have been shortsighted in its policy or merely hopeful of avoiding more controversy, a forlorn hope at best. But, in any case, Mr. Cogley's study is hardly a model of reportorial objectivity.

The report takes recourse to much undocumented and anonymous material; damaging allegations are made against specific persons without substantiating evidence. In at least two instances, Mr. Cogley's reporters did not ask those who were damned for their version of a specific incident. It was this same lack of elementary reportorial responsibility that was a reprehensible practice of "Red Channels." More unvarnished hard facts and less editorializing would have both strengthened its acceptance in those quarters where it might do the most good.

In light of the vastness of his subject, Mr. Cogley could not be expected to touch on all phases of blacklisting. But it is a pity he did not include a more penetrating analysis of Aware, Inc., at least some mention of former Communists who lied in order to obtain the support of honest liberals, a more generous acknowledgment of those business men who have sincerely sought to cope with blacklisting and an account of the indescribable tragedies that have consumed whole families during the long industry controversy.

Ironically, the Fund for the Republic study indulges in a bit of "clearing" in its own right. In using either the names or initials of some individuals, its version of their alleged political pasts is at variance with what has been cited elsewhere. The report may have the straight facts; a layman is hardly in a position to judge. But the report's reference to past political behavior pinpoints the true central problem of blacklisting once it starts. Even those most violently opposed to the practice find themselves sooner or later answering and fighting back on the blacklister's terms.

What will be the practical consequences of the issuance of the report? Every time the blacklisting issue is raised in the newspapers sponsors grow more sensitive and apprehensive. In recent months it is generally agreed that the blacklisting situation has been very much better, though by no means entirely eliminated.

In the long run, however, the more information that can be obtained about the problem the sooner it is apt to be resolved. There are at least two court cases pending. If they ever come to trial and the whole matter of blacklisting is spread out on the record for all to see, it could well be most illuminating and helpful. For the entire matter of blacklisting has been largely fought out, discussed and written about in an inhibiting vacuum of anonymity and darkness. That has always been the most frightening aspect of the difficult situation.

What a Blacklist Means: A Review of John Henry Faulk's "Fear on Trial"

November 22, 1964

The dark and ugly era of blacklisting in radio and television, the forbidding mid-1950s when a massive industry put itself in the hand of a few self-appointed patriots, is recounted in John Henry Faulk's report of his harrowing experiences in the jungle of accusation and suspicion.

"Fear on Trial" is an important book because it is by far the most detailed and specific recital of how the blacklist worked, the sinister chain of events that began with undocumented political charges against an artist, extended to economic intimidation of sponsor and broadcaster—and so often ended with the exile of the individual, without hearing or compassion. All the sordid ingredients of the period—the subordination of honor to expediency, the debasement of patriotism for commercial profit and the lasting agony of the blacklist's victims—are set forth in a capsule example of McCarthyism at work.

Yet "Fear on Trial" is also something of a disappointment. Mr. Faulk's voluminous material cries out for clearer organization, and he is not overly successful in bringing to life the other principles in the drama of tragedy and triumph of which he was a part. With more scholarly research and less haste he might have written the definitive history of vigilantism in broadcasting. He settled for a personal document that is of substantial interest as far as it goes, but falls short of the full opportunity that was his.

Mr. Faulk, of course, is the humorist who lost his job as a radio performer with the Columbia Broadcasting System after his name appeared in a pamphlet issued by Aware, Inc., a group that described itself as anti-Communist and sought to purge artists of which it disapproved. He decided to strike back and instituted a suit against Aware, Vincent Hartnett, who compiled the lists which generated panic on Madison Avenue, and the late Laurence Johnson, the supermarket owner of Syracuse, N.Y. Mr. Johnson threatened sponsors with loss of sales, if they used actors whose loyalty he questioned.

"Fear on Trial" is the diary of Mr. Faulk's ordeal—until six years later, he was vindicated by a jury award of $3,500,000 in damages. The heart of the book is the trial of his libel action—in which Louis Nizer, working for a fraction of his normal legal fee, relentlessly exposed the blacklisting for what it was, a cynical disdain of elemental decency that was couched in phony patriotic trappings and vicious disregard for fair play.

The heartening side of the book is the number of individuals, including Edward R. Murrow, Thomas D. Murray, Charles Collingwood, Mark Goodson, and David Susskind, who defied the TV-world's cowardice—and, in different ways, supported Mr. Faulk's one-man battle to assert the rights of the individual. On the distressing side is the way prominent corporations surrendered to the vigilantes, lest their ratings or income be disturbed.

It is not to detract from Mr. Faulk's courage to suggest that (in a legal sense) he was actually fortunate. He, at least, could establish a direct connection between loss of his job and the blacklist. Many other artists, some of greater stature, could not prove such a connection. Their tragedy was one that no lawyer and no court could alleviate. Their telephones simply stopped ringing. The dimension of their sufferings dwarfs anything related in "Fear on Trial."

Blacklisting's Effect: Censored Tape of Jean Muir's Remarks on '50s Travails Shown on ABC

January 15, 1965

The tape of Jean Muir's discussion of the blacklisting of actors finally reached the television screen at 9 o'clock yesterday morning. The American Broadcasting Company's censorship of her remarks took out virtually all pertinent facts and made it appear that the actress had been victimized by anonymous bogeymen. TV had a sorry 10 minutes on Channel 7.

Miss Muir was invited weeks ago to appear on the Virginia Graham show "Girl Talk," and was not advised that there would be any limitation on the scope of her remarks. But after the discussion was recorded the ABC lawyers held up the tape on Christmas Eve and then applied their scissors.

On the screen Miss Muir was heard describing how she suddenly was discharged as a "controversial" person in 1950. A handful of persons earlier had objected to her appearance on the screen because her name had been included in "Red Channels," a pamphlet purporting to have anti-Communist objectives, she said. Miss Muir then explained her personal ordeal that was to follow, first alcoholism and divorce and then full recovery of her health and sense of humor.

What a viewer did not hear from Miss Muir yesterday morning was the title of the show from which she was dismissed without a hearing; it was "The Aldrich Family." The viewer did not hear the identity of the sponsor that did the dismissing; it was the General Foods Corporation. The viewer did not hear which network concurred passively in her discharge; it was the National Broadcasting Company. The viewer did not hear the name of the individual to whom Miss Muir carried her protest in 1950; it was Clarence Francis, former chairman of the board of General Foods.

Attorneys for ABC Films, Inc., the subsidiary that produces "Girl Talk," justified the deletions on the ground of possible libel and damage to companies and individuals. It is not a layman's function to second-guess a lawyer perhaps, particularly when the exact transcript of Miss Muir's original remarks have not even been given to the actress, let alone anyone else. Miss Muir did see the cut version and raised no objection to its presentation.

But if there was any question of libel the remedy was simple. Miss Muir could have been asked to return to the studio and rephrase her remarks about the General Foods Corporation, NBC and Mr. Francis in such a way as to allow her to document her case within the everyday standards of fair comment and still calm the nervousness of ABC's lawyers. It is the total blackout of all names that is most unwarranted.

The censoring of the tape, known in the trade as "blooping," was very cleverly done and probably went unnoticed by most viewers. But whatever might accrue to ABC and "Girl Talk" for considering the issue of blacklisting in the first place was vitiated by the end result.

The great evil of the blacklisting of artists on the grounds that they were "controversial" and might hurt a sponsor's sales was the secrecy with which the practice was followed in broadcasting's highest and most respected circles. The conspiracy of silence, the self-same cloud of anonymity that reappeared yesterday, was the main feature of the industry's dark hour. Miss Muir and far too many others were made completely unemployable by unseen men relying on lists prepared by commercial patriots, some of whom peddled "clearances" for a fee.

The advance editing of "Girl Talk" did have the one reward of once again illustrating the futility of censorship. By deleting material facts, ABC has called attention to them far beyond what would have prevailed if the show had been quietly shown. But the important point is that once again, after 15 years, Miss Muir's individual rights have been made subordinate to cynical corporate pleasures. Surely by this time Miss Muir is entitled to civilized hospitality from television, not just its blooped courtesies.

Jack Gould to John Pope

October 13, 1971

Dear Mr. Pope:

I'll try to be as helpful as I can though one's memory can play tricks.

(1) Blacklisting in TV was primarily commercial in nature coupled with a few political overtones. It emerged at the time of McCarthyism and was based on threats not to buy a sponsor's product. Counter-Attack, as you know, was founded by ex-FBI agents, one of whom at least, I believe, genuinely thought there was a Communist under every bed. The compiler of "Red Channels" was Vincent Hartnett, who lost in court to John Henry Faulk but not before ruining his radio career. In

my judgment Hartnett was concerned mostly with the fees he charged agencies for "clearances."

At this point in history there were genuine Communists in TV, the theatre and Hollywood and I knew many of them. With the possible exception of one individual, now dead, I never regarded them as a menace to the country. Many show people at the time wore their emotions on their sleeves and were searching for their own way to alter the Establishment. This was and still is characteristic of show people and certainly they are not to be confused with dynamite throwers, etc.

The commercial element was introduced by the Syracuse supermarket operator named [Laurence] Johnson, who threatened to remove from his shelves products of manufacturers hiring those listed in "Red Channels."

If memory serves, the political element came when someone in Washington, possibly J. Edgar Hoover, characterized CBS as the Communist Broadcasting System. Of all networks CBS took the worst licks because they did employ the most liberals. Many of us in the trade did feel at the time that Jack O'Brian, then associated with the Journal-American, psychologically at least contributed to the death of [CBS correspondent] Don Hollenbeck.

(2) To the best of my knowledge Jean Muir is still alive. She suffered severe alcoholism after the "Red Channels" episode but subsequently straightened herself out. Ironically, she was married to Henry Jaffe, the attorney, who initially was very liberal and then subsequently wrote the by-laws and constitution for Aware, Inc. Later they were separated and, I think, divorced. He is an attorney and TV package producer on the West Coast; Dinah Shore is one of his clients.

(3) What little patriotism was attached to TV blacklisting was far outweighed by the fast-buck and purely commercial considerations. I recall asking the late Clarence Francis, then chairman of General Foods, if he ever lost any money from employing Jean Muir. His answer was, "No." Jello was her sponsor on "The Aldrich Family."

(4) "Red Channels" was the heart of those blacklisted in radio and it carried on into TV which was to prove the undoing of [Joseph R.] McCarthy, first by the Murrow show and then by the Army hearings. I know there were a few blacklisted who did not appear in "Red Channels" but at the moment I cannot recall them. Each network had a specialist in clearances. Many promising careers were wrecked because of lost momentum by being out of the spotlight for several years. Larry

Adler, the harmonica virtuoso, and Paul Draper, the dancer, have never been invited to appear on a network show.

(5) I was never seriously threatened either by Aware or Counter-attack, even though, I think, The Times was the first to break the story wide open.

[A paragraph in which my father gave John Pope the address of writer Allen Sloane has been omitted.]

Jack Gould to John Pope

October 31, 1971

Dear Mr. Pope:

Laurence Johnson was a rich and vain zealot. I believe his son-in-law or son was killed in the military service, which was the reason for his blind patriotism. At the same time he enjoyed the attention which was bestowed on him by the big-wigs of industry and communications.

Vincent Hartnett was the greedy one. He not only generated business for himself among the networks and advertising agencies but, I have been told, was quite willing to sell a "clearance" to someone mentioned in the Daily Worker or included in "Red Channels."

The true evil of Hartnett was that he interrupted the momentum of God knows how many careers. I don't think anyone who was blacklisted ever regained his old drive. Certainly, there were some Communists in "Red Channels" but I talked personally to many of them and could not find one determined to blow up the country.

As for the networks the situation varied at each chain. Moreover, at the height of McCarthyism, it must be remembered that advertising agencies still exerted great control over shows. The list of BBD&O [Burton, Barton, Durstine and Osborn], for example, carried enormous weight.

At CBS the most influential guy was Danny O'Shea, a former motion picture producer and a vice-president. In the case of [Allen] Sloane, for instance, he intervened with the Archdiocese of New York which, in turn, made arrangements for the FBI and Congressional committees to hear his confession. He was "cleared" independently of Hartnett.

CBS openly has a "loyalty oath" which was always widely misunderstood. The network didn't think the oath per se was worth too much. But after the oath had been signed and should it be disclosed an individual was involved in Communist or Communist-front groups he could be quietly dismissed for perjury. CBS had an ex-FBI agent constantly on the prowl—I forget the guy's name—because Columbia really had the jitters.

NBC and ABC had separate guys assigned to comb through cast lists, etc., but were much less noisy in their activities. At the moment I forget the names of the individuals but would suggest you contact Robert E. Kinter, former president of both networks. He is living in the Georgetown section of Washington. If you promise anonymity and can cope with alcoholic excesses from time to time I think he might help. We were very close friends so you can mention my name if it will help. He knows the score and has, of course, the added advantage of being a former newspaper man. I should warn you he is a close friend of LBJ's so stick to broadcasting.

I would be extremely surprised if you received any answers from the networks. The whole period was broadcasting's darkest chapter and they want to forget it. Such was TV's strength and novelty that to the best of my knowledge no one of influence was hurt in the slightest.

I have talked privately with most of the key figures at networks and some agencies and I believe all are now a bit ashamed. It was an extremely ugly period when a great many decent men succumbed to panic because of possible loss of income.

Your thesis is certainly timely because all the books I have read on the era have seemed second-rate to those of us who were in the midst of the matter.

Chapter Three

The Rise and Fall of Edward R. Murrow

A continuing story during my father's career as a television critic was the emergence of Edward R. Murrow of the Columbia Broadcasting System as one of the most powerful and articulate voices in the early years of television journalism. Dad covered Murrow's transition from an internationally known radio figure in the late 1940s with his *Hear It Now* program (done in partnership with Fred W. Friendly) to the team's debut on television on *See It Now* in 1951.

Just how close my father and Murrow were personally is hard to say. Dad's friendship with Frank Stanton was well known and probably made Murrow cautious about getting too close to my father. Murrow and Stanton were bitter rivals at CBS, where they clashed over news coverage, the use of polls, and the network's emphasis on entertainment profits. To say that the two men disliked each other was an understatement. Murrow and my father seem to have talked on the phone about industry issues, and Dad was well informed about the commentator's status at CBS.

During the 1950s Dad was a sympathetic observer as Murrow and Friendly took on Senator Joseph R. McCarthy (Republican from Wisconsin) in 1953 and 1954. My father's columns about Murrow's program on beleaguered Air Force Lt. Milo Radulovich and his later, more famous attack on McCarthy in 1954 enhanced the credibility of *See It Now* and its views. At the same time, my father warned of the dangers inherent in advocacy broadcasting from individuals less responsible than Murrow and Friendly. Dad later told interviewers that while Murrow deserved credit for his program, it was the televised Army-McCarthy hearings that proved fatal for the Wisconsin lawmaker. "That coverage did McCarthy in," my father remarked.[1]

While he liked and admired Murrow, my father recognized that the broadcaster was a shrewd businessman and entertainer. Murrow's program *Person to Person* anticipated modern celebrity journalism and paid its star handsomely for his weekly visits to the homes of the famous. Dad's columns address how Murrow balanced his own stardom with his instincts for hard-hitting journalism.

In the end, my father played a small but decisive role when Murrow's connection with CBS turned sour in the late 1950s. On October 15, 1958 in a speech to the Radio-Television Directors Association, Murrow delivered a blast against corporate sponsorship of network news and urged that more time be devoted to public service programming. In the wake of the episode, Murrow took a yearlong sabbatical. While he was away, television went through the scandal over quiz shows, an issue that Frank Stanton took on when as CBS president he addressed the same group to which Murrow had spoken a year earlier. Stanton saw his chance to curb Murrow's influence and get revenge for the commentator's attacks on his stewardship of CBS. Stanton promised that the network would avoid misleading practices in the future.[2]

A CBS public relations executive then alerted my father that Stanton wished to elaborate on his remarks. Calling his old friend, Dad learned that the strictures in Stanton's speech included Edward R. Murrow and *Person to Person*, which had sometimes used pre-arranged questions for its guests. The front-page story that resulted outraged Murrow and led over the next year to Murrow's departure from the network to join the administration of John F. Kennedy as director of the U.S. Information Agency. Murrow died four years later in 1965 of the effects of lung cancer.[3]

When Murrow left broadcasting in early 1961, my father assessed his impact on the medium in very favorable terms. Later in life he spoke of Murrow's "long and bizarre relationship with Bill Paley and how both were devoured by the sheer growth of CBS."[4] Dad felt an identification with Murrow because both men represented an idealistic vision of television news that left the medium poorer when it disappeared.

Edward R. Murrow's News Review "See It Now" Demonstrates Journalistic Power of Video

November 19, 1951

A striking and compelling demonstration of the power of television as a journalistic tool, lifting the medium to a new high in maturity and usefulness, was provided yesterday afternoon with the premiere of Edward R. Murrow's program "See It Now" (3:30 P.M. on CBS).

In its emotional impact, sensitivity and drama, the commentator's thirty-minute review of the week's news was in all respects a magnificent achievement—absorbing in its exploitation of video's technical capabilities and human and revealing in its understanding and point of view.

At the very opening of the program, Mr. Murrow did more to demonstrate graphically the potentialities of video than ever had been done before. For the first time the viewer sitting at home was able to see the waters of the Atlantic and Pacific oceans on the same screen. With a flick of the switch in the studio, a camera in San Francisco picked up the Golden Gate Bridge; then a camera in New York showed the Brooklyn Bridge.

Slowly the San Francisco camera switched over to Alcatraz Island and it was followed by a sight of New York's skyline. On the West Coast the scene changed to Telegraph Hill and the San Francisco skyline; back here the camera picked up the Statue of Liberty and the Narrows leading out to the Atlantic.

In less knowing hands than Mr. Murrow's, the simultaneous pick-ups on the two coasts might have been only an amazing stunt, but he also pointed the meaningful moral: television is a medium to be approached in humility.

The body of the news program was on film, much of it especially taken for the program, but, thanks to the editing of Mr. Murrow and his colleague, Fred Friendly, it was a far cry from a conventional newsreel. There were "shots" of Prime Minister Winston Churchill speaking in London, of the ordinary person's deep desire for peace. From the United Nations in Paris there was shown Foreign Minister Anthony Eden's affirmation of British support of honest disarmament proposals.

But it was a filmed colloquy between Mr. Murrow and Howard K. Smith, Columbia's correspondent in France, that gave the sequence a sense of immediate reality. Mr. Smith noted wryly that "mutual ill will is entirely unimpaired," but that more countries were bringing their international problems to the U.N., in itself a forward step for civilization.

On the home front, Mr. Murrow showed a hilarious bit of film involving Senator Robert A. Taft of Ohio, candidate for the Republican Presidential nomination. It was a close-up of the Senator's face while he was attending a dinner at which Senator Everett M. Dirksen of Illinois declared that the next President must be first an American and then a Republican. The look of complete satisfaction on Mr. Taft's face at that moment was a classic visual cameo. And Mr. Murrow let it speak for itself.

The last half of the program was devoted to a documentary film that CBS had taken in Korea. It showed all the hardship, good humor, and tension of the average soldier's existence at the front. The film was tough and real, but always thoughtful. And Mr. Murrow's sparing comments cut to the viewer's heart. When the film showed the GI's digging their foxholes, he remarked: "If you dig before dark, you have a better chance of living until light."

Then came the climax. One by one the soldiers stepped before the camera and merely gave their name and home town. Mr. Murrow reported on what had happened to the company since the film was made: fifty casualties. With searching eyes Mr. Murrow looked straight at the camera and said that some of the wounded might need blood. "Can you spare a pint?" he asked.

To television, in short, finally has come Mr. Murrow's rare feeling for the value of understatement in reporting the news and telling the facts as they are. Those qualities obviously were a source of inspiration for all who contributed to the success of "See It Now" and, more important, to the persons privileged to watch their efforts.

Television had a taste of its true glory yesterday.

Murrow's "This Is Korea" Film over CBS Captures Poignancy and Frustration of Life in Battle

December 29, 1952

A visual poem that caught the poignancy, frustration and resolution of life on the front lines of Korea was presented last night on "See It Now" by Edward R. Murrow in a special film over the Columbia Broadcasting

System's television network. It was one of the finest programs ever seen on TV.

Mr. Murrow and a large staff of CBS reporters and camera men shot the film in Korea on Christmas Day and the days immediately preceding. The film then was flown back to this country and edited by Fred W. Friendly in record-breaking time. When the film went on the air at 6 o'clock, it represented the culmination of months of preparation and an expense of at least $75,000, shared by CBS and the program's sponsor, the Aluminum Corporation of America.

The finished work, called "This Is Korea, Christmas 1952," was a masterpiece of reportorial artistry, a documentary that in its sensitiveness caught at the heart-strings of the viewer at home. For Mr. Murrow and his colleagues were only incidentally concerned with armaments, airplanes and guns; their interest was people and what these people did under the grim realities of an unfinished war.

Mr. Murrow and Mr. Friendly wisely did not attempt to tell any cohesive story of the war or put together the various parts of their film in any predetermined order. Rather they let the cameras catch the many facets of life both on the front lines and behind—a glimpse here and glimpse there. Together, the pieces fitted into a unified mosaic that gave the persons sitting thousands of miles away at home a sensation of participating in the ordeal overseas. It was an experience; it also was a lesson.

The brilliance of the film lay in the old-fashioned leg-work of Mr. Murrow and his associates. The sheer number of places and people visited in Korea bordered on the phenomenal. And it was the little items of authentic detail thus gathered that gave "This Is Korea" its quiet and understated impact. In more ways than one it was war seen in close-up.

The spirit of "This Is Korea" can only be related by listing some of the more vivid camera cameos that were shown: the girl in Korean Army uniform singing "Silent Night" as she flew over enemy territory; the French officer who kept shrugging his shoulders as he observed that no one knew how to end the war; the GI's singing "I've Got the Rotation Blues," and the sight of a wounded soldier being flown to a ship's hospital by helicopter.

Also, the Ethiopian soldiers playing their own version of field hockey; the Negro soldier smiling through his watery eyes as he extended Christmas greetings; the taciturn Britisher explaining how the war is really fought at night; the bitter complaints of everyone against the endless mountains; the conduct of religious services in the open as planes fly overhead; the picture of American soldiers giving presents to Korean children; the uncertain fate of mail intended for American prisoners, and, lastly, the sight of a patrol receiving its final instructions before trudging out to face the enemy.

As is the custom of "See It Now," the commentary of Mr. Murrow and the other CBS reporters was taut yet understanding, human yet free of the slightest trace of the maudlin. "This Is Korea" had that most elusive of qualities that always has distinguished "See It Now": exciting dignity.

Celebrity Time: Murrow Puts Cameras into Their Homes in "Person to Person"

October 7, 1953

If names make news, people make television programs. Fresh proof of the adage is afforded by Edward R. Murrow's new program, "Person to Person," which is being presented at 10:30 P.M. Fridays over CBS. By the simple process of taking the cameras into the homes of different personages, the presentation offers interesting TV.

"Person to Person" is a kissin' cousin of the NBC network's series of conversations with elder leaders in many fields. But where that series is done on film and has been mostly interested in an individual's general philosophy of life, "Person to Person" is done on a "live" basis and offers a brief glimpse of how people live, as well as what they think.

Technically, the new Murrow show is tricky, albeit not too intrusively so. All the bulky equipment for a "live" pick-up is set directly in the homes of the persons to be interviewed. Mr. Murrow is seated in a studio and looks at a large screen, framed as a window, on which he sees the person to whom he talks over a distance of some miles. The camera serves as Mr. Murrow's eyes, just as it does the viewer's.

For the premiere Mr. Murrow visited two homes. The first was that of Roy Campanella, the Brooklyn catcher, in the St. Albans section of Queens. The second was that of Leopold Stokowski, the orchestra conductor, and his wife, Mrs. Gloria Vanderbilt Stokowski, in Gracie Square.

The program opened in the living room of Mr. Campanella's home, and then switched to his trophy room in the basement. There, Roy casually displayed some of the awards he had won, talked about an ill-fated fishing trip, explained how many hours of sleep a star catcher needed (eight hours), mentioned his household routine and discussed the world series (the program was on the day he had hit the home run that won the third game).

The visit lasted only fifteen minutes, but at the program's conclusion a viewer did have the feeling that he had come to know Mr. Campanella. The catcher's warm personality and wonderful smile came over very vividly on the screen. And his casual chit-chat with Mr. Murrow brought out the human being behind the celebrity.

The visit to the Stokowski home made for an excellent contrast after the stop at Mr. Campanella's house. The celebrated couple explained that one end of their living room was reserved for Mrs. Stokowski's art, the other for Mr. Stokowski's music. Mrs. Stokowski showed several of her paintings and explained how they had evolved spontaneously from her inner emotions.

Mr. Stokowski played a few bars at the piano, expressed his preference for "long hair" in both his wife's coiffure and music, showed his somewhat disorganized studio and dutifully carried around a microphone. If the cameraman and Mr. Murrow slighted the maestro a trifle, they can hardly be blamed. Mrs. Stokowski is strikingly videogenic.

"Person to Person," however, will have to find ways of overcoming the stiffness and formality that were noticeable during the visit with Mr. and Mrs. Stokowski. The motivation behind the show should be a casual call, not a state visit.

In the advance announcements of "Person to Person" it was said that the program would concentrate on famous personalities. This Friday the cameras will be taken to the homes of Valentina, the fashion designer, and Col. Earl "Red" Blaik, West Point football coach.

Television already is too celebrity-conscious. "Person to Person" will be missing a real bet for fascinating viewing if it does not, at least occasionally, give some time to individuals who are not household names. The unsung doctor, teacher, chorus girl, construction worker, storekeeper and Wall Street clerk also could make absorbing interviews.

Up to now such persons usually have been seen only as Exhibit A on quiz shows; television could introduce no greater novelty than to show them as they really are.

Video Journalism: Treatment of Radulovich Case History by "See It Now" Is Fine Reporting

October 25, 1953

Edward R. Murrow's presentation of the case of Lieut. Milo Radulovich, who is threatened with dismissal from the Air Force because of anonymous charges of pro-Communist sympathies against his father and sister, was not just a superb and fighting documentary (10:30 P.M. Tuesday over CBS). It was a long step forward in television journalism.

The program marked perhaps the first time that a major network, the Columbia Broadcasting System, and one of the country's most important industrial sponsors, the Aluminum Company of America consented to a program taking a vigorous editorial stand in a matter of national importance and controversy.

The measure of Mr. Murrow's achievement, which occupied the full half-hour last week of his regular program, "See It Now," can only be judged against the background of broadcasting's usual approach to what it likes to call "public service."

Nine out of ten documentaries on the air work themselves into a great fury of indignation over matters about which there scarcely can be any argument. Juvenile delinquency is deplored and so is traffic in narcotics, poor schooling, failures to vote, etc.

Similarly, radio and TV are inclined to add the weight of their influence to the resolution of an issue after the matter already has been more or less settled. A community which overthrew rule by gangsters and politicians is wildly applauded, but when the town really needed help—in the midst of the battle—broadcasting all too often had been found timid and wanting.

It was this illusory and often deceptive approach to public service that Mr. Murrow and Fred W. Friendly, co-editor of "See It Now," unhesitatingly threw over. Instead, they embarked on a bold bit of enlightened crusading and offered their help at a time when it would count the most.

Both in word and picture the story of Lieutenant Radulovich was told factually, tersely and completely. Before the TV camera the officer explained how an Air Force trial board invoked the distasteful principle of "guilt by relationship." Though his own loyalty was not in question, he was deemed a "security risk" because of his sister's political activities and his father's subscription to a pro-Tito Serbian newspaper.

But the truly disquieting aspect of the case, which Mr. Murrow altogether properly emphasized, was the denial of even a semblance of a true trial. The evidence, including the identity of the accusers, was not revealed even to Lieutenant Radulovich and his counsel. They were expected to disprove the charges without being informed of their substance.

Mr. Murrow left no stone unturned to provide complete coverage. The viewer saw and heard not only the lieutenant, but his wife, his sister, his father and an attorney. There were "man-in-the-street" interviews with an anti-Communist union official who was convinced that the father had no pro-Red views, with a former American Legion official who disapproved of the Air Force trial methods, and with a woman who got up petitions in the lieutenant's home town of Dexter, Mich.

Especially vivid was the concluding sequence with Lieutenant Radulovich as he insisted that could not break his blood ties with his father and sister, that he did not see how he could be responsible for the views of other adults, that he wondered whether his own youngsters in later years would be adjudged "guilty by relationship." Would they bear the stigma of a father deemed a "security risk"? For these reasons, he explained, he would exhaust all avenues of appeal against the decision.

Mr. Murrow patiently explained that "See It Now" had been unable to obtain the Air Force's version of events, any more than newspapers had, but stressed that "See It Now" was ready to give full broadcast time if the Air Force later should choose to clarify matters.

Then, in measured words and with masterfully restrained anger, Mr. Murrow put the decision to his audience. What was to be the relation between the state and the individual in a day when we want to protect the security of the country but also the freedom of the individual? He admitted to no pat solutions but suggested that there was something all citizens could do. "Argue about it endlessly," he said.

The editorial position of "See It Now," in short was against the curtain of silence which so often has descended on difficult security questions.

For this inspired documentary, which saw the Aluminum Company forego its middle commercial, Mr. Murrow was at his journalistic best and with reason. He was dealing with a story that was alive and he reflected that intangible sense of excitement and urgency which comes with being on top of the news. "See It Now" demonstrated that there is no substitute for truly original reporting that is unafraid, perceptive and mature. Everyone connected with the program can be proud.

Murrow vs. McCarthy: "See It Now" on CBS Examines Senator and His Methods

March 11, 1954

Edward R. Murrow's television program on Senator Joseph R. McCarthy was an exciting and provocative examination of the man and his methods. It was crusading journalism of high responsibility and genuine courage.

For TV, so often plagued by timidity and hesitation, the program was a milestone that reflected enlightened citizenship on the part of the Columbia Broadcasting System and, particularly, the Aluminum Company of America who paid the bill to make it possible. No voice is braver than those who enable it to be heard.

On "See It Now" (10:30 P.M. Tuesday, CBS) Mr. Murrow brought vigor, conviction, and craftsmanship to the preparation of his indictment of the controversial legislator. His chief witnesses were Mr. McCarthy's own words, gestures, and mannerisms as recorded on film and sound tape. The Senator's most useful tools, Mr. Murrow suggested, were Congressional immunity and the "half-truth."

Yet the program was no less an indictment of those who wish the problems posed by the Senator's tactics and theatrics would just go away and leave them alone. Whether a viewer approves or disapproves of Senator McCarthy, he could hardly help but react to Mr. Murrow's challenge. That was Mr. Murrow's and television's triumph, and a very great one.

There need be no quibble about the point of view of "See It Now." By itself Mr. Murrow's program was strongly one-sided. But the alternative to not handling the story in this manner was not to do the story at all, by far a greater danger. The Senator seldom has shown relish for letting others do the cross-examination.

As it was Mr. Murrow made unmistakably clear at the program's outset that Senator McCarthy could have equal time to address himself to the points raised on the program. As the only person who can answer, Mr. McCarthy must decide whether to complete the record. Mr. Murrow can only invite, not subpoena. It will be interesting to see how the Senator pleads.

In "See It Now" Mr. Murrow and Fred W. Friendly, the co-editor of the program, took up the many facets of Senator McCarthy's activities in several stages.

The program's "working thesis," as Mr. Murrow called it, was that if the fight against communism was made into a fight against the two great political parties, one party soon would be destroyed and the Republic could not long survive. These words were taken from a speech by Senator McCarthy seventeen months ago.

Yet last month Senator McCarthy spoke of the "twenty years of treason" and said "those who wear the label of Democrat wear the same historic betrayal."

"See It Now" showed Senator McCarthy once explaining that his "cup and heart is so full" he could not talk. In contrast he was shown at no loss for words in describing a general as not fit to wear the uniform. Mr. Murrow took up the Senator's charge that the left-wing press was against him. Fifty large-circulation papers, including the most conservative, actually were against the Senator by a ratio of 3 to 1 on the Zwicker case.

Mr. Murrow presented on film Senator McCarthy's calculated quip accompanied by a giggle against Adlai E. Stevenson: "Strangely, Alger —I mean Adlai***" This was followed by detailed documentation that Mr. Stevenson had nothing to do with a barn in Lee, Mass., though the Senator had clearly implied it showed a Communist tie-up. Similarly, the irrelevancy and prejudice of much of the Senator's questioning of Reed Harris were detailed.

After documenting his case, Mr. Murrow offered his telling summary of its meaning. It speaks for itself:

> No one familiar with the history of this country can deny that Congressional committees are useful. It is necessary to investigate before legislating, but the line between investigating and persecuting is a very fine one, and the junior Senator from Wisconsin has stepped over it repeatedly.
>
> His primary achievement has been in confusing the public mind as between internal and external threats of communism.

We must not confuse dissent with disloyalty. We must remember always that accusation is not proof and that conviction depends upon evidence and due process of law. We will not walk in fear one of another. We will not be driven by fear into an age of unreason if we dig deep in our history and our doctrine, and remember that we are not descended from fearful men, not from men who feared to write, to speak, to associate and to defend causes that were for the moment unpopular.

This is no time for men who oppose Senator McCarthy's methods to keep silent, nor for those who approve. We can deny our heritage and our history but we cannot escape responsibility for the result.

The actions of the junior Senator from Wisconsin have caused alarm and dismay amongst our allies abroad and given considerable comfort to our enemies, and whose fault is that? Not really his, he didn't create the situation of fear, he merely exploited it and rather successfully. Cassius was right: "The fault, dear Brutus, is not in our stars but in ourselves."

"See It Now" Finale: Program Unexpectedly Ends Run of Seven Distinguished Years on CBS

July 8, 1958

An era in television ended unexpectedly last night; "See It Now," one of the medium's most distinguished programs, gave its final performance. A seven-year run, not just another season of TV, came to a close.

The demise of "See It Now" became known as the team of Edward R. Murrow and Fred W. Friendly offered a fascinating study of the rise of West Germany since the end of World War II.

Next year Mr. Murrow and Mr. Friendly will be engaged in the production of "Small World," a weekly half-hour series, which by means of film will present prominent figures in different parts of the world in a joint conversation.

Inquiry last night revealed that the title of "See It Now" is to be dropped, but that Mr. Murrow and Mr. Friendly may do a few long documentaries in the same general style.

"See It Now" has been on the air for seven years and has been noted for its willingness to deal in depth with controversial issues; its program on the late Senator Joseph R. McCarthy occasioned world-wide headlines. Mr. Murrow and Mr. Friendly have had virtual autonomy in their operation. Their new program, "Small World," will come under the aegis of CBS News.

But "See It Now" also has been a symbol of one of the TV industry's dilemmas. While its quality and contribution to a viewer's understanding of current affairs have been widely hailed, the program this season did not attract extensive sponsorship, even though it is very expensive to prepare. A somewhat tighter TV economy has forced review of many public service programs.

In CBS circles last night it was contended that dropping of the title "See It Now" did not mean that the Messrs. Murrow and Friendly could not duplicate their past successes under some other title. But skeptics noted that title changes sometimes can be indicative of fundamental policy changes in TV. Last night it was confirmed that the fate of "See It Now" had involved protracted high-echelon conferences at the network.

Whatever next season may hold for them, Mr. Murrow and Mr. Friendly dropped the curtain on "See It Now" in triumphant style. Their study of Germany, entitled "Watch on the Ruhr," was visual reporting of crispness and discernment.

The most vivid moment was the scene of a German audience leaving a performance of "The Diary of Anne Frank"; the theatregoers left in stunned silence after being reminded of the country's shame under Nazism.

"See It Now" briefly showed some of the horrors of the Hitler era and illustrated the great prosperity that West Germany since has earned. The program examined the economic, political and military ramifications of Germany's rebirth. Industrialists and Government leaders were interviewed, and there was an intriguing "bull session" with young students on the matter of reunification of East and West Germany.

"Watch on the Ruhr" is precisely the useful type of informative journalism for which "See It Now" always has stood. One can only hope that CBS next year will leave no stone unturned to assure that the Messrs. Murrow and Friendly can continue to deal in their own way with questions of substance.

"Harvest of Shame": Exploitation of U.S. Migratory Workers Is Documented on "CBS Reports"

November 25, 1960

The shocking degradation and exploitation of millions of human beings who pick the fruits and vegetables that are served on America's richly laden dinner table were shown last night on "CBS Reports" over Channel 2.

"Harvest of Shame," narrated by Edward R. Murrow, and produced by David Lowe, was uncompromising in its exposure of the filth, despair and grinding poverty that are the lot of the migratory workers who follow the sun from Florida to upstate New York and from Mexico to Oregon.

Mr. Murrow described the plight of the roaming laborers as "The grapes of wrath of 1960"; the program proved it.

Mr. Lowe, working under the over-all supervision of Fred W. Friendly, executive producer, spent months in following the fruit and vegetable pickers as they made their northward circuits. With his cameras he showed real-life scenes that could add up only to a terrifying blot on Democracy's escutcheon.

Humans were shown stacked vertically in trucks for trips of hours and hours while the products they picked were shipped in streamlined trains and refrigerated trucks. The hovels called homes, one-room shanties for large families working near Princeton, N.J., and Riverhead, L.I., were contrasted with the lush stables for race horses.

The faces of the migratory workers were their own eloquent editorial on a national disgrace. There were young women who looked like aged wretches; bright little children with no hope of a decent education; men and women, both white and Negro, with no apparent hope of experiencing minimum toilet facilities and youngsters waiting for the unspeakable meals that pass for nourishment.

"Harvest of Shame" stressed the role of "crew leaders" who recruit the migrant workers in the South and then truck them from state to state. But the chief blame was put on the so-called "farm lobby." The Secretary of Labor, James P. Mitchell, indicated that he been powerless to push forward the steps necessary to protect the mobile labor force.

Charles B. Shuman, president of the American Farm Bureau Federation, did not help his position by complaining over the possibility of Federal interference. The indignities visited upon the pickers made his words sound as if they came out of the Dark Ages, especially after a viewer had heard a mother of fourteen children explain how she worked in the fields from 6 A.M. to 4 P.M. Her total pay for ten hours under the broiling sun was $1.

One aspect of the migratory labor situation was not too thoroughly developed, namely the influence of the large chain grocery stores. One farmer said that food chains ultimately call the tune in the economics of fruits and vegetables, but Secretary Mitchell indicated that this was just an alibi by the farmers. The matter should have been pursued further.

The photography in "Harvest of Shame" was of exceptionally good quality; Mr. Lowe can be extremely proud of his accomplishment.

Mr. Murrow and "CBS Reports" left no doubt of where they stood. The commentator concluded by asking viewers who benefited from the labors of the "excluded Americans" to raise their voice in Congress, something very likely to happen.

Murrow Departs: Commentator Leaving Broadcast Post for Challenging Federal Job

February 5, 1961

The appointment of Edward R. Murrow as director of the United States Information Agency removes from the domestic broadcasting scene a man whose contribution scarcely can be exaggerated. To whatever extent television has found its voice of conscience, purpose and integrity it was as much the doing of Mr. Murrow as any other single individual in the medium.

In accepting the thankless post of head of government informational activities, including the Voice of America, Mr. Murrow brings a distinctive set of qualifications. His prestige and prominence, national and international, in themselves will endow the Voice of America with an importance that always has been distressingly lacking. What this country says to the world and more especially, how well it says it, has been a subject of official indifference that has bordered on the shocking.

If Mr. Murrow is not unaccustomed to the limelight, he undoubtedly will find the Washington glare very different from what he has known in the past. He can expect to make many appearances before Congressional committees, some members of which have delighted in making a football of the Voice. The American knowledge of the art of propaganda is so fragmentary that self-appointed experts abound in the subject and are eager to contribute their criticism.

While probably there is no ideal process of indoctrination for the novice on the Washington scene, certainly experience in the jungle of Madison Avenue should prove helpful. It is in that sphere that the commentator's record of achievement is doubly outstanding. Because, basically, it was his tough individualism that not only resulted in any number of memorable broadcasts but also served as a stimulating needle to an entire industry that did not relish a piercing provocation to stand up.

The genesis of Mr. Murrow as a broadcasting figure came in his unforgettable radio reports from London during World War II: his use of traditional British understatement gave drama and emotional content to the horrors of the air raids and the matchless courage of the English. But it was also at the same time that he played an instrumental role in putting together radio's most brilliant staff of reporters for the Columbia Broadcasting System.

After the war, between 1945 and 1947, Mr. Murrow had a brief flirtation with the higher-executive echelons of the network, but moving memoranda from the "In" to the "Out" drawer was not to prove to his liking. He reverted to the status of the working journalist just at the time that television began to emerge.

Almost alone of the commentators, Mr. Murrow chanced to be a TV natural. With his dark hair and strong facial features, he was highly videogenic; moreover his delivery was compelling. He met, in short, the test of personality. These factors may seem almost irrelevant but not in TV. His screen presence had the important virtue of making Mr. Murrow "commercial"; accordingly, he gained large enough audiences to interest sponsors.

With sponsorship came a power and independence that is denied to most TV journalists. Mr. Murrow quite readily might have luxuriated in his influence and taken the easy way out through expedient compromise. But the commentator happened to be a man concerned with the hour's pressing issues, a concern that was to find expression in the remarkable TV chapter known as "See It Now."

The full story of "See It Now," its beginning, middle, and end, may never be told, but its high-water mark was its frontal assault on the actions of the late Senator Joseph R. McCarthy, Republican of Wisconsin. Together with his partner, Fred W. Friendly, TV's most skilled practitioner in the field of documentaries and also a man of indomitable determination, Mr. Murrow and the TV medium stripped the mask of invincibility from the Senator.

What is not generally realized is that Mr. Murrow decided to go ahead with the program at a time when passions in the broadcasting industry were running wild on the issue of Communist sympathizers and dupes. It was the autonomy of the Murrow-Friendly operation, often the source of internal controversy within CBS, that got the vital show on the air.

In the tradition of the working journalist, Mr. Murrow always has taken a somewhat jaundiced view of TV business men, no matter how nobly motivated, in coping with the realities of reporting. While anything but a bad businessman himself, as evidenced in his share of the capital-gains deal on the sale of "Person to Person" to CBS, he has vigorously subscribed to the traditional separation of editorial and advertising functions. Even at the risk of hearing his operation described as an impenetrable fortress, he championed the cause of the network's news staff against all comers, a source of support that could be severely missed.

The influence of Mr. Murrow, however, did not stop with CBS If the history of public-service broadcasting in TV in recent years is traced back, it will be found that the success of his ventures was a primary motivating factor in arousing the National Broadcasting Company to greater efforts. Ironically, coincidental with his departure, it is CBS News that is in the throes of a reorganization, in part precisely because of the diffused leadership that he always felt was perilous.

If only because Mr. Murrow did pioneer vigorously for broadcasting of substance and controversy, he has been a rallying point for many gifted individuals of like viewpoint. Accordingly, his departure from the scene must in a way be regretted; for one reason or another the hard core of stimulating spirits in TV is sadly diminishing.

But if there is one area to hope that this is only a passing phase and new vigor will be forthcoming, it is in the inter-network rivalry in news and documentaries, the very cause for which Mr. Murrow held the banner aloft over a period of many lonely years.

In his directorship of the USIA, Mr. Murrow could not ask for a more challenging assignment. Parts of the Voice of America programming are first rate, but there is an undertone of strident preachment that is terribly wearing, beginning with the bombastic repetition of the Voice theme song, "Columbia, the Gem of the Ocean," which has a martial connotation that is avoided by every other country using the international short waves, including the Soviet Union.

While the Voice cannot be respected and trusted more than the fundamental foreign policies to which it must give global emphasis, there is much that can be learned from the subtlety and understatement of the British Broadcasting Corporation, probably the most widely used and highly regarded short-wave service of the Western world. Facts quietly and gracefully stated remain the best "propaganda" of all, a policy happily consistent with Mr. Murrow's public record and personal conviction.

Notes

1. Edwin R. Bayley, *Joe McCarthy and the Press* (New York: Pantheon Books, 1981), 209. My father gave Murrow more historical credit for the impact of the McCarthy broadcast in "Murrow and the Legacy of His 'Golden Moment,'" *Los Angeles Times*, March 4, 1979.

2. A. M. Sperber, *Murrow: His Life and Times* (New York: Freundlich Books, 1986), 574.

3. *NYT*, October 20, 1959; Sperber, *Murrow*, 576–579.

4. Gould memo, JLG Papers.

Chapter Four

The Influence of a Critic

My father always played down his direct influence on television as a critic, but on occasion he used his column to articulate his views on controversial issues. Three such cases involved some aspect of religion on the airwaves. He defended the embattled playwright George S. Kaufman in 1952 when he was dropped from a show for allegedly "anti-religious" remarks. Four years later Dad chastised the evangelist Oral Roberts for his use of faith-healing cases on television to promote the fortunes of his ministry. And in 1961 he criticized an atheist for his attacks on a person of strong religious views; in so doing, he provoked a lawsuit against himself and *The New York Times.* Though the lawsuit never came to trial, it had the productive effect of causing Dad to write a memorandum for *Times* lawyer Louis Loeb about how that particular review evolved. The memo gives insight into the general method he used in appraising performers and citizens who appeared on television.

On two other occasions my father, by his own account, had his greatest impact as a critic. In 1956 he assailed the networks for their failure to cover the proceedings of the United Nations Security Council during the Suez crisis. His column "Disgrace of the Networks" aroused a wave of approving comments from the public. Network executives changed their programming, at least temporarily. My father rarely saved any of his mail. He kept all the cards and letters he received about this column.

In 1959, when a New York station planned to cancel its dramatic program *The Play of the Week,* my father challenged his readers to save the program. Again the mail came in (and again he kept it), and the program survived for more than a year. In the end, the economics of television triumphed over the words of the critic, and the program disappeared. Nonetheless, Dad believed that his advocacy of quality television in this case represented one of the best moments in his tenure at *The Times.*

Kaufman Incident: "This Is Show Business" Dismisses Panelist for Pre-Christmas Quip

January 4, 1953

How frightened and susceptible to pressure can television get? The firing of George S. Kaufman from the panel of "This Is Show Business" because of his quip about "Silent Night, Holy Night" is a far greater and more serious mistake than any the playwright may have made.

If only because the sequence of events in the Kaufman incident stretched over a period of some days, it would seem pertinent first to recount what actually happened.

On the performance of "This Is Show Business" on Dec. 21, which was at a time when practically all programs were observing the Christmas theme, Mr. Kaufman held down his usual post on the panel of theatrical celebrities. And in the course of the show, he made the following remark:

"Let's make this one program on which no one sings 'Silent Night.' "

The program had not even finished before the Columbia Broadcasting System began to receive telephone calls of protest. These were followed by letters addressed both to CBS and the American Tobacco Company, sponsor of the show.

Exactly how many protests were received is not certain, but one person in a position to know estimated "a couple of hundred." Mr. Kaufman had been told perhaps 400 or 500.

Assuming that the protests reached the figure of 500, and that the audience of "This Is Show Business" might have been 10,000,000, this would mean that roughly one twenty-thousandth of those who saw the show felt sufficiently concerned to write or call.

However, the protests were sufficient to lead the Columbia network, which controls the program package, to ask Mr. Kaufman "not to appear" for the final three performances of the program. "This Is Show Business" had been announced to leave the air at the end of this month even before the Kaufman incident occurred.

The burden of the protests was that Mr. Kaufman's remark, coming at the very height of the holiday season, was in poor taste and that it was "anti-religious."

When he finally had a chance to explain his position more fully, however, Mr. Kaufman was specific as to what he had in mind when he made the ad lib.

"This was not wittingly an anti-religious remark," he said. "I was merely speaking out against the use and overuse of this Christmas carol in connection with the sale of commercial products."

In retrospect, Mr. Kaufman no doubt probably wished he had not made the quip. Perhaps he did not choose either the best place or the best time to raise the issue of the overcommercialization of the Christmas spirit. If some earnest and well-intentioned members of the audience felt offended, then at the very least he did not explain himself adequately. One failing of the professional gag man is that he can be too anxious to be witty. Perhaps this was the real explanation.

To use his remark, however, as reason to bow to the cries of "off with his head" was in no way justified or desirable. Let's concede that Mr. Kaufman is—and always has been—something of a controversial personality. His is the bitter and pointed school of wit that is the complete antithesis of the sweetness-and-light approach. Sometimes he's been even a bit boorish on the air.

But American humor has fallen on sad days indeed if no longer is there a place for the sourpuss. So what if Mr. Kaufman's personality does not radiate a happy and childlike joy? A great many viewers could argue that he was only of the truly mature wits before the cameras; frequently he was.

Behind his acerbic observations there often lay a great amount of intelligent criticism and a case in point was his feeling about the overuse of "Silent Night." To suggest that his viewpoint was "anti-religious" is absurd. Actually, it was much more "pro-religious."

This year television producers started making use of Christmas music extraordinarily early—right after Thanksgiving. For three weeks it was on the air almost morning, noon and night. The lovely and sacred carols, which, after all, are of the church, in some instances were put to uses little short of shocking.

One such example, which, incidentally, took place on CBS, was a trite play about a governess who falls in love with a rich count. The story had not the remotest connection with Christmas, yet for the happy ending there were heard in the background the strains of "Silent Night." Is it "anti-religious" to ask that the meaning of Christmas be treated with reverence and discernment?

There were many ways in which CBS and American Tobacco could have handled the Kaufman incident without setting the unwise precedent of firing him out of hand. A simple explanation on Mr. Kaufman's part this Sunday would have served nicely.

But now television has advertised to the world that it is an easy mark for any small group which wants to exert its will. A comparative handful of protests apparently can induce almost a state of panic among some executive echelons. No thought is given to the overwhelming majority of millions who either concurred in what Mr. Kaufman was trying to say or were not sufficiently disturbed to ask for his scalp.

The consequences of this policy can only harm television. People who hold views that don't please "all of the people all of the time" will be afraid to speak lest they be sacked in the morning. But they will not suffer in the long run; only television will. The decision to fire Mr. Kaufman is but a symbol of the terrifying vacuum into which TV is retreating in needless panic.

The irony is that this policy of appeasement on the part of television's leaders is the worst possible way to achieve their goal: freedom from controversy. If a network gives ground in one direction, there will be always other groups asking that it give ground in other directions. Appeasement can only feed on itself. And as was true in Mr. Kaufman's case, the repercussions cannot be hidden behind a curtain of silence, as CBS tried to do. The facts will out and then there is more controversy than ever.

On Faith Healing: Preacher's Timely TV Miracles Raise Questions of Stations' Standards

February 18, 1956

For all the attention and publicity accorded to Billy Graham, there is another evangelist who appears to be edging him out on television and radio. The gentleman in question is the Rev. Oral Roberts, and his presentations would seem to pose a matter of fundamental policy for the broadcasting industry.

Brother Roberts, as he identifies himself, was in the news last week, it will be recalled, after he abruptly ended a tour of Australia because of the hostile reception he received in the Australian press. His program last week, incidentally, overlooked this turn of events and spoke of his trip in most glowing terms of success.

The evangelist makes his headquarters in Tulsa, Okla., but he is seen and/or heard over more than 400 TV and radio stations. He is understood to spend about $20,000 a week for the purchase of time. He does not directly solicit funds but makes it unmistakably clear that he cannot continue on the air without "generous letters" from his audience.

The program of Brother Roberts is divided into two parts. The first part is devoted to a most impassioned delivery of a sermon. The second part—and the one quite different from any other TV presentation—is devoted to faith healing.

No one will dispute that faith can play an enormously vital part in hastening recovery from bodily ills. Similarly there need not be questioned the existence of miraculous recoveries that seemingly cannot be explained by medical science.

But it is quite another matter to pass miracles on a weekly basis and to claim on the screen without even the most rudimentary proof, permanent cure of an endless variety of ailments.

Last Sunday evening Brother Roberts called up four persons to be helped. A woman said she had a swollen foot, the result of blood poisoning, and a bone infection. Doctors had been unable to cure it, she explained. Brother Roberts struck her head sharply with the palm of his hand. The woman cried "Hallelujah!" She said she was recovered and stomped her foot to prove it.

Another person receiving the ministrations of Brother Roberts was a man who said he had suffered from deafness and impaired sight. He explained that his hearing had improved just by attending the meeting; he said that God's presence just suddenly went through him. Brother Roberts put his hands on the man's ears and eyes. Then he gave him a hearing test. The man could hear a whisper.

The man then told Brother Roberts he had learned of the evangelist's work by watching and listening to him on television.

The climactic moment of the program was the case of a small boy who suffered from double club feet.

The youngster was held in the arms of a woman relative and before Brother Roberts invoked his power of faith, the youngster exclaimed with the help of some coaching, "Boy, am I a lucky duck?" He was going to be made well, he said.

Brother Roberts took the boy in his lap. As he placed his hands vigorously on the boy's feet he stressed that "the ligaments had been cut." Under such circumstances, Brother Roberts added, only a miracle, nothing else, now could enable the boy to walk. "Lord, when I put this child down, he's got to walk," he said. The boy scampered off the stage.

The TV presentation, according to the announcer, was "sponsored by Oral Roberts." In short, here was the case of a man buying time on the air to present his own assured miracles. To have failed obviously would have made totally incongruous the evangelist's guarded closing appeal for further financial support.

Evangelists long have been part of the American scene and no doubt always will be. So long as they adhere to purely religious objectives, their appearance on the home screen may be beneficial and worthwhile. Faith can come to men in different ways, and only the intolerant would presume to judge which is best.

But faith-healing would seem a different matter. To allow the enormously influential medium of television to be used week after week to show undocumented "miracles," with all their implied aspersions on the competency of medicine, seems contrary to the spirit, if not the letter, of the industry's code governing mature and responsible broadcasting.

Enlightened leaders of both the clergy and the medical profession recognize that theirs can be a fruitful partnership, that often one may achieve what the other cannot. But this has nothing to do with a gospel preacher making his own extemporaneous medical diagnoses and claiming magic results unsupported by the slightest shred of rational evidence. Brother Roberts, it may be noted, carefully avoids rigid comparative tests before and after his miracles.

From watching Brother Roberts on the screen there can be no question that, in so far as the evangelists on TV are concerned, he has gone a step further than the others. To try to heal a man's soul and restore his faith is one thing. But for a man to ask TV viewers to hold up their babies in front of the screen while he extends his hand to the camera, with a crystal-clear inference that this will heal the infant of bodily ills, is hardly an edifying use of a mass medium.

If Brother Roberts wishes to exploit hysteria and ignorance by putting up his hands and yelling "Heal," that is his affair. But it hardly seems in the public interest, convenience and necessity, for the TV industry to go along with him.

The outlets in this area carrying Brother Roberts are Channel 9 at 11:30 P.M. Sundays; Channel 13 at 8 P.M. Wednesdays; and Channel 8 (New Haven) at 8:30 A.M. Sundays. Of these respected stations it must be asked whether they are allowing their standards of religious broadcasting to be determined by a faith healer merely because of his ability to pay for time. If so, their behavior is infinitely more distressing than anything Brother Roberts has done.

Disgrace of the Networks: Chains Ignore Session at United Nations

October 31, 1956

The gigantic network broadcasting industry—radio and television—disgraced itself yesterday. Neither the National Broadcasting Company, the Columbia Broadcasting System, nor the American Broadcasting Company, with the facilities to enlighten a nation in its own home, carried the crucial late afternoon and evening session of the United Nations Security Council.

On the network television outlets it was the usual run of soap opera, giveaway, movies and commercials; on radio, it was disk jockeys, etc. In short, the national electronic communications system made an absolute mockery of its obligation to serve the public interest. It was stupid, selfish and irresponsible. When the chips were down the networks lived in their narrow, narrow world.

In television there was one notable local exception, WPIX, the outlet owned by The Daily News. It carried live the heart of the discussion at the U.N. It did a tremendous job, marred only by its failure to cover adequately the evening session, including the French and British veto of the American resolution.

On radio there was only one local exception—the ever-reliable WNYC, owned by the City of New York. It carried everything from start to finish. If ever there was justification for the tax-supported municipal outlet, it came yesterday. Commercial broadcasting cannot be relied upon.

After 10 o'clock last night, only a single frequency modulation station, WNYC-FM, available to just a minority audience, was broadcasting from the U.N. WNYC, the standard station, had to sign off at 10 because of a Federal regulation that it must not disturb rural listeners to WCCO, Minneapolis, a CBS affiliate. Both WYNC and WCCO operate on 830 kilocycles.

In short, not one of the city's twenty standard stations nor one of its seven video outlets broadcast the Council deliberations. This was the bleak record in the late evening in the world's largest community, the home of the United Nations.

The value of the WPIX telecast cannot be exaggerated. It was a dramatic, instructive and frightening primer in one of the most complex turning points in history. To the viewer fortunate enough to see the coverage on Channel 11, the involved issues, the points of view of large and small powers and the contrasting personalities of the Council delegates were made vividly and comprehensively clear.

Before one's own eyes there occurred the hard-to-believe chain of events that found the Soviet Union and the United States on the same side, Britain and France defending their ultimatum to put troops along the Suez, the brilliant exposition of the Israeli position and the Egyptian appeal for action against Britain and France. The world suddenly seemed to have gone topsy-turvy; thanks to WPIX, a viewer could see it happen. Or, in the case of WNYC, hear it happen.

The WPIX telecast was one that should have been broadcast from coast-to-coast; here was a situation—man's own struggle to avoid a holocaust—which the electronic medium was designed to cover. Here was a chance to report history in close-up, to enable every citizen, old and young alike, to see destiny unfold.

David Sarnoff, chairman of the Radio Corporation of America, NBC's corporate parent; William S. Paley, chairman of CBS, and Leonard Goldenson, ABC president, are the men who should search their consciences this morning.

Of what use are this country's superb communications facilities if they are not put to work on behalf of the people who own the airwaves? How is a nation to appreciate fully the gravity of world affairs if nothing is allowed to interfere with broadcasting's subservience to the middle commercial? How can the President of the United States impress the world with our concern if we ourselves sit benumbed at home in front of old movies?

Television broadcasters always excuse their inaction on the basis of cost; it is time they stopped whimpering and acted as grown-ups. Every journalistic medium has high costs when an emergency occurs; it is part of the overhead that goes with the privilege of having access to the country's minds.

If television economics are in such deplorable state that the networks cannot properly play their part in a crisis it is time the leaders of broadcasting had a long, hard look at their operations. If television is to be only a parlor carnival, let it say so and stop its pompous proclamations about being in the field of communications. If television does want to be a branch of the Fourth Estate, let it act that way.

P.S.: In erecting its headquarters, the United Nations thought of television and installed the necessary equipment for use by broadcasters. These facilities were available yesterday. The networks simply don't have an excuse for their behavior.

More on U.N.: Networks Make Limited Progress in Their Coverage of World's Realities

November 2, 1956

The television networks made limited progress last night in the way of more respectable coverage of the United Nations, but they still did not allow the world's realities to disturb unduly their commercial habits.

In his telecast Wednesday evening, President Eisenhower indicated that the hopes of the United States for peace were vested in the United Nations General Assembly. Last night, Secretary of State John Foster Dulles detailed before that Assembly the American viewpoint.

The chains did not agree. Apart from customary bulletins such as they normally give the news, their minds were on other matters while the Secretary was asking the support of the nations of the world.

The National Broadcasting Company presented Guy Lombardo and his orchestra and later Dinah Shore. The Columbia Broadcasting System was on its toes with the latest installment of "Sergeant Preston of the Yukon." The American Broadcasting Company met TV's fierce competition with "The Lone Ranger."

By a crowning irony, viewers watching NBC and CBS received a complete exposition of the position of Britain. But commercial programs denied them a chance to hear, as it happened, an explanation of their own country's position. Excerpts on film were shown later.

In fairness, it should be noted that the networks were caught in a dilemma that highlighted a very genuine journalistic problem in TV. The answer of Adlai E. Stevenson, Democratic Presidential candidate, to President Eisenhower's address came at exactly the same time as the Secretary was on the air.

Having pledged to Mr. Stevenson the time, the chains could not change at the last moment. But WOR-TV, an independent outlet, did show that it was possible to switch back to the United Nations immediately after Mr. Stevenson and catch some of the meatiest portions of the Secretary's statement. Later on CBS cameras picked up the evening session of the Assembly.

There were encouraging developments, however, on the broadcasting news front. First and foremost was the action of Consolidated Edison in meeting the cost of the fine full coverage provided by WPIX, which led the way in recognizing the United Nations during the present crisis. The company's public-spirited move contributed genuinely to the community's well-being; the utility merits praise and thanks.

On radio the situation was vastly improved over earlier days. ABC said it planned full coverage of the Assembly evening session; so did WOR-FM and, of course, the reliable city-owned outlets, WYNC and WNYC-FM. CBS and NBC radio also were much more attentive.

WQXR, the radio station of The New York Times, also was on its toes, in coping instantly with the time conflict between Mr. Stevenson and Secretary Dulles. By tape recording, it presented the text of the Secretary's speech immediately after Mr. Stevenson finished.

What imagination can accomplish was illustrated in the case of KRUX, Phoenix, Ariz. On a short-wave set it picked up the running commentary the United Nations radio broadcasts to the far corners of the world.

TV Can Be Good, Too: "The Play of the Week" Is a Case in Point

November 22, 1959

In a season marked by scandals and many programming disappointments, there is one shining feature that, more than volumes of words, reaffirms the exciting potential of television. It is the local attraction entitled "The Play of the Week," seen over Channel 13.

"The Play of the Week" is much more than an important event in television; in a larger sense it is a significant occurrence for the theatre as well. At long last the artistry, independence and taste of the legitimate stage have been transferred with integrity and respect to the home screen.

The maturity of "The Play of the Week" was never better illustrated than by the current production of "The Waltz of the Toreadors," which may be seen in its last performance from 3 to 5 o'clock this afternoon.

Jean Anouilh's study of a tiring profligate is presented in all its hilarious naughtiness, a truly sophisticated and gay exploration of the subject of sex. It is worldly wise, cynical and specific; more to the point, it is an intellectual romp of the first order.

Hugh Griffith, who had the lead in one London stage production, is absolutely perfect. Mildred Natwick, as the shrew, is altogether divine and the supporting company, including Beatrice Straight, James Valentine and John Abbott, join in the fun with zest and subtlety.

But "The Waltz of the Toreadors" is not merely an isolated smash for "The Play of the Week." Its opening bill, Judith Anderson in "Medea" was a towering accomplishment. Thereafter there have been "The Power and the Glory" by Graham Greene; "Burning Bright" by John Steinbeck; Ivan Turgenev's "A Month in the Country," with Uta Hagen, Alexander Scourby and Luther Adler; and two original short works by John Mortimer.

Obviously, this is not only the most consistently brilliant TV dramatic series of this season but quite probably for many seasons past. And it is ironic that such a notably forward step in video's evolution should come not from a network with all the money in the world at its disposal but from an independent outlet that discovered an old truism; give theatre people a chance to do work in which they can take pride and satisfaction and they won't ask for the economic moon.

Because the story of "The Play of the Week" is both an invigorating and reassuring demonstration that, while the woods may be filled with avaricious and thoughtless souls who put the buck before the play, somewhere and some place there will turn up a band of individuals who find a way to hold up the theatre's colors with dedicated pride.

One of these individuals is Ely Landau, head impresario of Channel 13 (WNTA-TV). He is not, it should be said instantly, a man who hates money. But he is a gambler in the honored tradition of the show business: he is staking a very considerable sum on the hunch that, given time and determination, quality in TV can be made profitable.

As is now generally known, Mr. Landau adopted the format of playing a vehicle every weekday night and on Sunday afternoons, which for the busy viewer is a great convenience. This would not have been possible, it is to be noted, without the advent of tape. By the repeated shows Mr. Landau can prorate his overhead and also achieve a cumulative total audience of significant proportions.

Also the tapes of the shows ultimately may be syndicated on other stations in the United States and in some foreign markets. When these added rewards come in, the acting company will receive their share.

While the economic arrangements for "The Play of the Week" are necessarily important, the artistic factors are even more so. One of Mr. Landau's basic philosophies is that TV must adapt itself to the requirements of the program that it undertakes to present, not assume that the whole world must march in some goose step that happens to fit the financial convenience of TV.

Accordingly, the play determines the length of "The Play of the Week," though actually it falls comfortably within a two-hour running span. This means there is not the confounded editing of bits and pieces of a playwright's labors that on the networks so often robs a drama of its original intent and vitality. One of the joys of "The Play of the Week" is that there is time for actors to give a rounded and total performance. And the writers are fully heard.

Under these circumstances it is small wonder that the people of the theatre are rallying to the cause of "The Play of the Week." The ever-busy David Susskind is frequently at the helm, but many of the finest talents of the Broadway stage are participating. The American Federation of Television and Radio Artists also deserves unreserved applause; it is giving Mr. Landau every conceivable assistance in the belief that what helps TV theatre will help a labor union.

The only dark shadow across the project is the refusal of the Music Corporation of America to permit some of the stars it represents to appear on "The Play of the Week." But then M.C.A. always has been something of a bore.

Madison Avenue Case Study: "The Play of the Week" Faces Doom Jan. 30

December 29, 1959

Some of the finest theatre of the current season has been found on television, not Broadway. It has been presented on the Channel 13 project known as "The Play of the Week" which, for set owners in New York, has been an island of civilized viewing fare.

But "The Play of the Week" no longer can be regarded merely as a television program. In its broadest sense the presentation is a new cultural asset of the community, a heaven-sent means of extending the riches of adult theatre into countless homes in the metropolitan area.

With daring and boldness, station WNTA-TV in effect has set up a revolving theatre company of dedication, integrity and competence. Its value assuredly is not less because it does not happen to be housed in a concrete building that is part of some new center; its standards reflect credit on the theatre and electronics alike.

But the magnificent undertaking of Channel 13 is now in jeopardy, and its fate should commend itself to all those concerned with the well-being of the arts. Ely Landau, the station's overseer, confirmed yesterday that the series might have to be terminated on Jan. 30 because of the maddening economies peculiar to TV.

If the worst should happen, it will not be for want of sacrifice by the people of the theatre. The program's stars, including Helen Hayes, who starred last night in "The Cherry Orchard," and Judith Anderson, whose superb "Medea" began the series, have all worked for a pittance—a standard fee of $650, which covers thirteen days of rehearsal and three back-breaking days of taping before the cameras.

The problems of "The Play of the Week" constitute a case study of the working of the immutable rating laws of Madison Avenue.

The budget of "The Play of the Week" is of the order of $42,000; for a few shows it has gone substantially higher. To approach the break even point, Channel 13 has fixed a charge of $500 for a spot announcement, or $3,500 for one advertisement during each of the play's seven performances. It would take twelve spots a night to meet the investment; Channel 13 has not always had six.

The ratings explain why. The potential audience for any television program in the metropolitan area is roughly 4,500,000 homes equipped with TV sets; the general assumption is that there are two viewers to a set, or a possible total of 9,000,000 persons.

With one production the seven performances of "The Play of the Week" were estimated to have been seen in a cumulative total of 1,000,000 homes. This meant that for the sponsor it cost him $3.50 to get his sales message into 1,000 living rooms. With lower ratings the "cost per thousand homes," which is one of the quantitative tests of advertising efficiency, could and did jump to $4 or $5.

On the other hand, if a sponsor bought a spot in, say, a re-run of "Highway Patrol" or a wrestling match, which have larger audiences and lower production costs, it might cost him only $1.20 to reach 1,000 homes. The WOR-TV program "Million Dollar Movie," which gives sixteen performances of the same film in a week, estimates its cost per thousand at $2.

For advertisers and their agencies interested solely in counting noses the differential speaks for itself; "The Play of the Week" appears to be overpriced.

In coming days, however, the determined Mr. Landau plans to come up with further statistics touching on one of the least-publicized aspects of the rating issue; the composition of TV audiences.

He has received one survey that shows 93 per cent of the audience for "The Play of the Week" as comprised of adults. It is no secret that some high-rated network attractions actually are made up predominantly of youngsters whose influence over the family purse strings hardly matches their control of TV sets.

But the difficulties of "The Play of the Week" point up the problem that at some time and in some way the leaders of TV, particularly sponsors and advertising agencies, will have to face. It may be sound advertising to compare Miss Anderson in "Medea" with a rigged wrestling match, but socially, ethically and culturally it is preposterous.

Actually the figures registered by "The Play of the Week" are of the utmost significance if viewed in a different frame of reference. If a full-length play is watched in 500,000 homes, or by audience of 1,000,000 persons, this is the equivalent of a Broadway run of upward of two years.

Surely, this is a gain that socially cannot be minimized. The cost of going to the Broadway theatre is now so prohibitive that a venture such as "The Play of the Week" is much more than a mere advertising matter;

it is a vitally needed means of assuring an expanding entente between the public and the living theatre.

Ultimately, if broadcasting and advertising cannot find ways of regularly accommodating such qualitative fare, it may be inviting a reconsideration of pay-as-you-see TV. Certainly, there seems something wrong when it is realized that if each person watching "The Play of the Week" were willing to pay 10 cents apiece, or 5 cents an hour, there would be no problem over the program's future.

Meanwhile, those who have enjoyed "The Play of the Week" and believe in its purpose can render tangible aid. Is a season of perhaps twenty-six plays with fine casts worth a 3-cent postcard to WNTA-TV, 10 Columbus Circle, to demonstrate that there is a sizable audience for grown-up television? The viewer must help too.

"The Play of the Week": Demise of Drama Series Has Economic Moral

June 11, 1961

The suspension of "The Play of the Week," which scored so many notable firsts in the presentation of qualitative drama on the home screen, is bound to come as a disappointment to thoughtful viewers. Its loss underscores the continuing need for deeper study in solving the riddle of television's mass economics.

The news of the lay-off, which in all probability will turn out to be a permanent one, was not entirely unexpected. The program's fate immediately became uncertain when the owners of station WNTA-TV announced their need for cash to retire short-term obligations and invited bids for the Channel 13 outlet that has been the program's home.

By ironic coincidence, a group of individuals who would be the first to join in the applause for "The Play of the Week" is scheduled to take over the outlet. It is the committee of public-spirited citizens, working through the National Educational Television and Radio Center, that plans to convert Channel 13 to noncommercial educational TV.

As part of his appraisal of the over-all operations of National Telefilm Associates, Inc., Charles L. Glett, the concern's new president, said last week that a detailed study would have to be made of the operating economics of "The Play of the Week." The examination, he noted, could not be completed until mid-September, which made any new shows for next season "very remote." Worthington Miner, who has been executive producer of "The Play of the Week," feared the project was now a dead issue.

For a time it had been hoped that the advent of an educational channel would not mean the termination of "The Play of the Week"; there were reports that new productions would be seen over Channel 5, which does plan to present re-runs of some of the program's past successes, such as the brilliant "Medea," "Tiger at the Gates" and "The Iceman Cometh."

But Mr. Glett explained the financial aspects of "The Play of the Week" would have to be analyzed in terms of its success as a syndicated feature in other cities. The substantial costs of such a venture must be recouped in showing elsewhere; a single station in New York could not alone meet the total budgets for two-hour plays with top casts.

One of the imponderables of "The Play of the Week" is the question of its survival if the educational group had not bid for WNTA-TV. The former chairman of National Telefilm, Ely A. Landau, who resigned for the express purpose of trying to get the station for himself, was convinced that he could have kept the series going without interruption.

But even though Mr. Landau made the highest bid, it proved to no avail. The citizens group had a telling ace in reserve—the sympathetic encouragement of the Federal Communications Commission. Sale of the station to a commercial bidder such as Mr. Landau—David Susskind also lost out for the same reason—would have meant long hearings before the FCC.

Mr. Landau has reason to be disillusioned. Independent stations that made little effort to raise TV standards will continue to offer their re-runs of network half-hours or old movies while the outlet that he nurtured so diligently has passed out of his hands.

The answer, of course, is that the educational group had to bid for the only station that was put up for sale; not to have done so would have meant the loss of an opportunity that could lead to nationwide benefits in the field of educational TV. These considerations necessarily had to take precedence over a project that, no matter how worthy, still was subject to the uncertainties of the commercial marketplace.

Conceivably, by the time these lines appear—if not, probably within a reasonable period thereafter—the educational citizens committee, of which John D. Rockefeller 3d is one of the members, will announce formally its purchase of WNTA-TV.

Under the present economics of educational TV, there is hardly a chance that even if the fifty-odd noncommercial stations pooled their resources they could afford the budgets common to "The Play of the Week." A program running to the order of $50,000 a week would be out of the question for any extended period of time.

Yet in the environment of commercial TV the obstacles are formidable. Even with the sympathetic aid of the labor unions, the familiar set of conditions—the minority of audiences for quality drama, the overhead inherent in two hours of running time, the substantial production and talent costs—combines to make survival of "The Play of the Week" precarious. And for a variety of reasons no program has access to every play of which a viewer might think; the size of casts and the demands of playwrights can be determining factors, among many others.

Pay-as-you-see TV might seem a solution, but for the present that method is still only in the dream stage with its economics far from resolved.

Yet the overriding problem remains: the medium of television has no difficulty in financing the pap but the challenge of doing quality remains as great as ever. Mr. Miner, for one, believes there is a crying need for an altogether fresh look at the economics of distributing quality TV.

Surely, one can be hard put to think of a more worthwhile project for an educational TV network than doing the finest in drama, which, if announced beforehand, could be integrated into a variety of courses on many different school levels.

One admissible procedure in educational TV and agreeable to the FCC is the award of grants by corporations; their names can appear on a noncommercial station but there can be no formal advertising. If sponsors who make profitable sales use of the TV medium were to chip into a common pot for drama on a noncommercial network, it might readily resolve the financial problems.

"The Play of the Week," being an eminently human undertaking, had its noble moments and its off-nights. But the principle for which it stood assuredly is worth preservation and furtherance. If a free economy one way or another cannot solve the problem of sustaining quality then it is not very free.

Lively Panel Show: Betty Furness Is Spry Hostess on WNTA

August 2, 1961

Amid the doldrums of summer television, a touch of much-needed spice and controversy is being furnished by Betty Furness. The actress and erstwhile custodian of refrigerator doors is demonstrating on Channel 13 that she is also an efficient and quick-witted moderator of the liveliest panel show on the air at the moment.

Miss Furness is officiating on the nightly outing called "At Your Beck and Call," which recruits a group of individuals of widely dissimilar professions and interests and subjects them to a running fire of questions submitted by set-owners at home.

The format could hardly be construed as an ideal means for dealing in much depth with the multitude of subjects that arise between 8 and 10 P.M. But there is no gainsaying that the show on many evenings does sustain interest and moves quickly. In fact, the questions submitted by the audience in a great many cases are admirable for their directness and humor, and Miss Furness passes them along with zip and relish.

The program of Monday evening was typical in its over-all construction if not in its specific tone. The guests were Henry Viscardi, Jr., executive vice president of Just One Break, Inc.; John Lansing, a private detective; Dr. David Roginsky, specialist in internal medicine, and Joseph Lewis, president of the Freethinkers of America.

Mr. Viscardi discussed his work in aiding the physically handicapped and stressed the importance of religious faith both in his life and in the lives of those whom he has aided. In mentioning his birth without limbs, he noted that his mother always had an ennobling explanation. Since there had to be crippled boys in the world, God had especially chosen the Viscardi family to take care of one.

In juxtaposition to Mr. Viscardi's remarks, the observations of Mr. Lewis were unfortunate, not because of their point of view but because of the manner of their delivery. If freedom of religion is carried to its logical conclusion, it must accommodate not only those who believe but also those who disbelieve. Miss Furness and Channel 13 were on sound ground in giving him a hearing.

But even a freethinker is not immune to the code of good manners. In casting aspersions on the efficacy of prayer and challenging God's presence because there are blind, mute and crippled among us, Mr. Lewis struck a note bordering on the sadistic. It was as if he were more determined to jolt and shock than persuasively advance his philosophy.

Moreover, Mr. Lewis tended to detract from the intellectual appeal of his argument by his accompanying emotional display. His performance hardly suggested that an atheist is entirely at peace with himself.

Dr. Roginsky gently dismissed the medical value of supplementary vitamins for most Americans who enjoy three good meals a day—a point of view that may have been of interest to the vitamin sponsor on Channel 13. His opposition to the views of the American Medical Association was voiced in warmly human terms. Mr. Lansing good-naturedly discussed the private eye.

In handling the varied guests, Miss Furness admittedly may not always be everyone's hostess. She is so businesslike, so much the competent woman executive, that the thought of shared champagne by candlelight is not likely to intrude unduly on a viewer's concentration. But her alertness, brevity and slightly edged barbs reflect a mental tidiness that can be very much preferred to distaff gushiness.

Jack Gould to Louis Loeb

October 19, 1961

Mr. Loeb:

Mr. Lewis's excerpts from my article omit a fact that was basic to my criticism of his performance.

Mr. Viscardi is, of course, limbless. On the program he explained how much he had been helped all his life by a strong religious faith. He also explained quite movingly how his mother had felt God had chosen the Viscardi family to look after one of the world's handicapped children.

It was against this background that Mr. Lewis very stridently contended that if there truly was a compassionate God he would not people the world with the handicapped, the blind, etc. It was this performance which I thought in wretched taste and quite unnecessary to his presentation of the case for atheism.

Of course I was moved neither by malice nor anything else, which would seem clear enough in my support of his right to state his case. I think my conclusions were warranted on the basis of his performance by which he invited public attention.

I would add that personally I am a strong believer in running letters of dissent from opinions. Our columns have been open to Mr. Lewis as to anyone else but over the many weeks since the program he has not chosen to avail himself of this forum.

If you need further data I am at your disposal. I'm not sure whether this [sic] is a tape recording of the program anywhere but Miss Furness would be cooperative.

Chapter Five

A Critic's Likes and Dislikes

The job of television critic meant that my father dealt with a staggering variety of entertainment and news programs during his twenty-five years of watching video offerings. Any selection of columns from his work about performers, specials, and news programs must be to some degree arbitrary. This chapter presents notable examples of his opinions about famous television programs and personalities, especially when his judgment proved controversial (Elvis Presley), when he advanced the early careers of future stars (Johnny Carson and David Brinkley), or when he discussed the fate of an important or long-running show (*Omnibus* and *Today*).

Dad's review of the premiere of *The Today Show* in 1952 and his critical comments about Elvis Presley in 1956 are among his most quoted writings. His observations about *Today* had a constructive effect on what Sylvester "Pat" Weaver and his colleagues at NBC were doing with their new concept. As one of the early staff members of *Today*, Clifford Evans, wrote to my father on March 2, 1972: "We were faulted for just about everything and the review hit us very hard. But we thought you were right. We had over-extended ourselves—not in our thinking, but in our planning and in our execution." In conclusion, Evans added, "While you may not have known it, we were grateful to you for 'murdering' us on 'Opening Day.' "

In addition to my father's negative assessment of Elvis Presley, this chapter provides a look at some of Dad's personal favorites—Mary Martin, the young Johnny Carson, and the forceful and outspoken Howard K. Smith. His comments on Richard Nixon and "the Checkers speech" and his analysis of the appeal of Lucille Ball shed light on two noteworthy aspects of television during the 1950s. His lament about the end of *Omnibus* indicates how his hopes for television were eroding by the end of that decade.

Comment on "Today": NBC's Early Morning Show Needs Some Work

January 20, 1952

> A new era in television dawned today.
> NBC STATEMENT

> Assurance was felt that a revolution was taking place in the television industry.
> NBC STATEMENT

> The studio will become the nerve center of the planet.
> NBC STATEMENT

Gosh, something must have happened up at Dave Sarnoff's. It did too! Television at breakfast. After weeks of preparations and communiques the National Broadcasting Company unveiled last week its much-awaited effort to add the hours between 7 and 9 in the morning to the television day.

The two-hour marathon is called "Today"; its basic theme is the presentation of news in just about every shape, form and manner possible, and its intriguing problem is to try to lure man, woman and child to Channel 4 during the busiest and most confusing hours of the family's daily routine.

Manifestly, "Today" is a spectacular gamble and at this early stage the only safe course is to hedge all bets on its future. Breakfast-time TV has been a commercial success in some cities outside of New York and it may be that Sylvester L. Weaver, the restless NBC vice president who in large measure conceived "Today," may hit the jackpot. He has before.

But if tentative conclusions about "Today" are in order, then the jargon of the show business provides a singularly apt summary of the program's present status: it needs a lot of work. Indeed, on the basis of its first four days of presentation, "Today" was a disappointment, albeit a disappointment which should not be too difficult to overcome.

"Today" requires a great deal of explanation, which perhaps is what is fundamentally wrong with the program at the moment. In the RCA

Exhibition Hall on West Forty-ninth Street the network has built what it calls a "communications center" especially for the program.

This large room, which is shown on the screen, holds every conceivable type of equipment: monitoring screens which show remote visual pick-ups from other cities; tape recording machines; press association teletypes; bulletin boards with "still" news pictures and the front pages of newspapers from cities across the country; banks of desks and typewriters; phonograph record players; assorted control panels for patching in short-wave circuits from overseas, and, everywhere, miscellaneous microphones.

Presiding over this maze of gadgetry is Dave Garroway, the leisurely gentleman from Chicago, who for the most part runs the show. He is aided by Jim Fleming, the erstwhile editor of that excellent radio program, "Voices and Events," who handles the reading of the more important news, and Jack Lescoulie, who serves as a sports specialist and general utility infielder.

NBC is assuming that during the most hectic hours of the morning the average person is not going to look in for more than twenty or thirty minutes at most, which is probably a thoroughly safe assumption, and the format of Today is patterned in general on the continuous newsreel.

First, there is a two-minute capsule summary of the news, based on a headline in a New York newspaper and some photographs; then there may be an interview with the author of a new book or a drama critic reporting on a first night; a phonograph record, or an out-of-town pick-up showing people going to work, and next, a fuller news report by Mr. Fleming. At intervals there are "recesses," which NBC hopes before too long will be occupied by contented sponsors.

Because of the hours at which it is presented, "Today" also is riding two horses at once. It is hopeful that much of the program can be appreciated by the ear alone so as not to interfere with the morning rituals of shaving, getting breakfast, and going off to school or work.

Thus far "Today" has been excessively pretentious and ostentatious and unreasonably confusing and complex. With all the variety of equipment around them, the Messrs. Garroway, Fleming and Lescoulie give the appearance of baffled fathers on Christmas morning who are intrigued with a new set of electric trains but are not quite sure how they work.

Everyone on the show is self-conscious and overawed by all the technical devices with which they are surrounded, yet what appears on the screen is not a great deal different from what has been seen on a number of other shows, notably Ed Murrow's "See It Now." "Today," in short, is the slave rather than the master of its own inventiveness and ingenuity.

The preoccupation with gadgetry makes for a program which the viewer must watch and cannot only hear; there's so much confusion on the show that a listener feels compelled to look to find out what's going on. When he does, it's often not worth the time. Old-fashioned radio has its points in the morning.

Indeed, one of the great problems of "Today" on its first week was it tendency to build to a succession of anticlimaxes. There was much hoopla about going to Washington, but what was shown? A parking lot, first empty, and, an hour later, full. There was a melodramatic radio pick-up from abroad; it was snowing there.

The establishment of the communications center was a sound idea, but its technical magic will be most vivid if it is just shown on the screen, not endlessly discussed. Too often "Today" tries "gimmicks" just for the sport of it when actually greater simplicity would give the program added authority.

Mr. Garroway is doing an excellent job as an informal presiding official, but he should be relieved of running technical errands and allowed to assume a more detached perspective on the whole proceeding. From such a position he might be able to contribute more of his observant commentary and wit, the latter being a quality which "Today" especially needs.

Surprisingly enough, "Today" also is rather sketchy with the hard news of the morning, and in this regard is not as complete as many radio news programs. Mr. Fleming's assignment could be expanded to good advantage and he should not be hurried.

All in all "Today" is a challenging experiment for which Mr. Weaver deserves real credit, and no doubt he will soon have an answer as to how many persons are going to look at TV first thing in the morning. In the meantime, since he is to some extent making his debut in the journalistic field, he could help his show by adopting as a rule of thumb a healthy skepticism of publicity handouts, especially his own.

The Nixon Telecast: Personal Story Brings High Drama to TV

September 28, 1952

After Senator Richard M. Nixon's defense of his personal trust fund of $18,000 last Tuesday evening, there can be no further doubt about television's influence on the political scene. On all major counts his was a remarkable performance peculiar to the video age.

The telecast by the Senator was easily the moment of high drama in the campaign thus far; the plot and setting were a playwright's dream. A handsome and youthful figure, with his pretty wife at his side, sat in a lonely studio before the cameras. He had thirty minutes in which to argue his case before a jury of millions and stave off personal tragedy. Whatever he did was history in the making.

For the initial fifteen minutes the Senator was very effective. Amazingly self-assured under the circumstances, he sat quietly at a desk, looked directly at the camera and with understatement began the recital of his affairs. If he never addressed himself directly to the moral issue of the fund that aroused a national furor, he spoke earnestly and persuasively. He gave his audience a sense of sharing his personal ordeal.

The second half of the program saw Senator Nixon succumb to theatrics. The story of his children's love for their little cocker spaniel which they had received as a gift was an awkward sequence to be injected into a candidate's discussion of his qualifications for the Vice Presidency.

Senator Nixon then took a tack which seemed to dilute even further the impact of what had gone before. In launching into a routine campaign speech attacking his opponents and effusively championing General Eisenhower, who was to decide his political fate, there was somehow lost the element of poignancy and personal crisis that was felt during the program's opening.

Even with these limitations, however, there can be no gainsaying that the program had the high emotional content that in television and radio always has won a broad response. The glimpses of Mrs. Nixon, the little details of their family life and the climactic appeal for support were unusual in political broadcasting from a studio, certainly on the level of the campaign for the country's second highest office.

But if Senator Nixon hardly can be blamed for turning to his own advantage the emotionalism and melodrama inherent in his unprecedented situation, the important point to remember is that the extraordinary circumstances are not likely to be duplicated again.

Hence it must be hoped that other political leaders will not regard the Nixon type of program as a pattern for the future use of television under normal campaign circumstances. Because if impetuous partisans should misinterpret the broadcast as merely a magic format worth copying, the consequences could be perilous to Democrats and Republicans alike.

There is a very real danger in superimposing the methods of show business on politics. Chiefly, these methods can result in misleading oversimplification of vital issues and the substitution of emotion for information, slogans for reasoning and glamour for understanding. Especially in a visual medium having easy access to the nation's mind, the problems of government must be presented soberly with the hope to inform, not just to divert.

The philosophy of broadcasting that Hooper and Nielsen popularity polls justify the means may have at least a commercial plausibility in the entertainment world. But governmental issues hardly lend themselves to dignified, calm and judicious determination by the code of the returned box top.

There are many legitimate ways in which television can and has contributed wholesomely to the political field. From the voter's standpoint the most rewarding is the televised press conference, where a candidate has to stand on his feet. It still is the most revealing of a candidate's personality, opinions, and knowledge of issues. Other variations may serve much the same purpose.

Where the risk comes is when the world of politics steps over the line into the purely entertainment sphere. Then politicians try to become actors or campaign topics turn up as plays or vaudeville sketches.

At the time such practices may seem harmless in themselves and justified if there is a chance of influencing a few votes. But here the political world could profit from the experience of broadcasting. In radio it was the disheartening truth that once the bars were lowered a little here or there on certain programming practices a whole succession of compromises quickly followed. And the pattern is repeating itself in some phases of television.

Now—not tomorrow—is the time to hold the line against television turning politics into a coast-to-coast vaudeville show or a daytime serial.

Because if that happens it would be but a short step for video to become the platform of the irresponsible demagogue. Then television's power could be frightening.

Sweeping and Imaginative in Conception, "Omnibus" of Ford Foundation Makes Video Debut

November 10, 1952

The TV-Radio Workshop of the Ford Foundation made its debut on television yesterday afternoon with a program called "Omnibus." There is only one word that fits the occasion: bravo!

Rarely has there been one presentation so sweeping and so sensible in its imaginative concept, so disdainful of video's traditional inhibitions and so gloriously triumphant in its execution. It is what television has needed for a long time.

"Omnibus," which is being shown each week at 4:30 P.M. Sundays over the CBS network, runs a full ninety minutes and on its premiere had so many treasures that they can only be taken up individually.

Easily the most exciting and arresting segment was the appearance of Rex Harrison and Lilli Palmer in "The Trial of Anne Boleyn," written especially for the program by Maxwell Anderson. Here was the stimulating and adult theatre for which TV is starved.

In his television playlet, Mr. Anderson admittedly drew rather liberally on his earlier full-length success, "Anne of a Thousand Days," in which Mr. Harrison appeared. What he did actually was to do the trial scene that, in his Broadway play, took place off stage.

But in the trial scene as done on television, Mr. Anderson wrote with a compactness, sensitivity and earthiness all too seldom seen on the screen. And as brought to life by Mr. Harrison and Miss Palmer in superb portrayals of Henry VIII and Anne, it was a poignant and powerful delineation of human relations.

A new play, "The Bad Men," was contributed by William Saroyan. It was a typical Saroyanesque fairy tale—plotless and formless yet entrancing in its mood and love of people.

His setting was a railroad and his cast a railroad clerk, two Indians, a little boy enamored of the West, and a bitter girl. Out of this bewildering mosaic Mr. Saroyan, as by now is his familiar way, fashioned his own version of a Good Samaritan. It was appealing theatre.

The opening portion of the program was devoted to Martyn Green in brief excerpts from "The Mikado." If the emphasis was somewhat more on Mr. Green than on Gilbert and Sullivan, it was a spirited introduction to "Omnibus."

For bringing "The Witch Doctor," a short film showing a Haitian voodoo dance, to the mass audience of TV, the Ford Workshop deserves the thanks of all. It is an impassioned poem of movement that in its stark simplicity represents striking use of the cinema art.

Tying together all the diverse parts of "Omnibus" is Alistair Cooke, the author and radio commentator for the British Broadcasting Corporation, and he is ideal in the assignment. His style is diffident and casual yet both thoughtful and amusing as circumstances require.

There are many other individuals deserving of mention: Alex Segal for his direction of the Anderson play; the interpretation of Russell Collins as the stationmaster in the Saroyan work, the conducting of Lehman Engel of the Mikado excerpt, and William Spier, the overall producer of "Omnibus."

But something also should be said in behalf of Robert Saudek, executive producer of the Workshop, who translated the Ford Foundation's dream into impressive reality. He is off to a fine start in the television experiment that could have a profound and constructive influence on the whole medium in many different ways. The measure of the program's success is that its potential influence cannot be summarized in one writing.

Why Millions Love Lucy

March 1, 1953

> In the comical trials of Lucy and Ricky Ricardo TV audiences recognize the exasperation and warmth of their own lives.
> *New York Times Magazine*, March 18, 1953

Last week's signing of a record $8,000,000 contract to keep "I Love Lucy" on television another two years was economic confirmation of the obvious. The weekly TV adventures of Lucille Ball and her husband, Desi Arnaz—"and/or" Lucy and Ricky Ricardo—clearly are not susceptible to the usual mundane standards of appraisal. By every reasonable criterion they are something very special.

Not since the heyday of the fifteen-minute broadcasts of "Amos 'n' Andy," which back in the Nineteen Thirties brought American home life to a halt every evening, has a program so completely caught the interest and affection of the public. "I Love Lucy" is probably the most misleading title imaginable. For once all available statistics are in agreement: millions love Lucy.

"I Love Lucy" is as much a phenomenon as an attraction. Fundamentally, it is a piece of hilarious theatre put together with deceptively brilliant know-how, but it also is many other things. In part it is a fusion of the make-believe of the footlights and the real-life existence of a glamorous "name." In part it is the product of inspired press agentry which has made a national legend of a couple which two years ago was on the Hollywood sidelines. In part it is the fruit of the perennial unpredictability of show business.

But whatever parts make up the whole of "I Love Lucy," the most trenchant fact is that week after week upwards of 40,000,000 persons tune in Lucy and Ricky at 9 o'clock (Eastern Time) on Monday evening. What makes them do it? What has Lucy got?

The distinction of "I Love Lucy" lies in its skillful presentation of the basic element of familiarity. If there is one universal theme that knows no age limitations and is recognizable to young and old, it is the institution of marriage—and more especially the day-to-day trials of husband and wife. And particularly on television, which plays to the family circle sitting in its own home, it is the single story line above all others with which the audience can most readily identify itself.

"I Love Lucy" has no monopoly on the humor inherent in marriage; the idea is as old as the theatre itself and television channels are cluttered with rival shows rather pathetically hoping that the "Lucy lightning" will strike. But what seems to escape most of these imitations is the extraordinary discipline and intuitive understanding of farce that gives "I Love Lucy" its engaging lilt and lift.

Miss Ball and Mr. Arnaz always know what they are about. Every installment of "I Love Lucy" begins with a plausible and logical premise. Casually the background is laid for the essential motivation: Lucy vs. Ricky. Only after a firm foundation of credibility has been established is the element of absurdity introduced. It is in the smooth transition from sense to nonsense that "I Love Lucy" imparts both a warmth and reality to the slapstick romp which comes as the climax. The viewer has a sense of being a co-conspirator rather than a spectator in completely unimportant yet amusing high-jinks.

"I Love Lucy," in other words, is marriage projected in larger-than-life size but never so distorted that it loses its communion with the viewer at home. By the art of delightful exaggeration Lucy and Ricky put marriage in sharp focus.

As sheer farce, "I Love Lucy" has the fragility of this form of make-believe, and what the show would be without Miss Ball is a prospect about which no one should think. Unquestionably, she is the unrivaled top TV comedienne of today, a complete personality blessed with a very real and genuine comic artistry. How she was ever wasted as a sexy glamour girl in the motion pictures passes all understanding anywhere except Hollywood.

Miss Ball's gifts are those of the born trouper rather than the dramatic school student. First and foremost is her sense of timing; in this respect she is the distaff equivalent of Jack Benny. Maybe it is a roll of her big eyes. Maybe it is the sublime shrug which housewives the world over will understand. Maybe it is the superb hollow laugh. Maybe it is the masterly double-take that tops the gag line. Whatever it is, it comes at that split-second instant that spells the difference between a guffaw and a smile.

But the most durable and recognizable quality conveyed by Miss Ball—perhaps it is the real heart of "I Love Lucy"—is wifely patience. Whatever the provocation or her exasperation, she is always the regular gal and the wonderful sport. On stage and off, Miss Ball is a person.

Mr. Arnaz, alias Ricky, is a success story in himself. Before TV he was known primarily as an orchestra conductor. The very qualities which presumably hampered his advance at that pursuit were turned to advantage on "I Love Lucy."

His rather marked accent and his unprofessional style of performing were wisely left alone. The result was a leading man far removed from the usual stereotyped stage husband. It was a case of awkwardness being recognized as an asset. Today—after two seasons in his role—Mr. Arnaz is rapidly becoming a competent actor.

As Ethel and Fred Mertz, the landlords, neighbors and friends of the Ricardos, Vivian Vance and William Frawley consistently turn in performances that are veritable cameos of resignation to the unpredictable ways of Lucy and Ricky. Would that the supporting casts of most other TV shows were half as good!

Probably no event in recent theatrical history has occasioned as much national suspense as the birth of a son to Lucille and Desi. By careful advance filming of the script the TV Ricardos also welcomed a new arrival. The two events managed to coincide on the same day because the child was delivered by Caesarean section. But it was plain luck that the birth of a boy happened to be exactly as called for in the script.

The expected birth of a child, including the mother's obvious condition, seldom, if ever, has been used as the basis for an extended comedy series. There were a number of protests. But most viewers welcomed the tasteful and tactful handling of the sequences and certainly the humorous side was recognized by every parent. And, unlike so many shows that stand still, doing the same thing over and over again, "I Love Lucy" now has a limitless supply of comedy material in bringing up the child.

Perhaps that's the explanation of why millions like "I Love Lucy." It's very human—and so are we.

Delightful "Peter Pan": Marriage of Media Is Noted in Inspired Video Offering

March 13, 1955

There was no question of the news in television last week; it was Mary Martin's radiant "Peter Pan." The electronic excursion into Neverland was perhaps television's happiest hour. In spirit and laughter a whole country joined hands with the little boy who wouldn't grow up.

Monday evening on the National Broadcasting Company's network was an exhilarating tonic. In a day when the realities of life press in only too relentlessly, upwards of 65,000,000 persons could feel the indescribable glow of fairyland. The magic of TV and the wonder of make-believe were joined in an experience not soon to be forgotten.

What made Peter Pan so supremely delightful? Miss Martin, yes; many times yes. Cyril Ritchard as Captain Hook, too. Sir James M. Barrie as well. But there was something elusive and indefinable, a quality and a heart. Call it a sublime fusion of skill and inspiration.

In the rejoicing over the telecast of "Peter Pan" considerable emphasis understandably has been placed on the importance of the NBC triumph to the whole future of TV. The ramifications are bound to be many, varied and beneficial. But lest it be forgotten, Monday night was not only a television night. It also was a theatre night.

The greatness of the "Peter Pan" telecast stemmed from a marriage of media under ideal circumstances. The advantages of "live" television and the advantages of living theatre were merged as one. Alone neither medium could have offered the miracle of Monday evening.

The grace, infectious buoyancy and inventiveness of "Peter Pan" were not born overnight. The premiere on Broadway was preceded by months of planning and toil by many hands. There were the weeks of rehearsal and then the run.

The living theatre—bumbling, economically inefficient and bewildering darling that she is—has managed in the age of mass media to hold on to something vital and precious: the time to be creative. Television will never survive without her.

The importance of having the time to be good was apparent in the heavenly flying through the air of Miss Martin, in her glorious performance that had spontaneity and yet was so professionally perfect and assured. The dances of Jerome Robbins? How different in their originality from the TV norm! And the style of Mr. Ritchard, so sure and deft and such magnificent fun.

There were, in short, many jewels, each brought to its own distinctive sparkle by patience, imagination and fantastic hard work. Could they be mined in the hurry-up land of TV with its cruel rating systems? Not yet at least.

Television's role—different but no less vital than the theatre's—was to take these cherished gems and hold them forth for a nation, not a handful of persons to see. Under the guidance of Fred Coe, NBC did just that and used the camera as the creative tool that it is, complementing and heightening the craftsmanship of the theatre.

Many persons who attended the Broadway performance and saw the TV version have remarked that the Monday night performance seemed the better of the two. Perhaps one explanation may be that with TV everyone had a perfect front-row seat and, in most instances, saw "Peter Pan" with their children, the only real way, incidentally, to see the Barrie play.

But the influence of TV certainly didn't stop there. It's almost hard for the mind to grasp that people of every walk of life were sharing a joyful evening at the theatre. This was no rare treat just for those with the ability to pay a box-office price or for those in the right geographical location. Thanks to television, the proscenium arch of Broadway was moved to wherever there was a home screen.

The National Broadcasting Company is entitled to unstinting praise for its wisdom and vision in forgetting formula-thinking in television and opening up its schedule to accommodate "Peter Pan." In the jargon of the trade it may be called "big television" but far more accurately it is sensible television, even elementary television.

"Peter Pan" came in the nick of time. In late months television has been increasingly preoccupied with film, with the use of television as a sort of neighborhood movie house of the air. Films will always play a part in TV, but true TV is live video—the actuality, reality and immediacy of a living and breathing performance that happens as you see it.

Excitement. That was what "Peter Pan" had, the excitement of the theatre. Television has its own brand of excitement, but it isn't quite the same. Usually the TV brand doesn't quite have that same intangible status of an event, an occasion, which makes theatre-going the delight that it is. The telecast of "Peter Pan" did have that status.

Now a viewer can only offer a prayer that television will not try to formularize its trips to the theatre or make them so often or mechanically that they become reduced to just another video format. The flexible NBC policy is exactly right: Do the unusual when the opportunity arises, but don't try to force it. Don't make theatre-going on TV a routine; make it something to be anticipated.

The theatre and television need each other, artistically and economically. Happily, they already are complementary, not competitive. As the years go by many ways will be found in which they can cooperate, with incalculable benefits to both. "Peter Pan" has advanced brilliantly the union of the arts; this is a union that must be continued.

Johnny Carson: CBS Offers Answer to That Man Gobel

July 8, 1955

The Columbia Broadcasting System may have a comer in a young man named Johnny Carson, who now has his own show at 10 o'clock Thursday evenings. He a humorist of the quiet, unhurried school and he has a most engaging smile and personality. With help, he could go places.

CBS apparently intends to use Mr. Carson as its answer to George Gobel on the National Broadcasting Company network. The construction of last night's show was disconcertingly similar to the pattern of Mr. Gobel's program—the trick opening, the off-beat pattern, the musical interlude and then the sketch on home life.

Such copy-catting is a serious mistake in [sic] altogether the wrong way to go about advancing Mr. Carson's career. The young man is no Gobel; he has neither the uncanny timing nor the performing experience. To invite comparison is only to do a disservice to Mr. Carson.

What Mr. Carson does have is a singular youthful charm and an impish twinkle in the eye. He seems like the proverbial nice guy down the block. To capitalize on this asset manifestly is the CBS assignment; last night Mr. Carson was not fortified with sufficiently strong material or an adequately competent supporting company.

The best part of the show was Mr. Carson's delivery of a report on the teen-age problem, which included the statistic that there were 27,000,000 boys and girls who were in absolutely no trouble at all last night. The country's high schools, he further suggested, were becoming nothing but breeding grounds for education. It is this sort of a line that Mr. Carson can throw away effectively.

The rest of the show, unfortunately, was only too typical summer video fare—a routine girl vocalist, a conventional jazz unit and a sketch about a guest who did not know when to go home.

CBS might be well advised to give Mr. Carson more inspired directorial guidance and a brisker script. He would seem worth the investment, if only because he is a such a warm and pleasant individual on the home screen.

New Phenomenon: Elvis Presley Rises to Fame as Vocalist Who Is Virtuoso of Hootchy-Kootchy

June 6, 1956

Elvis Presley is currently the entertainment world's most astonishing figure. The young man with the sideburns and the mobile hips is the rage of the squealing teen-agers and his records are a hot item in the never-

never land of juke box operators and disk jockeys. By any reasonable standards of success he is big business.

Mr. Presley made another television appearance last night on the Milton Berle show over Channel 4; indeed the entire program revolved around the boy. Attired in the familiar oversize jacket and open shirt which are almost the uniform of the contemporary youth who fancies himself as terribly sharp, he might possibly be classified as an entertainer. Or, perhaps, quite as easily, as an assignment for a sociologist.

Mr. Presley has no discernible singing ability. His specialty is rhythm songs which he renders in an undistinguished whine; his phrasing, if it can be called that, consists of the stereotyped variations that go with a beginner's aria in a bathtub. For the ear he is an unutterable bore, not nearly so talented as Frankie Sinatra back in the latter's rather hysterical days at the Paramount Theatre. Nor does he convey the emotional fury of a Johnnie Ray.

From watching Mr. Presley it is wholly evident that his skill lies in another direction. He is a rock-and-roll variation on one of the most standard acts in show business: the virtuoso of the hootchy-kootchy. His one specialty is an accented movement of the body that heretofore has been primarily identified with the repertoire of the blond bombshells of the burlesque runway. The gyration never had anything to do with the world of popular music and still doesn't.

Certainly, Mr. Presley cannot be blamed for accepting the adulation and economic rewards that are his. But that's hardly any reason why he should be billed as vocalist. The reason for his success is not that complicated.

Witty Commentator: Brinkley Enlivens NBC Convention Coverage

August 17, 1956

A quiet Southerner with a dry wit and a heaven-sent appreciation of brevity has stolen the television limelight this week at the Democratic National Convention. He is David Brinkley, who together with Chet Huntley has been providing the National Broadcasting Company's running commentary from Chicago.

Mr. Brinkley quite possibly could be the forerunner of a new school of television commentator; he is not an earnest Voice of Authority imparting the final word to the unwashed of videoland. Instead of the pear-shaped tones he has just a trace of a soft Carolina drawl. He contributes his observations with assurance but not insistence.

But, during the many long hours in Chicago, where at times it has seemed there has been only a national convention of commentators, Mr. Brinkley's extraordinary accomplishment has been not to talk too much. He has the knack for the succinct phrase that sums up the situation. Sometimes his incisiveness has been such as to catch camera men and directors off-guard; he's finished his trenchant commentary but out of TV habit they wait for more.

It is Mr. Brinkley's humor, however, that is attracting audiences. It is on the dry side and rooted in a sense of relaxed detachment from all the political and electronic turmoil around him. With a neatly turned sentence or two he frequently manages to put a given convention situation in an amusingly civilized and knowledgeable perspective.

Mr. Brinkley is the regular Washington correspondent on NBC's nightly "News Caravan," but this is his first important break. He was born thirty-six years ago in Wilmington, N.C. He worked for The United Press in Nashville and on Southern newspapers. He joined NBC in Washington in 1943 and in 1949 took over the "News Caravan" spot.

The sudden rise of Mr. Brinkley on the national scene and the introduction of Mr. Huntley—the two work well as a team, incidentally—is the first real change in the network news situation in a long while. This convention marks the first time that the Columbia Broadcasting System, with such established stars as Edward R. Murrow and Eric Sevareid, has had real competition from NBC in the matter of news personalities. So far NBC has had a little the edge.

The CBS pre-eminence always has been something of a sore point with NBC, but now even NBC might enjoy the irony of how it found a solution. Picking a chap from its own shop and then leaving him alone. But the larger significance of the happenings in NBC news may lie elsewhere. Who would have thought good old gray NBC could relax and laugh a little?

Elvis Presley: Lack of Responsibility Is Shown by TV in Exploiting Teenagers

September 16, 1956

Television broadcasters cannot be asked to solve life's problems. But they can be expected to display adult leadership and responsibility in areas where they do have some significant influence. This they have hardly done in the case of Elvis Presley, entertainer and phenomenon.

Last Sunday on the Ed Sullivan show Mr. Presley made another of his appearances and attracted a record audience. In some ways it was perhaps the most unpleasant of his recent three performances.

Mr. Presley initially disturbed adult viewers—and instantly became a martyr in the eyes of his teen-age following—for his strip-tease behavior on last spring's Milton Berle program. Then with Steve Allen he was much more sedate. On the Sullivan program he injected movements of the tongue and indulged in wordless singing that were singularly distasteful.

At least some parents are puzzled or confused by Presley's almost hypnotic power; others are concerned; perhaps most are a shade disgusted and content to permit the Presley fad to play itself out.

Neither criticism of Presley nor of the teen-agers who admire him is particularly to the point. Presley has fallen into a fortune with a routine that in one form or another has always existed on the fringe of show business; in his gyrating figure and suggestive gestures the teen-agers have found something that for the moment seems exciting or important.

Quite possibly, Presley just happened to move in where society has failed the teen-ager. Certainly, modern youngsters have been subjected to a great deal of censure and perhaps too little understanding. Greater in their numbers than ever before, they may have found in Presley a rallying point, a nationally prominent figure who seems to be on their side. And, just as surely, there are limitless teen-agers who cannot put up with the boy, either vocally or calisthenically.

Family counselors have wisely noted that ours is still a culture in a stage of frantic and tense transition. With even 16-year-olds capable of commanding $20 or $30 a week in their spare time, with access to automobiles at an early age, with communications media of all kinds exposing them to new thoughts very early in life, theirs indeed is a high degree of independence. Inevitably it has been accompanied by a lessening of parental control.

Small wonder, therefore, that the teen-ager is susceptible to overstimulation from the outside. He is at an age when an awareness of sex is both thoroughly natural and normal, when latent rebellion is to be expected. But what is new and a little discouraging is the willingness and indeed eagerness of reputable business men to exploit those critical factors beyond all reasonable grounds.

Television surely is not the only culprit. Expose magazines, which once were more or less bootleg items are now carried openly on the best newsstands. The music-publishing business—as Variety most courageously has pointed out—has all but disgraced itself with some of the "rock 'n' roll" songs it has issued. Some of the finest recording companies have been willing to go right along with the trend, too.

Of all these businesses, however, television is in a unique position. First and foremost, it has access directly to the home and its wares are free. Second, the broadcasters are not only addressing themselves to the teen-agers but, much more importantly, also to the lower age groups. When Presley executes his bumps and grinds, it must be remembered by the Columbia Broadcasting System that the even the 12-year-old's curiosity may be overstimulated. It is on this score that the adult viewer has every right to expect sympathetic understanding and cooperation from a broadcaster.

A perennial weakness in the executive echelons of the networks is their opportunistic rationalization of television's function. The industry lives fundamentally by the code of giving the public what it wants. This is not the place to argue the artistic foolishness of such a standard; in the case of situation comedies and other escapist diversions it is relatively unimportant.

But when this code is applied to teen-agers just becoming conscious of life's processes, not only is it manifestly without validity but it also is perilous. Catering to the interests of the younger generation is one of television's main jobs; because those interests do not always coincide with parental tastes should not deter the broadcaster. But selfish exploitation and commercialized overstimulation of youth's physical impulses is certainly a gross national disservice.

The issue is not one of censorship, which solves nothing; it is one of common sense. It is no infringement on the medium's artistic freedom to ask the broadcaster merely to exercise good sense and display responsibility. It is no blue-nosed suppression of the proper way of depicting life in the theatre to expect stage manners somewhat above the level of the carnival sideshow.

In the long run, perhaps Presley will do everyone a favor by pointing up the need for earlier sex education so that neither his successors nor TV can capitalize on the idea that his type of routine is somehow highly tempting yet forbidden fruit. But that takes time and meanwhile the broadcasters at least can employ a measure of mature and helpful thoughtfulness in not contributing further to the exploitation of the teen-ager.

With congested schools, early dating, the appeals of the car, military service, acceptance by the right crowd, sex and the normal parental pressures, the teen-ager has all the problems he needs.

To resort to the world's oldest theatrical come-on just to make a fast buck from such a sensitive individual is cheap and tawdry stuff. At least Presley is honest in what he is doing. That the teen-ager sometimes finds it difficult to feel respect for the moralizing older generation may of itself be an encouraging sign of his intelligence. If the profiteering hypocrite is above reproach and Presley isn't, today's youngsters might well ask what God do adults worship.

Tribute to "Omnibus": Expected Loss of Program Brings Call for Similar Experimental Shows

July 30, 1958

The National Broadcasting Company's confirmation of earlier reports that "Omnibus" faces an uncertain future is bound to be disquieting. Television has so few outlets for experimental programming that a further reduction in the scope of Robert L. Saudek's pioneer project must be regretted.

At the moment, a series of golf matches will take over a portion of the Sunday afternoon time heretofore occupied by "Omnibus"; Sam Snead and Cary Middlecoff will supplant Leonard Bernstein and Joseph N. Welch.

Meanwhile, NBC says it "hopes" to offer perhaps four "Omnibus-type" of presentations within the framework of a series of specials on Friday and Sunday evenings. Moreover, the network says, it is "exploring the possibility" of doing some "Omnibus" productions at other time periods.

Perhaps something will be worked out, but the vague phraseology of the network is not inconsistent with the process of erosion as it usually applies to a TV venture facing difficulties. "Omnibus," after seven years on the three networks, seems in considerable danger of disappearing.

Under the circumstances, the simplest and most tempting course is to upbraid NBC. But an examination of the network's problems on Sunday afternoons and evenings would appear to have some pertinency.

"Omnibus" is an expensive show and this year NBC will offer on Sunday nights a new series of dramas, many of them originals, which assuredly will be a welcome development. Unfortunately, as of this writing, the drama series is a long way from being sold out and appears to be having much the same sponsorship problem as "Omnibus."

Concededly, the drama presentation is not a replacement for "Omnibus," which explored other fields beside straight theatre. But the record should show that while NBC is curtailing one program of substance it is adding another in good evening time. The over-all picture, in short, is not entirely one-sided.

But, on the other hand, "Omnibus" always has been something more than a mere program; in many ways it has been a major symbol of a venturesome spirit in an industry beset by many forces that dictate pursuit of safe and proven ways. As only one example, the "Omnibus" dramatic editorial against capital punishment last season simply could not have been expected on other TV shows.

Except for "Omnibus," in fact virtually the whole burden of experimental TV programming has been borne by Sunday morning programs; indeed, presentations offered by religious organizations and "Camera 3" offer more adult leeway in theme material and more inventive production technique than any other group of offerings.

But on a larger scale it has been "Omnibus" that has primarily held aloft the banner of experimentation. Granting that the industry's agenda for next season does seem more promising than last year, television nonetheless always must find room for continuing trial of new program forms, ideas and talents.

In other art forms the disappearance of a particular undertaking generally is not too serious; before long the slack is taken up by a similar project, which may have the added advantage of embracing fresh points of view. But in only a very few years the TV viewer has witnessed the passing of "The Search," "See It Now," "Wide Wide World" and "The Seven Lively Arts." There have been replacements to be sure, but not of the same individual character.

It is now so late in the television selling season that a regular fall niche for "Omnibus" seems virtually out of the question. But at least efforts should be made to preserve its identity, even on an irregular basis, so that it may have another chance next year. That much "Omnibus" surely has earned.

Forthright Radio News Program: Smith's Analysis of Alabama Violence Shows Real Role of Commentator

May 28, 1961

In broadcasting's coverage of the violence in Alabama no program has been more forthright and clear than the radio commentary of Howard K. Smith, chief Washington correspondent for the Columbia Broadcasting System. He had the advantage of being in Birmingham during the first assault on the Freedom Riders, but even so his remarks had the ring of hard-hitting common sense reminiscent of the late Elmer Davis.

Mr. Smith's talk, delivered last Sunday evening over the CBS radio network, painted an exceptionally vivid picture of the forbidding atmosphere of extremists taking over the center of a community while the police looked the other way; in fact it was a description not excelled by any of the newsreel films shown on television.

But the CBS reporter went beyond the surface brutality and suspension of law and order to deal in strong editorial terms with the deeper issues. He decried the "baseless myth" that Supreme Court rulings are not the law of the land. He noted that the United States cannot insult the 65 percent of the world's people who are non-white by condoning white supremacy.

Mr. Smith, himself a native of Monroe, La., went on to observe in conclusion:

"The emptiness of what the South fears needs exploring with a searchlight. No community that, for example, has finally accepted token integration has suffered from it. In fact there's evidence that a burden of tension and of unconscious guilt falls from the white man when the falsehood of racial supremacy is abandoned.

"The high Negro crime rate, which is a fact, cannot be met and stopped until the Negro ceases to be a depressed and deprived American.

"To those who suggest all this is going to take time, the answer from the news all over the world is this, 'we have not got the time.' The basic question may soon well be, 'Do we really deserve to win the cold war?' "

That his views will not receive unanimous approval in the South is, certainly, keenly appreciated by Mr. Smith, who knows first-hand the depths of the resentment over unsolicited opinions from the North. But it does broadcasting credit that one of its trained journalists should speak his mind so uncompromisingly.

By any reasonable standard of interpretation Mr. Smith did engage in unadorned commentary of a sort that once contributed so importantly to the diversity of ideas broadcast over the sound medium. It is precisely such a display of conviction, of determination to influence society's course for good, that does build respect for the world of broadcasting.

Yet the policy of CBS News with respect to commentary does seem ambivalent. What apparently is deemed good for radio is not deemed suitable for TV. Some months ago Mr. Smith's nightly commentary from Washington was dropped and never replaced.

More recently—in fact, just a matter of days before the radio program—Mr. Smith appeared as narrator on "CBS Reports," the program that offered interviews with white and Negro citizens on the problems besetting Alabama.

After the TV program there were reports that Mr. Smith had been disturbed by the decision of higher network officials to temper some of his remarks and indeed that he had hoped his participation in the film could be edited out entirely. As events were to prove in only a matter of hours, the gravity of a situation that Mr. Smith likened to a dictatorship was not exaggerated.

The individual who tuned in Mr. Smith's successive TV and radio appearance naturally cannot be privy to all the editorial considerations that may have governed both presentations. "CBS Reports" was more concerned with a broad sampling of opinion on the segregation issue; Mr. Smith's analysis hit directly at the hard news and included his personal views. A case could be made for different objectives in news presentations being handled differently.

Yet whatever the assorted ramifications of CBS's long-standing policy with respect to commentary, a policy that consistently gets rather badly bent in application, one fact remains: the dominant broadcasting medium of today—TV—did not enjoy the full benefits of what Mr. Smith had to offer. Night-time video, with its large audience, heard a diluted Smith, while Sunday night radio, with a very much smaller potential audience, heard Smith at his best.

In the context of the requirements of today it might behoove all three of the networks to reappraise their fundamental approach with respect to commentary on TV. In the course of their programs, Chet Huntley and David Brinkley manage to incorporate an editorial aside on occasion, but they hardly have enough time to do the job of which both are capable. The American Broadcasting Company has one of the widest ranges of commentary on radio but nothing of consequence on TV.

To judge by the recent unpleasantness in Washington, one of the complaints against TV is the sterility of the average nightly fare. But would not one of the simplest and more exciting remedies for this state of affairs be the presentation by the networks of their equivalents of Walter Lippmann, James Reston, Arthur Krock, Marquis Childs and David Lawrence in an evaluation of the meaning of the day's happenings.

Men of journalistic stature might well take the place of vapid weather girls who use five minutes to say it is raining outside but will be clear in the morning. The good that might be accomplished in generating thought and controversy on major issues could be enormous and a rotating stable of commentators, including some from the South, could be something to look forward to each evening.

Straight reporting of the news is only part of TV's job; the other part of the task in enabling the public to make up its own mind is the presentation of opinions with which a set owner may agree or disagree.

Chapter Six

The Quiz Show Scandals

The rise of the prime-time quiz show to immense popularity during the mid-1950s was a television phenomenon that my father followed with his usual attention. When the quiz programs first gained a wide following, he praised the use of ordinary citizens as contestants. He wrote with enthusiasm in 1955 about the opera expert Gino Prato and his success on *The $64,000 Question*. He called the program "one of the most cleverly contrived shows of many a year." He has as yet no idea of how right he was. By 1956 he was complaining that the quiz programs had become "mostly talk" as producers sought to limit the amounts any contestant might win in a single week. As Dad noted, the actual cost of these major quiz shows is very low by television standards.

Two years later, the first public revelations of scandal were beginning to be heard. My father laid out for readers of the *Times* on September 7, 1958, the internal pressures on the makers of quiz shows that had fostered an atmosphere of deceit on such shows as *Twenty-One* and *Dotto*. His discussion of the "carry-over" of successful players showed that a drive to maximize ratings and to keep costs down led to manipulation and fixing of results. According to at least one law enforcement figure in the probe, Joseph Stone, my father's column provided a timely education for the attorneys looking into the quiz programs during the fall of 1958.[1]

When the scandal erupted in its full dimensions during the last months of 1959, Dad dealt with the revelations surrounding Charles Van Doren, the Columbia professor of English whose "brilliance" on *Twenty-One* turned out to have been bogus. Yet my father refused to level all of the blame at television alone. His columns in October and November 1959 addressed larger issues of journalistic ethics and patterns of corruption throughout the mass media. His remarks did not reshape any network practices, though they might have influenced how some reporters at the *Times* behaved. Four decades later, many of the shady techniques about which he wrote are now staples of journalism, show business, and academic life. My father would not have been surprised at that outcome, but he would have been disappointed.

Man in the Street: The Public Often Can Outshine TV Stars

August 14, 1955

The past week in television has reaffirmed one of the most elementary yet most often ignored principles of good television: there's no people like non-show people. The TV that deals with actuality, with real unglamourized people behaving as themselves, is still the most fascinating TV of all.

Though "The $64,000 Question" is one of the most cleverly contrived shows of many a year, the program's success rests in great measure on its ability to capitalize on the TV medium's unique power; to hold the mirror up to life as it is revealed spontaneously before a viewer's eyes. This is the uncanny wizardry of TV, totally different from either stage or screen; yet it is amazing how infrequently this magic is put to fruitful use.

Long after "The $64,000 Question" has disappeared and been forgotten, it is just possible that the quiz show will have succeeded in persuading TV producers that they have overlooked their most obvious yet inexhaustible supply of material: people.

Watching Gino Prato, the cobbler, decide how far he should go in pitting his knowledge of opera against a fortune was the intriguing come-on of "The $64,000 Question" for the last month. But what also made Prato an entrancing figure overnight was his own personality, modesty, pluck and intelligence. A nobody, in short, turned out to be a warm and intriguing guy.

Curiosity about other people, about new persons one may meet, is a fundamental human instinct, and it is the nature of video to sharpen it. Yet, if there are programs that do endeavor to satisfy this curiosity, there are only too many that miss their opportunity, either wholly or partly.

Take quiz shows in particular. Run down the list. One sees for the most part the same chronically familiar set of faces, the rather specialized group of individuals who likely as not are celebrities in TV and not any place else. Some are fine, but why not a new tack for a change?

In a country of 160,000,000 the woods must be filled with Gino Pratos, Mrs. Kreitzers and Patrolman O'Hanlons. Why not, for a change, some rotating panels of everyday people who are new to the viewer? For that matter, let's bring back something on the order of "Information Please" with Gino Prato, Mrs. Kreitzer and Patrolman O'Hanlon for a starting panel. Phooey on the celebrities. They're not needed so much in the TV age. TV can make its own, if it only will, and in the process impart some added and continuous excitement to viewing fare.

TV errs grievously in its tendency to make its guests fit into some predetermined studio mold; what TV needs is the freshness and element of the unexpected from the outside world. A small yet meaningful illustration is John Daly's habit of answering for the participants on "What's My Line?"

Except in absolutely necessary cases he should let the guest take over completely. Since Mr. Daly is a sound reporter, after the game is over couldn't he probe a little into the lives of the non-celebrity guests? The guests often are interesting persons, but a viewer hardly gets to know them.

Surely every viewer can recall one of TV's most common occurrences: An absorbing person is on the screen; then the TV interviewer sits there with egg on his face and doesn't know what question to ask next. If the video prima donnas could forget their own magnetism and do a little reportorial digging, they would find a gold mine in many a John Doe.

What applies to quiz shows also applies to discussion programs in many instances. The majority of the participants on these presentations are Congressmen, officials and authorities.

But there are others, too, in the United States who have opinions on life. Just once couldn't there be a discussion on a pressing national interest by a farmer in Kansas, a factory worker in New England, a professor from New Orleans and a doctor from Los Angeles? Television is being expertized almost to death. It would be a novel experience to hear more often what the people think, to expand to a half-hour what a show such as "Today" often does in abbreviated style.

Television complains continually that it doesn't know where its material will come from next and in desperation repeats itself *ad nauseam.* Yet, meanwhile, it overlooks the bottomless reservoir of intelligent people in the world who could be brought to the home screen with their varied faces, personalities, viewpoints and backgrounds. With a little imagination they could be used in limitless formats. All that's required is the interest and willingness to go out and find them. They're certainly there.

Quizzes Mostly Talk: "$64,000 Question" and "Big Surprise" Use Less than Half Their Times on Queries

September 26, 1956

Holding a stopwatch on two of the most celebrated quiz shows—"The $64,000 Question" and "The Big Surprise"—reveals that the quiz itself doesn't even consume half of the time the program is on the air.

A number of viewers have noted recently that the so-called giveaways are indulging increasingly in time-consuming stage waits. Coupled with the rather ample volume of commercials it sometimes seems as if the questions had become almost incidental.

Last night on "The Big Surprise," which was presented at 8 o'clock on Channel 4, a total of thirteen minutes was concerned directly with the business of answering questions. Four minutes were devoted to commercial plugs. The rest of the half hour was consumed by miscellaneous chit-chat, including remarks by a "Mrs. X," a refugee from Russia, who expressed fears for her safety.

On "The $64,000 Question," which was seen at 10 P.M. on Channel 2, almost exactly the same total of time—thirteen minutes and fifteen seconds—could be associated directly with the game. The remaining thirteen minutes again were given over to incidental remarks, including Randolph Churchill's awkward epilogue.

Some exchanges between the master of ceremonies and a guest on a quiz show are both necessary and appropriate; in the case of a new participant there should be an explanation of his or her background.

But when the questions themselves do not constitute even 50 per cent of a quiz show the producers are spreading themselves pretty thin. Of course, there is a sound economic purpose behind their strategy. The actual costs of these major quiz shows is very low by television's going standards. Many weeks pass before a participant hits a sizable amount, which bring the average weekly cost down below that of a half-hour TV film.

Incidentally, the four minutes of commercials exceed the television industry's so-called code of self-regulation. That rather meaningless document calls for only three minutes of advertising in a half hour. Network leniency often has let it run a half minute longer. Now there has been an extension beyond that. Adding to the commercialism are the signs bearing the sponsor's name or trade-mark, which are spread liberally around the studio and repeatedly caught by the camera.

It is perhaps of more than passing significance that one of the oldest and most successful of the quiz programs, "What's My Line?," pays the most attention to the game itself. And in all its years on the air it still hasn't raised its top price above $50. Other shows might take the hint and put the quiz back in the quiz program.

As a postscript to the timing of commercials, let it be noted that last night's NBC news program (at 7:45 P.M.) offered three minutes and fifteen seconds of advertising during its fifteen minutes on the air. Who exactly does subscribe to that so-called code?

Under Suspicion: Investigation of Quiz Shows Shakes Viewer's Faith in TV's Integrity

September 7, 1958

Television has run into early-fall difficulty. The quiz shows, which represent $100,000,000 or so in annual time sales and production costs have come under the dark cloud of suspicion; it seems quizzes are part of show business. At the moment nearly two dozen are on the air.

The viewer's passive faith in the integrity of the home screen purportedly has been shaken by the abrupt and awkward cancellation of "Dotto," which disappeared in the wake of a complaint that some of its wholesome contestants were given the answers before the questions.

Adding to the set owner's disillusion has been a set of rather erratic allegations that "Twenty-One" was not an awesome citadel of total recall but an electronic offshoot of a boardwalk carnival. Charges that the

Monday evening divertissement was "fixed" or "rigged" were met by rebuttals taking the form of libel suits and recorded conversations alleging blackmail and other psychiatric irregularities.

District Attorney Frank S. Hogan promptly took an option of the quiz scandal. The Democratic nominee for the United States Senate, who later in the season should become a more familiar figure on the parlor medium, indicated that in another week he might be able to decide whether any TV quiz producer was a prospect for a state-supervised isolation booth or merely a deft manipulator of public credulity.

Network executives understandably have their fingers crossed that time and TV's narcotic influence will persuade set owners to forget insinuations that broadcasters deal in packaged phoniness.

The current unpleasantness stems from the innovation that projected "The $64,000 Question" into the limelight. The public may have been impressed by the reward in five figures, but within Madison Avenue's realistic confines greater attention was accorded what is now known as the "carry-over."

The weakness of primitive quizzes was that their formats did not permit building interest over a period of weeks. "The $64,000 Question" corrected this defect by having a contestant return again and again.

By having a contestant make repeated appearances, he became fixed in the public mind and could be exhaustively publicized. Moreover, he imparted a sense of continuing identity to a show which otherwise only had a master of ceremonies as a familiar weekly feature. All these factors translated themselves into higher ratings, which for the sponsor interested in selling his product, represented the crucial test.

The longevity of a television contestant, in other words, had a direct connection with the basic sales function of the video medium. During the peak of the hoopla which each major quiz experienced for a time there arose an increasing emphasis on how many weeks a contestant was on the air. Some shows purposely adopted or altered formats to afford contestants the possibility of longer and longer runs. Then the publicity clamor was directed toward constantly increasing total winnings.

Last week the rating value of the "carry-over" was succinctly acknowledged by Dan Enright, co-producer of "Twenty-One," in explaining why he gave Herbert Stempel, a former contestant, an advance on his winnings. "We needed Stempel on the show," he said.

Economically, introduction of the "carry-over" was immensely attractive because a program could talk about huge sums interminably but only pay them out infrequently. The longer a contestant stays around, the lower is the program's weekly average cost.

But a companion problem of the "carry-over" format, which was quickly adopted by most of the quizzes, was that for all practical purposes it introduced the "star system" into the half-hour rating periods. If a rating was to be enhanced and excitement and interest increased, a quiz could not tolerate the lackluster dog who unfortunately was endowed with more knowledge than personality. The big brain may have its revered place on the secluded campus but on television it must be complemented by a more marketable commodity such as sex appeal.

In short, the principle of careful casting was applied to many quiz shows, and producers began to walk a delicate chalk line between conflicting pressures. On the one hand, contestants should meet the test of typicalness to preserve a viewer's sense of vicarious association with the individual on the screen, which takes the form of either admiring or loathing a contestant. On the other, a contestant could hardly be a walking vacuum without disastrous consequences in the next month's Trendex.

Accordingly, many—though by no means all—quizzes accepted the necessity of some "control" of contestants. An applicant for a spot on a daytime quiz, for instance, might be asked as many as 500 preliminary questions before being accepted. After this brainwashing session a producer had a fairly complete understanding of the contestant's capabilities, what he could or could not answer. One young lady who achieved considerable national renown as a quiz expert earlier had served as a guinea pig in testing sundry formats for a package producer.

A concomitant of obtaining reasonably engaging contestants has been to choose question categories that would heighten the factor of contrast. It would be one thing for a kindly old lady to hold forth on the intricacies of tatting but much more intriguing if she were a connoisseur of the machinations of the Mafia.

"Dotto" was accused of furnishing answers to selected contestants, and naturally this proved disturbing in a business that has enlisted the services of reputable banks and armed guards to disabuse viewers of the notion that there might be backstage hanky-panky.

But pending the receipt of more information than is available at the moment, the sin of "Dotto" ultimately may be construed as one more of degree rather than principle. There do exist some circumstances that appear to warrant a measure of skepticism.

For an example, it has been contended—and not convincingly refuted—that some contestants have been afforded a sabbatical in which to become proficient in a given area before appearing on the air. Admittedly, this is a far cry from outright fraud, but neither is it exactly cricket.

Long before the present sound and fury began a contestant on two major quiz shows—not yet a party to the publicity proceedings—remarked in writing on the coincidence that some of the questions asked in his "screening" re-occurred on the air. Moreover, he contended, he later learned that his rival was given a question that she had been unable to answer in a "screening." The latter person lost.

Cynics in the show business also have questioned the use of established theatrical stars on quizzes. It is argued that celebrities who depend on the affection and applause of the audience are not apt to run the risk of appearing in public as complete boobs. If nothing else, astute theatrical agents are not likely to condone a situation where their clients might stand helpless from Maine to California, egg dripping from their unhappy faces.

Another inevitable factor of "control" is a show's budget. A sponsor buys a quiz program with the clear understanding that his weekly outlay will run to a regular figure. Were a profusion of geniuses to appear simultaneously and receive maximum monetary satisfaction, the rules of the game inevitably would need tidying up.

But the chief problem in the realm of quizzes is the profusion of such programs. Competition necessarily is exceptionally severe and new twists must be imparted to the basic format. With some quizzes explanation of the rules has become so complicated that there is barely time left for the commercials.

Television already has begun to display its sensitivity to the flurry of current charges. Masters of ceremonies are taking extra pains to play up their integrity, and quite possibly there will be an increasing trend to quizzes that are rooted in pure luck rather than education by rote. Interestingly enough, shows which place primary emphasis on a game, not big money with repeat appearances of guests, have proved the most durable.

But many realists say that with a television sponsor's traditional distaste for anything controversial—let alone suspect—the quiz fad will die quickly. One agency executive said last week "their day is done."

Indeed, even before the outbreak of the present situation, the ratings for quizzes indicated that they were inviting indictment on charges of boredom and repetition. Meanwhile, under the criminal code, it would seem a matter for legal authorities to decide whether there has been "fixing." But under the theatrical code there indubitably has been "staging."

A Plague on TV's House: Rigged Quiz Shows Viewed as Symptom of the Age, with Many Guilty Parties

October 12, 1959

The investigation by the House Special Subcommittee on Legislative Oversight of rigged quiz shows is symptomatic of the age of corner cutting. The admitted participants in the backstage hanky-panky are headed for a lonely exile, the fall guys for a mode of life rooted in opportunism. But there is guilt enough to be spread around among the many; it should not be reserved only for the select few.

The public, which would have been the first to scream if that little shoemaker had not won, has seen again that a superior education is not of itself an automatic assurance of moral fiber. Perhaps now the eggheads will be more lenient toward the hucksters, who at least have the grace to acknowledge in advance that they will not be deterred from pursuit of the buck.

The attitude of the networks and sponsors in the current inquiry is a dismal one. Their plea that they were "deceived" along with everyone else is not persuasive. Dark gossip about rigged games circulated in the industry for weeks before the scandal broke. But the ratings were booming and no one wanted to learn the worst.

Actually a television show does not reach the air without the constant involvement of representatives of networks, advertising agencies and sponsors; their relationship with the package producer is sustained and extremely intimate. They are also present at all shows.

Accordingly, the realities of the TV life do not allow the suggestion that none of these worldly wise individuals had the slightest inkling that quizzes were arranged for maximum suspense, that guests were chosen with the view toward their publicity potential and that unattractive personalities were unceremoniously dumped. These objectives could not have been achieved without careful control of the entire show, including questions and answers.

But if many industry individuals, including some of far higher stature than have been named in the Washington inquiry, felt that they were merely going along with the prevailing standards, who can say them naught?

Many members of Congress see nothing wrong in owning stock in broadcasting stations while weighing legislation that affects broadcasting; yet heaven help the appointee who fails to divest himself of a possible conflict of interests. The Federal Communications Commission has had its share of embarrassments in recent months.

The significance of the quiz scandal does not lie in the individuals involved. Rather it is an illustration of an influence of TV that has been little appreciated.

Before TV's introduction there was an essential line of separation between the necessary function of selling and mankind's innumerable other interests and pursuits. But with television everything and everybody—thoughtful people, creative artists and the human being's greatest treasure, his realm of ideas—frequently and often almost imperceptibly, have become mere instruments of merchandising. Here, there and the other place are signs of little erosions of old-fashioned values.

As vice presidents of the leading advertising agencies testified only last summer, today's norm is the contented sponsor whose all determining goal is to sell his product. But no longer is this dominant philosophy applied only to the advertising over which the sponsor properly should have complete control. It also governs the content and form of TV's cultural output. Only news and public-affairs programs are still exempt from the salesman's purview.

What has resulted is a world of continuing and unrelenting compromise that all parties have come to accept as part of the price of commercial success. It is, of course, inexcusable to offer a phony game as an honest one, and the charges of perjury resulting from the scandal are a matter of utmost seriousness.

But television cannot enter a blanket disclaimer of responsibility; keeping everyone in the pressure cooker of higher ratings was bound to lead to trouble. The fact that an entire industry kept mum until the situation leaked must speak for itself.

It may be another generation before anyone can appraise accurately the effect of the economic inflationary cycle upon the nation's culture; rising costs plus the need for constant expansion do put a cruel premium on success, which in TV means be popular or perish.

Meanwhile, the talk in Washington of devising new legislation to avoid a repetition of the quiz episode seems as forlorn as it is unnecessary. Men, not laws, are determining in the matter of environment and conscience. But when the hearings close something useful should remain: a mirror in which to have a look at one image of 1959.

Journalists' Junkets: Quiz Show Headlines Raise Question of How Clear Is Conscience of Press

October 27, 1959

The television industry, for the moment somewhat bruised by the scandal over quiz shows, is nursing a small resentment against the press. Not because of the headlines that inevitably are part of the exposure of the fixed quizzes. But rather because they feel substantial elements of the Fourth Estate are not entirely qualified to don the mantle of unsullied virtue.

What many responsible individuals in TV have in mind is a practice that is prevalent in many areas of American business, not just video, but could not exist without the tacit consent and knowledge of the world of journalism. In the parlance of the newspaper trade, the practice is known as "the junket."

The junket is an arrangement whereby a business pays all the expenses of a newspaper man to cover an event of direct financial interest to the company. The word "expenses" is totally inclusive: de luxe transportation between the newspaper man's home office and perhaps some location thousands of miles away, the finest accommodations at the most costly hotels, the best meals and liquors, a continuous round of parties, laundry, taxis, etc.

Tradition demands that discussion of the junket always be done in a low voice. Companies that pick up substantial tabs for newspaper men do not wish to raise a hue and cry; they must live for a favorable press and a pleasant public climate. Similarly, as the economic beneficiaries of the junketing era, the gentlemen of the Fourth Estate are prone to shyness in the matter.

The quiz scandal, which apparently is going to lead to fuller disclosure of many things beside prefabricated intellectualism, inevitably has affected the status of the junket.

Veteran video hands, who for weeks now have been hearing that they are the twentieth century's original sinners, are not quarreling with the duty of the Fourth Estate to champion motherhood. They merely contend that what goes on backstage in the newspaper business is not without pertinency in a consideration of contemporary ethics.

Lest they be drawn and quartered by writers who are inclined to insist on having the last word, the people who know about junketing, which includes everybody in TV, prefer that no questions be tape recorded.

But, measured by any standard, junketing is a very prevalent practice in TV. Directly involved are the scores of newspapers, trade papers, magazines and press associations that authorize employees to participate. The financing of the junkets is done not only by networks but also by sponsors, advertising agencies, individual stations, airplane lines and hotels.

One TV organization, for instance, sends upward of sixty newspaper men, which means critics, columnists, reporters and editors, to Hollywood every year. The expense-free stay is usually four or five days, but this can be extended by the newspaper man if he wants to persuade a second firm to subsidize a second week. The newspaper man, incidentally, can go at his own convenience.

Another approach, which goes back to the motion picture industry's lusher days, is to import whole planeloads of newspaper men—eighty to 100 is not unusual—for several days of meeting celebrities and listening to executives reiterate the company line. The mass method not only assures saturation of the press; it also denies newspaper space to the competitors of the sponsor of the junket.

Since journalists have the usual trouble with spouses who feel they never get out of town, some junkets are designed to preserve domestic harmony. Wives and husbands—sometimes even the children too—often may arrange a change of scene on the cuff.

One of the accepted rituals of junketing, of course, is for all concerned to make quite clear that the writer's independence is in no way jeopardized. Bemused public relations experts in and out of TV, are content to let the Fourth Estate rationalize the problem but they are not clumsy at threading the needle.

Why, they inquire, will a newspaper think a story warrants coverage if someone else pays the bill but not if the publication must meet the cost of assigning its own man? Does a newspaper man think he is being invited because of his enchanting personality or because of his position? Why would junkets continue if the company that picked up the bill did not feel it had a determining influence over what appeared in the paper? To keep up with TV, might not the press identify which of its articles were done on a sponsored or sustained basis?

In this regard one episode is amusing. A TV company gently ferried a newspaper man from the West Coast to Paris and back. Patiently, the firm waited for its usual reward. Not a line appeared. The reporter reasoned the party had everything but news. The novice now heads tomorrow's list of the disinvited.

In junketing, as in everything else, there are scattered exceptions to the normal practice, but TV's masters of gamesmanship are not so easily thwarted. There is, after all, the companion tradition of "the Christmas loot," the practice of showering holiday presents upon the high and low in journalism.

Where, it is asked, is the publication without at least one staff member who did not preserve the Yuletide harmony by his willingness to be remembered? Not too many years ago a broadcasting trade publication took a bold editorial stand in the matter: Send the loot to the newspaper man's home. It's a nuisance to have the stuff delivered to the office.

The loot of Christmas in TV runs to substantial sums; one typical organization shells out about $25 worth of merchandise for each of 150 newspaper men. Yesterday, it was learned, an influential concern in the industry plans this season to abandon the practice.

Moreover, throughout the year, a smaller stream of gifts filters into newspaper offices; some are of fairly substantial value.

All in all, TV folk agree their own mode of living has left much to be desired. But they just wonder whether perhaps others have not yet got around to their own fall housecleaning.

The Quiz Scandal: Legal and Moral Issues of Van Doren Affair Said to Need Resolution

November 4, 1959

The case of Charles Van Doren is bound to be discussed for a long time. The educated young man inevitably is going to pay a high price for his sordid participation in the rigged game of "Twenty-One."

He has lost his job at Columbia University and yesterday he was dropped by the National Broadcasting Company. Naturally, no one wishes to see him subjected to indefinite persecution. At some point he is entitled to the repenter's second chance.

But the emotional wave of sympathy for Mr. Van Doren, engendered in part by the TV medium itself, is not a reassuring commentary on today's sense of values.

In his testimony Mr. Van Doren sought to paint a picture of a weak man caught in the clutches of some of video's confidence men. Up to a point this may have been the case.

But it must not be overlooked that his situation extended far beyond TV. He went before grand jury, took the oath to tell the truth and lied. And similarly, it cannot be overlooked that he waited until the very last moment to recant and then only under the pressure of events.

Other individuals of far lesser station and intelligence have found themselves in the same dilemma, but they have been forced to pay the price without having the chairman of a Congressional committee say, "God bless you."

The point takes on some pertinency in the light of Mr. Van Doren's description of the harrowing personal ordeal that he suffered. Yet over the week-end he apparently was not so totally unmindful of the publicity implications of his presentation in Washington that he could not find time to write a newspaper man what amounted to a plea for special understanding.

Indeed, it remains to be seen whether the aftermath of the scandal is not going to prove just as distasteful as the actual rigging of the contest.

As of the present, the record still shows that a duly constituted grand jury, one of the basic foundations of a democratic society, was treated almost with contempt. To judge by the available evidence, apparently many witnesses felt that going before a grand jury was just another little quiz game to which the answers could be rigged in advance.

District Attorney Frank S. Hogan has indicated that he is not yet finished with the matter and perhaps there are legal difficulties that preclude further action.

But at the moment much more than the TV industry has been tarnished. The seriousness of the grand jury's investigative role has been beclouded. The action of the court in impounding the jury's presentment at the behest of programs now acknowledged to be rigged must puzzle the layman.

For many youngsters addicted to television the Van Doren case may be their first exposure to a genuine moral issue. If only for their benefit, it would seem wise to tidy up any remaining loose ends and not allow hysteria or emotions to confuse show-business trickery with the solemnity of due process of law.

Formula for TV: Quiz Scandal Shows a Need for New Rules

November 8, 1959

What can—or should—be done about television in light of the quiz scandal?

With the pattern of rigging shows and the confession of individual participants now spread on the public record, attention has turned inevitably to the question of whether the medium needs new ground rules. Suggestions have included establishment of a noncommercial network, greater government regulation, and elimination of the advertiser from actual preparation of programming.

Implicit in all the proposals are not only a belief that some steps are needed to prevent a repetition of the quiz situation but also a more basic dissatisfaction with programming as a whole.

Accordingly, the problem of TV's future essentially divides itself into two parts: (1) What type of schedule on the home screen would meet the test of public interest and necessity; (2) How can it be achieved?

In all the high emotion of the moment a measure of calmness is needed with respect to TV's shows. There can be no excuse for displays of sheer brutality and violence that exceed all reasonable requirements of good entertainment; this is an undeniable blot on the medium. And no one can deny that there is a high degree of mediocrity.

But at the same time TV is not composed entirely of madmen. One of the primary functions of the medium is solely to entertain. Many viewers who have done a day's work simply want to be diverted; they do not want to be uplifted, educated or anything else. The adventures of "Peter Gunn" or "Maverick" have an altogether legitimate place in the output of a mass medium. To scrap popular fare that appeals to a huge audience would be sheer folly and in itself an abdication of responsibility.

But where TV has erred is in its assumption that its obligation to the mass must be the overruling consideration in an ever-increasing number of instances. What has happened, in short, is that TV has lost a sense of proportion and balance in its programming. Under the rising commercial pressures the element of diversity simply has tended to be ignored more and more.

Immediately, however, a companion question arises: who is to determine such a balance? How many Westerns should there be? Is it more in the public interest to have a weekly series of poor live dramas or an occasional dramatic series seeking higher quality? How much discussion of political matters should there be, say, on a Wednesday night?

Determination of balance gets down to the basic matter of control of the schedule. Where does control lie? The answer is that it has been virtually nonexistent. There has never been even a minimum set of standards that everyone in the industry knew had to be observed. Individual networks have sought to establish their own policies, but frequently the forces of competition had dictated a string of compromises. What happens to standards, for example, when one network puts on a good sustaining series and immediately a second network retaliates by offering another Western?

It is this fundamental vacuum that not only explains many of TV's current reforms but also makes rather academic many proposals for reform. A favorite gambit, for instance, is that networks should assert control over sponsors and agencies. But what value is this if the networks simply prepare those types of shows that will interest advertisers? The theoretical separation of advertising and programming is also no guaranteed cure-all: would not the programs be designed to attract the spots?

Obviously, there is no pat formula to assure minimum standards, but there is a procedure that could be adopted and it might at least point the way.

First, the networks should be required to spell out the categories of programming they plan to do. In other words, they should make some sort of commitment as to how they propose to use the airwaves. Let them determine their own measure of balance in programming, not by government direction, and for once the public could have some insight into the ratio between one type of program or another.

But such a declaration should not be presented in the form of a so-called "sample week"; this device enables a station to crowd one type of programming into less favorable hours and others into peak viewing periods. Balance, if it is to mean anything, must be done across the board, within the morning, afternoon and evening segments of each programming day. Application of the philosophy of balance on such a basis could virtually reshape TV.

It is at this juncture that a revitalized Federal Communications Commission should step into the picture. Annually, it should ask the networks to come to a hearing and show that their freely made promises have been matched by performance. In the case of persistent and obvious variations between pledges and performances then, the networks would have only themselves to blame if the FCC reviewed its licensing procedure or Congress felt new legislation were required.

At present networks become almost hysterical over the thought of being licensed directly; under existing rules only the individual station affiliated with a network is licensed for a three-year period. But some licenses of individual stations affiliated with networks run out each year. Since one of the networks is the prime source of programming for most stations, would not the programming intentions of the chains be pertinent to renewal of the licenses of affiliated stations?

Both the TV industry and the FCC have been equally remiss in not facing up to the matter of programming intentions. It is not censorship, only common sense, for the government to ask the user of public property—the airwaves—what he proposes to do with it and then ask him to demonstrate that he kept his word. Such a procedure at the very least would meet one acid test: the public would have the means of knowing what was going on.

Assessing Effects of Life under the Table: Influence of "Payola" on Culture Weighed

November 20, 1959

Call it "payola," "kick-back," "pay-off" or "ice." The semantic nuances vary from one branch of show business to another, but the practice of buying or giving commercial favors on an extra-curricular basis has been part of the entertainment world for years.

Probably the most novel aspect of the present concern over payola—the melodic definition employed in Tin Pan Alley and environs—is the display of interest by the House Special Subcommittee on Legislative Oversight and District Attorney Frank S. Hogan. Traditionally, life under the table has prospered in the shade offered by official indifference.

On the other hand, Government officials are not undeserving of a considerable compassion. The kickback has been so gracefully refined that it may be legal. All one does is welcome a partner who is not wanted.

From the standpoint of the public weal, however, the current inquiries do have a significance transcending such legalities as "commercial bribery." Most hanky-panky in the business world is a relatively private moral problem. But in the case of radio and television, payments made in the dark may have a strong cultural influence affecting the nation as a whole.

The present concern for payola in the recording industry actually stems from a fight that has been going on for years.

The dispute originates with many of the country's foremost composers—the writers of Broadway and Hollywood hit tunes—who have been dismayed to witness the dominance of rock 'n' roll on the nation's airwaves.

If the investigations establish that disk jockeys, who are a decisive factor in influencing sales of records to the huge teen-age market, took bribes to plug rock 'n' roll, the repercussions could be formidable.

In the recording world payola may come from a variety of sources. The publisher of a tune may pay for favored treatment on a disk jockey program. Or the record company may foot the tab. Or it may come through a distributor. The money goes to whichever individual selects a tune, either a program director or a disk jockey. That there are honest "deejays" goes without saying, but payola on a national basis is believed to be substantial.

But Dick Clark, an idol of the rock 'n' roll teen-age set, may have taken something of a bad rap in publicly being "exposed" as one who owned an interest in music publishing and record firms. The American Broadcasting Company has ordered Mr. Clark to divest himself of any conflict of interest.

If Congress is going to pursue this area realistically then it will find that many singing stars have a "conflict of interest" at some point. Innumerable singers own "a piece" of a music publishing house and favor songs of that house in their repertoires. And ages ago it was common practice for some singers to insist that, in exchange for plugging a tune, they be listed as a co-author of the number, a neat dodge that could mean royalties for years.

Cynics in broadcasting wonder, however, whether the disk jockeys are not relatively small fry when it comes to pay-offs. A more enticing area may be with the packaged shows. The big question is this: Might pay-offs have some bearing on quality?

In some advertising agencies one man may have enough influence to decide whether producer A or B will be the beneficiary of a million-dollar commitment to purchase a film series. The skeptical world of Madison Avenue finds it hard to believe that the lucky winning producer does not understand some of the reciprocal amenities that may be observed. In other instances, it is said, the agency man may be cut in more formally, regularizing the procedure for the benefit of the Internal Revenue Service.

Wherever an executive in broadcasting holds great powers in either granting or denying the wishes of an eager solicitant, say in the construction of scenery or the making of commercials, the possibilities of supplementary revenue are not entirely nonexistent.

A first cousin of these arrangements is either a "tie-in" or a "cut-in." An ambitious soul may have a fine idea for a program but to get it on the air may mean becoming a reluctant associate of a network, talent agency, sponsor, et al.

The uproar over hidden commercials—sly plugs for concerns and products not directly involved in sponsorship of a program—amuses veterans in show business. In a stage play if a star holds up a given brand of Scotch, it should be good for a case of Scotch every week through the show's run.

The Hollywood motion-picture industry is a past master at the hidden commercial. It's old stuff, for instance, to arrange for use of a particular make of automobile. In exchange, those who make it feasible find that the manufacturer places a new model at their disposal for some years. To avoid tax complications, the experienced Hollywood folk request that the car be registered in the manufacturer's name.

In television, with its giveaway shows, etc., the hunting has been much more lucrative. Both in Hollywood and New York there are companies that specialize in planting surreptitious commercials, and the rates for such service are well established.

Comedians and masters of ceremonies can be tremendously cooperative, but at other times they may be unfairly accused. Commercials have become such a part of the American idiom that they may lend themselves to legitimate satire; some plugs are designed with that possibility in mind. The substitution of "like" for "as" in a cigarette commercial was genuine inspiration, thanks not to payola but to humorless intellectuals.

Whatever the varied methods of the mass media, they derive naturally enough from the mother of the theatrical arts—the living theatre. With smash hits and impatient big shots who want to display their influence there always has been an enticing margin between the price on a ticket and the price paid in the black market. How this difference—known as ice—has been split among parties with an interest in a success is a question that makes Broadway's engaging extroverts a study in diffidence.

But when the sins of the entertainment field are held up for review, its partisans have a good question: Why just pick on show business?

Note

1. Joseph Stone and Tom Yohn, *Prime Time and Misdemeanors: Investigating the 1950s TV Quiz Scandal—A DA's Account* (New Brunswick, N.J.: Rutgers University Press, 1992), p. 54. See also Kent Anderson, *Television Fraud: The History and Implications of the Quiz Show Scandals* (Westport, Conn.: Greenwood Press, 1978) and Terry Smith, "Jack Gould and the Quiz Show Scandals: How *The New York Times* TV Critic Covered One of the Biggest Media Scandals of the Fifties," seminar paper, Ohio University, June 1, 1992, courtesy of Terry Smith, JLG Papers.

Chapter Seven

Children and Television

One subject to which my father devoted extensive critical attention was television programming for children. With three young sons of his own during the late 1940s and early 1950s, he witnessed first-hand the impact of the new medium on the behavior of his family. In an age before remote channel changers, we sat too near the screen and wore out the dial that moved from one channel to another. He also noticed our preference for horse operas (Westerns) and science fiction over educational offerings. From the outset of his tenure as a television critic, Dad argued that broadcasters had a clear obligation to provide high-quality programs to younger viewers. That meant recognizing the special needs and vulnerabilities of children and not exploiting their credibility and trust.

More often than not, my father found that children's shows fell into the same bad habits as their adult counterparts had. Violence, commercialism, and low taste usually won out over sensitivity and responsibility. When he found praiseworthy shows such as *Kukla, Fran, and Ollie* or *The Howdy Doody Show* in its early days, he was gratified and enthusiastic. His support for *Howdy Doody* led my brother Richard and me to attend one program, and somehow(!) we happened to be the children picked out to box with Buffalo Bob Smith and Clarabell that day. By 1956, however, Dad had curdled on *The Howdy Doody Show;* it had become "wretched." He responded well to *Ding Dong School* except when its star, Frances Horwich, ventured into the outright plugging of vitamins and other products. On the other hand, when he saw what he regarded as a purveyor of trash and excess in Pinky Lee, he could be scathing.

My father's priorities for children's television were consistent. The networks owed youngsters decent shows at accessible times that instructed as well as entertained. Violence should be minimized and frightening topics avoided for the very young. Parents had a large role to play in selecting what their children watched, but broadcasters had a duty to think about more than profit and loss when it came to shows for children. Throughout the 1950s Dad lobbied for these values, but he recognized at the end of the decade that the economic pressures of television had diminished the initial promise of children's shows in much the same way that they had adversely affected adult offerings. Since contemporary children watch more television than ever and face a dearth of programs aimed at their needs, my father's comments about the early years of children's television have not lost their relevance to contemporary concerns.

Kukla and Ollie: Burr Tillstrom's Puppets Have a Spirit and Personality Unique in Video

March 27, 1948

With the opening of the coaxial network cable last January, one of the Midwestern shows to come eastward was "Kukla, Fran and Ollie" (7 P.M. Monday through Friday over NBC video). Though its local arrival was greeted with more enthusiasm than was accorded any of the other Chicago attractions, its welcome none the less was on the conservative side.

Now that there has been an opportunity to get to know the three principals of the show much better, it is obvious that "Kukla, Fran and Ollie" cannot be treated so casually. Without any question whatsoever it is the most charming and heart-warming excursion into pure make-believe that is to be found in television today—a program which in its taste, imagination and wonderful fun probably has almost as many adult fans as it does young admirers.

"Kukla, Fran and Ollie" technically falls into the classification of a "puppet show," but to regard it as such is to do the program the gravest of injustices. It is no more a conventional bit of puppetry than Mickey Mouse was a usual cartoon figure. Through the sheer artistry of its creator, Burr Tillstrom, the program has acquired a personality and a gay spirit which is utterly engaging and in terms of viewing, completely habit-forming. "Kukla, Fran and Ollie" has the verity and innate appeal of the ageless fable, yet it is projected with all the timeliness and know-how of contemporary theatre. On all counts it is uniquely television.

For the uninitiated, "Kukla, Fran and Ollie" requires a little explaining. The "Fran" is Fran Allison, an actress who usually is the only living person seen on the screen. With complete naturalness she serves as a sort of mother, sister and girl friend of the little figures in the enchanting and whimsical world of Mr. Tillstrom's imagination. For the most part Miss Allison merely stands to one side of the puppet stage and talks with the figures as they are most skillfully given voice and animation by Mr. Tillstrom. Yet, even with the lack of movement, she sustains superbly the illusion that the little figures are entirely real.

And very real they are. The mainstay of the proceedings is Kukla. In appearance he is a cross between a gnome, underfed brownie and a pet gray squirrel. In character he is the perennial worrier who always is afraid that each afternoon's adventure will end disastrously. If he is a little the world-weary cynic, he also boasts the proverbial heart-of-gold, being devoted to the friends who constantly exasperate him.

Of his friends the closest is the most wonderful dragon of all time—Ollie. Ollie has the mouth of an alligator but the traditional tooth of the dragon. He is the Peck's Bad Boy of the piece—a vain, humorous and lovable scamp who has a knack for getting in hot water and a better knack for getting out of it. He boasts a faculty for doing a double take or bellowing a stage guffaw which is completely hilarious.

Kukla and Ollie have much with which to put up. Among others, there are that young rabbit named Fletcher, who when company is coming insists that his floppy ears be freshly starched; Madam Oglepuss, a fugitive from high society; Beulahwitch, the old hag who can't do anything right but ride a broomstick in the wrong direction, and Cecil Bill, the world renowned stage manager, who speaks a jargon of his own.

It is within the framework of these characterizations that Mr. Tillstrom displays a theatrical craftsmanship which easily makes him one of the most truly creative influences in television. Day in and day out, he devises situations which are so far above the general run of children's fare that at the moment he is without serious competition in either television or radio.

Primarily, Mr. Tillstrom employs a form of presentation which is thoroughly comprehensible to even the very young members of his audience, but he never makes the mistake of being condescending or underestimating their intelligence. With a taste that is absolutely impeccable, he directs his satirical glance at all manner of subjects. At the same time he gets over a host of important educational values by the simple expedient of being amusing and never once getting near the word "education."

Mr. Tillstrom's adventurous ways may best be judged by the record. Once he called upon Kukla and Fletcher to execute a Chopstick Concerto for the piano and xylophone, replete with four movements. Again he went into opera, with Ollie and Madame Oglepuss performing "Hi, Diddle, Diddle" as an "answer" to a man named Mozart. Poor Ollie, incidentally, had to play the cat, dog and cow. On other occasions Kukla and Ollie built a television station and showed how Hollywood made a film.

In each case Mr. Tillstrom's work was thoroughly adult in its diverting subtlety and in its sharp yet agreeable spoofing of established institutions. At the same time each piece was funny and informative in its own right for the youngsters who had no interest in deeper meanings.

Too, what that rascal Ollie can do to the professional critic should make him the envy of all of show business. Miss Harriet Van Horne of The World-Telegram several weeks ago made the mistake of casting several very feminine aspersions on Ollie. Ollie, completely and volubly heartbroken, decided on the air not to send her a Valentine. A few days later The World-Telegram critic ran another story praising Ollie without reservation. To conserve newsprint The New York Times declares for Ollie now.

Hail Howdy Doody! He Triumphs over Mr. X, Survives Mr. Y and Always Delights the Youngsters

November 14, 1948

No mistake about it, it's Howdy Doody time. With a platform favoring double ice cream sodas for a dime, school once a year and plenty of movies, the earnest young boy who is the favorite of the Peanut Gallery finished third behind Truman and Dewey, racking up ten times the number of votes accorded Wallace. By a margin of 10,000,000 ballots, more or less, he snowed under that infidel Mr. X, who, upon investigation proved to be Howdy's twin brother, which made him Double Doody.

As the duly elected president of the boys and girls of America, Howdy is reigning supreme on television each afternoon at 5:30 as he prances before the NBC cameras under the knowing guidance of Bob Smith. Though plagued for the moment by the incessant questioning of Mr. Y, Howdy in all the wonderful make-believe of puppet imagery is still the first exclusive and most amiable creation of video-land.

Howdy came to life a little less than a year ago, a rather sprawling, awkward puppet who was heard only once a week. But within a matter of days he proved to be the proverbial smash, the delight of untold youngsters along the Eastern seaboard who sympathized with his distinctive character—a sort of cross between Dopey and Charlie McCarthy. Now he belongs to the elite of broadcasting: he is heard "across the board" Monday through Friday.

Mr. Doody, as he is never called, is the handiwork almost exclusively of Mr. Smith, who in a twelve-month period has exhibited a gift for dealing with children that is truly phenomenal. Previously identified only as the proprietor of an early morning chatter and song show a la [Arthur] Godfrey, he proved upon exposure to Howdy to be that rarest of souls: a man who avoids any hint of condescension toward the younger generation and makes the boys and girls feel partners in the spirited high-jinks of his wooden alter ego.

Thanks to Mr. Smith, those high-jinks are sparked by one of the most imaginative minds in broadcasting. For the Howdy Doody show is blessed with incredibly superb gadgets and, most importantly, a point of view which always is wholesome yet never stuffy.

Consider the honk-a-doodle. This is a much-needed machine which takes the honks of a mother goose and reproduces them in English. It can also work the other way around. Also, there's the forerunner of the Schmoo, the flap-doodle, which Howdy uses when he needs anything. And who couldn't feel sympathetic, too, toward Clarabell, the clown, whose vocabulary consists of shaking her head or blowing two affirmative toots on an automobile horn? Howdy's world is truly grand.

Interlarded with the engaging nonsense and pure fantasy, however, is an astonishing amount of information and education for the youngsters. Last Tuesday the visitor to the show was an Air Force colonel and of course that old bothersome Mr. Y wanted to know what made an airplane get up in the air. The resultant explanation was clear, succinct and enlightening, even for an adult.

Or take Howdy's heroic victory over Mr. X in the election. Without ever saying so, Mr. Smith offered what was a primer in democracy, explaining how to mark a ballot and the rules of an election contest in a free country. But it was all done with gaiety and harmless suspense so that it did not seem like education at all. Just now the irrepressible Howdy is embarked on a campaign to persuade his followers to collect old toys and take them to the nearest firehouse, where they will be repaired and put in shape for other boys and girls.

On all important moves affecting Howdy Doody, Mr. Smith is careful to consult the members of the Peanut Gallery, consisting of several rows of seats occupied each afternoon by visitors at the studios. His ability to prevail upon shy youngsters to speak up often makes for some of the most viewable cameos seen anywhere on the video screen. And in keeping a verbose lad within bounds, he displays all the suavity of the sophisticated night club master of ceremonies silencing a heckler.

In his spare moments, too, Mr. Smith thinks nothing of offering in the popular vein a polished performance at the piano or rattling off a set of lyrics which first the small fry and then the big fry of the household are apt to find themselves repeating days later.

In the extraordinary versatility of his performance, Mr. Smith may have hit upon the answer to the academic do-gooders who bemoan the influence of the comics and the thriller radio shows and, as a substitute, would jam old-fashioned tales into unwilling ears. The more constructive solution as suggested by the success of Howdy Doody is to offer something wholesomely different, something which is equally stimulating to the youthful imagination yet is not furnished in what children might regard as a demeaning manner. For many, many reasons, in fact, hail Howdy Doody!

Video and Children: Parents and Broadcasters Have Separate Roles

January 8, 1950

What is television doing to children? That provocative question again has come to the fore with the disclosure by several school principals that some youngsters are neglecting their homework in favor of the sundry attractions to be seen on the screen. Where there is a competition between the text book and the cathode tube, so the scattered reports of the educators show, scholastic marks are apt to tumble downward and the pupils may show up in class with rings beneath their eyes.

That there is a problem in the relationship between the younger generation and television probably will not be seriously disputed by any family which has had a set for some time. The existence of a continuous show in the parlor necessarily plays hob with the routine that existed before the arrival of the set. And what the child sees—and his reaction to what he sees—can be of enormous importance educationally, socially and emotionally.

But what is chiefly distressing about the present controversy over TV and the child is that it is being argued in terms of superficial extremes, as was the case in the debate between Al Capp and Norman Cousins on last Tuesday's "Town Meeting." If the experience in radio is a criterion, this will not prove particularly helpful in the long run.

Well-meaning organizations, perhaps with an eye on a headline here or there, are issuing statements which sweepingly condemn almost everything in television and lay the full burden of all sins at the broadcaster's door. In turn, the broadcasters here are taking refuge in irrelevant popularity ratings and are complaining that the "do-gooders" do not understand the "practical" aspects of their operation.

Obviously, nothing is to be gained by a continuance of "blaming the other fellow." The proper and constructive use of television in behalf of children can come only if both the parent and the broadcaster recognize that theirs is a mutual yet different responsibility and each must do his part, realistically and fairly.

If they are willing to face up to the truth, the average television parents must concede that they themselves in part brought about their child's preoccupation with television. A television receiver becomes an exceptionally handy "baby sitter" if parents want a little relief from youthful spirits at the end of a day or on a rainy afternoon or weekend. Later they may find the habit difficult to break.

Similarly, parents do not always concern themselves as they should with what a child sees on television or hears on the radio. Where parents may exercise adult direction as to what films their child sees or what comic books he may read, often they fail to participate to the same extent where broadcasting is concerned. The set in the house is just "on" without any conscious parental thought as to what may be coming out of it. In a very real sense, the adults in such cases are making the mistake of delegating their parental responsibility to the broadcaster.

If parents wish their child to acquire certain tastes and interests, they must take the initiative to develop their child's selectivity in tuning in. They will find far greater rewards if the share the experience of "finding" such a show as "Mr. I. Magination" or "Kukla, Fran and Ollie" rather than arbitrarily imposing a blanket censorship on cowboy films.

The decision on how long a child should look also must fall to the parents, who are the only ones to know whether TV is disrupting a homework schedule or excessively exciting a youngster just before bedtime. If they traditionally have believed that a night's sleep was a prerequisite to a job well done or that schoolwork came before too much moviegoing or stamp-collecting, it is hard to see why television should make any difference. Video is only something to see; it is not a way of raising children.

The coming of TV actually puts the parents on their mettle to see that there is a balance in the family's activities. If the parents feel that there is too much television in the house, then they must answer the further question: What efforts are they making to provide alternative diversions in the home? It is all very well for the articulate parents' group to complain of the lack of variety in programming on the air. But at the same time such a group also should recognize the need for variety in "home programming" by parents.

Great as is the parent's job, the broadcaster's responsibility toward children who look at television is even greater. Since he is entrusted with the attentiveness and interest of the younger generation for long periods of time, he must meet the obvious obligation of filling that time not only entertainingly but constructively and wholesomely.

Western pictures and puppet shows currently dominate the schedule for children and certainly they have their place, if only because they do have the substantial audiences which sponsors want. But this in itself is no excuse for the paucity of alternative types of shows. If the broadcaster seemingly can always reapportion his budget so that he can come up with one more bit of vaudeville, he could do the same in the children's field. Television's programming problems do not arise only from its limited budget of the moment. How it spends what money it has is the acid test of its programming intentions.

Television certainly sells itself short when it offers at an early evening hour, either here or in the Midwest, the doings of a vampire, as the CBS "Suspense" did; or a gruesome use of the knife, as the NBC "Lights Out" does, or a closeup of hands itching to strangle somebody as the DuMont "Hands of Murder" does. Such distasteful episodes, if presented at all, should come later in the evening when adults predominate in the audience.

But even more important is the fact that such excessive items of horror cannot be justified by the familiar argument that they "have an audience." If television really wants to get itself a following in a hurry, it simply has to summon the services of a strip teaser. Good taste and common sense keep the burlesque queen off video and they should do the same in the case of the mystery show producers who lose their heads.

No thoughtful viewer expects television to satisfy all tastes hour after hour and competitive considerations necessarily will continue to dictate some unfortunate juxtapositions in the program schedules. But the viewer is not being unreasonable in expecting that the broadcaster will do his utmost in achieving balance in his own individual schedule and will not drift carelessly or selfishly with the changing commercial tides. By self-discipline the television broadcaster will not only be serving his own best interest. He also will be serving the interest of parents and their children.

A Boy's Question: School Youngster Raises an Issue for Video

April 29, 1951

Public School 612, at 113 East Eighty-seventh Street, is a school for boys who have run afoul of the law or otherwise become involved in serious trouble. Its student body, embracing youngsters of the age level of grammar school and junior high, includes boys who have rolled drunks, drawn knives on store proprietors, engaged in hold-ups and participated in killings.

Last week as part of its regular assembly program, the school held a discussion on television. The families of virtually all the boys are on relief, but the majority have TV receivers at home, in itself a telling commentary on the times. Be that as it may, however, the boys proved intimately acquainted with the programs on the air and asked questions reflecting unusual alertness and intelligence.

After the formal program one boy had his own question to ask privately. He was dressed in dungarees and polo shirt. He had both a smile on his face and a twinkle in his eye and his sandy hair was appropriately tousled. He could not have been more than 9 or 10 years old. It was hard to believe that the boy might not have been a playmate of one's own son, let alone a lad with a record.

But it was with the directness of youth that the boy came to the point. There was no teacher in the room, just himself, three of his classmates and this writer. His question was as spontaneous as it could possibly be.

"Mister," the boy said earnestly, "the cops and teachers keep tellin' us that crime doesn't pay and all that. If they're right, how come television puts on so much crime stuff and shows how to do it?"

Here was no fancied theory of the penologist, sociologist, reformer, educator or a duly appointed committee assigned to make an exhaustive study. It was the overwhelming and terrifying logic of the true authority, the child who had been in trouble and could not reconcile what society told him to do with what society did.

What was the answer? As fortune would have it, the bell summoning the children to lunch rang before there was time for anything more than hurried generalities. But now, some days later, the two searching brown eyes are still there and cannot be evaded. For the boy, anonymous, troubled and wondering, is right, terribly right. He deserves an answer.

Under the guise of many different formats, television's schedules are lopsidedly heavy with "crime stuff." It is not just that the mystery thriller or the crime story does and should have its place in the realm of theatrical make-believe, which is something the boy in his personal situation admittedly might have difficulty in appreciating.

But he unerringly put his finger on the sore spot in two words: so much. Crime stuff is not represented solely in the excessively vivid shows specializing in horror and the macabre. It is to be found everywhere in the plethora of old movies which stress the glamor of racketeers and in the violence which is part and parcel of the Westerns. Even the very best in TV drama often goes in for the psychological murder thriller in one form or another.

A careful examination of the television schedules in New York will more than bear out the contention of the boy at P.S. 612. From mid-afternoon until late at night some place on the dial there usually can be found a show—"live" or film—which has for its motivating characters persons who handle a gun or flout the law. Hour after hour, it continues in a steady diet brought right into the home for the youngster to see.

And in their competitive drive to gain audiences and find the different "twist," what is the great incentive of the producers of these shows?

It is to come up with the crime that is done in a slightly different way or with the criminal or sleuth who is just a bit cleverer. The goal of the producer may be a better show, but the reasoning of the boy is not faulty; the net effect is to "show ya" how it is done in increasingly varied ways.

But to get to the boy's main point: "how come?" On the record of broadcasting there can be only one realistic reply: Crime pays handsomely. The mystery show is perhaps the quickest, easiest and cheapest way to get a substantial audience. It sells the sponsors goods and the viewers lap it up.

If the boy is to be answered honestly, obviously society as a whole must accept a large share of the blame. How can adults reconcile their admonition to youngsters that the criminal's way of life is evil and to be scorned if at the same time they sit hypnotized night after night watching a criminal's doings? If grown-ups unduly glorify the criminal for purposes of profit and escapist diversion, who is to point the finger at the child who steps over the law in pursuit of the same objectives? If the parent is indifferent to racketeering, is it the child who is supposed to sit on the Kefauver committee?

The television station owners, sponsors and advertising agencies altogether misunderstand their function in broadcasting, however, if they believe the indifference of a large segment of society gives them an excuse to adopt a similar attitude. Since they are privileged to have access to the public mind, they have accepted a unique and new responsibility which permits of no alternative but constructive leadership. To take refuge behind the alibi of merely giving the public what it wants without regard to the social consequences, is cultural subversion of the worst sort.

Television enters the home with an intensity, vividness and regularity heretofore unknown and is watched by children of all ages and, it should be stressed, at all hours. The sponsors and the broadcasters are creating new habits and new interests in the younger generation and they have a deep obligation as citizens, parents and business men to do all within their power to direct the new medium into wholesome channels. Above all, they must recognize that TV is vastly more than just a salesman: it is a teacher.

Crime and mystery shows always will be an integral part of television's fare and certainly the television industry cannot be expected to be guided by the needs of a minority boy who is in trouble. But the overemphasis on stories of violence and lawbreaking in television has exceeded all reasonable bounds and is little short of shocking. There are many other types of stories which can and must be shown in far greater volume.

Up to now each television broadcaster has insisted that his own operations in the crime show field were not too bad and that he could not be responsible for the industry as a whole. That line of expedient reasoning will not do. The broadcasters must recognize that they are bound to be judged in part by the cumulative effect of the actions of the industry as a whole. Certainly this will be the case when even the more thoughtful broadcasters thus far have lacked both the personal and corporate courage to champion openly desirable standards with a view to influencing the laggards.

It is up to television to straighten itself out, just as the boy at P.S. 612 is trying to do.

Pinky Lee Show Turns Children's Hour into a Conspiracy against Parents

November 8, 1954

The Pinky Lee show for children is a conspiracy against parents. Presented at 5 P.M. Mondays through Fridays over NBC, the program is a tasteless, witless and crude half hour that calculatedly exploits behavior in children that sensible mothers and fathers do their best to curb.

By trade Mr. Lee is concededly not a child psychologist but a hoofer, singer and comedian. As a new idol of the tots, he's never had it so good. It is only human nature for him to enjoy whatever good fortune comes his way. If he didn't put on the program somebody else would. The responsibility for Mr. Lee's show must rest therefore with those at NBC who have charge of such matters.

There is no deep mystery about the goal of Mr. Lee's program: It is to sell goods. But what is distressing and irritating in the extreme is the program's callous assumption that this end justifies the use of any means. Mr. Lee's show is a veritable blueprint of what not to do during the children's hour.

Lest it come as an astonishing surprise to network executives, the hour of 5 o'clock is a critical one in the child's life, not to mention the mother's. The youngster already has had a busy, full and tiring day. His next assignment is to have dinner. It is a logical period for a child to unwind and slow down.

Mr. Lee's program is dedicated to precisely contrary objectives. The screen lights up and there is hysterical bedlam—screaming and wild jumping up and down by Mr. Lee. He induces little children in the studio to do the same and, even worse, their mothers. The whole operation is a sort of organized frenzy designed to whip children into a high emotional pitch. In the parlance of today's youth, it amounts to a TV invitation to "hack around."

The specifics of last Friday's program tell their own story. There was a variation on the old German vaudeville act in which Uncle Weiner and Uncle Schnitzel use their protruding stomachs to push Pinky back and forth across the studio. The two uncles also jam handfuls of popcorn into the mouth of Pinky. Pinky then spits out the popcorn on the studio floor.

The main part of this particular sketch, incidentally was devoted to the agonies of having a tooth removed, which presumably helped make the life of American Dental Association just that much easier in dealing with child patients.

The Friday sponsor was the manufacturer of a candy roll. What's more natural than to hold out the roll of candy and persuade a child in the studio to lunge for it with his teeth. Perhaps nothing more than persuading a mother to do the same for the edification of children from coast to coast, which is exactly what Mr. Lee did.

The great climax of Mr. Lee's program was a straight give-away. Three mothers competed in putting balloons into wire baskets. For this major accomplishment the winning mother was burdened down with gifts—a new suit, travel case, et cetera and et cetera. Even the losers were similarly honored. So were the children who were beside themselves with excitement over their "mommies" getting a TV handout. Is this a philosophy, a way of life, for children from 4 to 8 years?

Mr. Lee states on the air that he is reliving his childhood: This is not true. There was no television in Mr. Lee's childhood: He had a chance.

NBC's offense is by no means unique. On the very day recently that CBS officials were piously testifying in Washington about their record in regard to crime shows, a monstrous crime offering, eliciting many protests from parents, was shown locally to children over WCBS-TV.

In these cases the answer is always the same: The welfare of its product is being put above the welfare of the child. This is not the true art of American advertising, which has brought forth many fine TV achievements, including shows for youngsters. This is commercialism run amuck. It's time the whole dreary business was cleaned up.

Peril in Small Pills: Pushing of Vitamins by "Ding Dong School" Indicates Deficiency in Commercials

December 23, 1955

Two matters concerning programs for children are on today's agenda. One concerns Dr. Frances Horwich, principal of television's "Ding Dong School" and the other Miss Katherine Copeland, the guiding spirit of "Talkaround."

"Ding Song School" currently is being sponsored by the manufacturer of vitamin tablets. The commercial is being delivered by Dr. Horwich in precisely the same studied tempo in which she discusses toys, helping mother or being a good child.

Yesterday Dr. Horwich looked soulfully at the screen and put the question directly to her audience, which consists of youngsters of pre-kindergarten age.

"You take them (vitamins) every morning like I do?" Dr. Horwich inquired. "I hope so."

Then came the demonstration. Out of the bottle she took two pills and put them on a cardboard plate.

"They're a very pretty red color," said Dr. Horwich, later adding: "They're small. They're so easy to swallow."

In conclusion, Dr. Horwich urged the youngsters to make sure when they visited the drug store with their mothers that they picked out the right bottle.

To put it as mildly as possible, Dr. Horwich has gone a step too far in letting a commercial consideration jeopardize her responsibility to the young children whose faith and trust she solicits.

First and foremost, there is the simple factor of safety. Small children should be kept away from pills of all types and should not be encouraged to think of them in the same context as toys. Lots of different kinds of pills are "pretty" and "red" and "easy to swallow." What kind of talk is this to pass on to impressionable infants? Dr. Horwich simply cannot realize how alarming her words sound on the home side of the screen. The less said about pills the better.

Secondly, it is not for television to decide if tots do or do not need pills. Whether a child has a vitamin deficiency is better determined by a parent after consultation with a physician rather than the National Broadcasting Company. Thirdly, use of a child's credibility to club a parent into buying something is reprehensible under the best circumstances. But in the case of a product bearing on a child's health it is inexcusable.

As for Miss Copeland, she is scheduled to leave the Columbia Broadcasting System network on Jan. 1. Such an event cannot come to pass without protest. Her program, "Talkaround," is an altogether superior offering.

Thanks to Miss Copeland's skill, "Talkaround" really gets to the heart of the thoughts and problems of teen-agers. For both old and young it is informative and helpful. Not the least of the attractions of "Talkaround" is that it is one program on which teen-agers speak from their own knowledge and experience. Somewhere on TV "Talkaround" merits its own niche.

Juvenile Audiences Suffering from Chains' Delinquency in Planning

December 2, 1956

The decision of the National Broadcasting Company to terminate the morning program of Dr. Frances Horwich has brought to the fore again the perennially difficult problem of television for children. After a run of nearly four and a half years, the "Ding Dong School" for pre-kindergarten viewers is to close Dec. 28.

The abandonment of "Ding Dong" of itself might not be too serious. Not even a children's presentation can be guaranteed a perpetual engagement and the program's exploitation of a young child's trust to peddle commercial products was not always too edifying either. "Ding Dong" had many supporters; it also had its share of critics.

But what is disturbing about the cancellation of "Ding Dong School" is that it is not going to be replaced by another presentation for youngsters. In its efforts to catch up with the profitable daytime operation of the Columbia Broadcasting System, the NBC chain is inserting one more woman's program. The tots are simply being disenfranchised.

As matters stand at the moment, the situation with regard to children's programming is not as impressive as it should be. With the departure of "Ding Dong School" the NBC network will not have any live programming for small children from Monday through Friday. CBS has "Captain Kangaroo" as a show at breakfast time, but nothing in the post-school hours. The American Broadcasting Company has the daily "Mickey Mouse Theatre," which sometimes has worthwhile segments.

The weekends are better. CBS has several commendable ventures: "Let's Take a Trip," "On the Carousel" and "The Big Top," among others. NBC presents the excellent Mr. Wizard, which helps to compensate for the wretched Howdy Doody. Here in New York on WPIX, there is that other favorite of many, "Shariland." There are, of course, many cartoon shows.

There are two related difficulties that have a bearing on children's programming. First and foremost, what is a child? Is he a 6-year-old or a 16-year-old? For maximum effectiveness a children's program must be pinpointed toward some specific age group, and few of them are. Because economically both networks and sponsors pursue maximum audiences, the approach of many children's programs is so broad and diffuse that it never fully satisfies either the young or the old.

As a way out of this dilemma there has been extraordinary emphasis this season on what in the trade is called the "family adventure series." The most successful example is probably "Robin Hood," which theoretically lures the youngsters to the home screen and has enough action to appease parents and older brothers and sisters.

The corollary to this aspect of serving the wants of children is the inescapable fact that many children do not like children's programs. One consequence of the video age is the astonishing—and frightening—degree of sophistication acquired by youngsters at a very early age. Since they see so much television intended for general adult consumption, they are understandably impatient with the note of condescension that generally creeps into purely children's fare. A travelogue may be terribly wholesome, but a child does not have to be very old to appreciate more the violence and action of a Western. The child viewer, in short, graduates with great facility to the slick trash relished by his elders.

Yet only the incorrigible academic snob who refuses to acknowledge TV's existence would deny that children obtain a vast amount of incidental information from the home screen. Their exposure to news programs, documentaries and plays may be taken for granted, but nonetheless, children are more aware of the outside world, thanks to television, than were most of their seniors at a like age.

If only because children as a group constitute television's most loyal and avid audience, the medium cannot minimize its share of responsibility in contributing to their well-being.

One fundamental weakness of the television world is its apparent belief that children's programming must be set off by itself; actually, superior children's programming will attract an adult audience.

An obvious example is the Children's Newsreel. Prepared with simplicity and clarity, such a program offered daily in the late afternoon could play a vital role in enabling the younger generation to keep up with today's confusing events. Its value to schools could be incalculable if it became an established fixture. This viewer saw such a program as presented in London by the British Broadcasting Corporation; some parts of it were fascinating for all ages.

Similarly, the serial technique has not been intelligently explored. Not the routine Hollywood cliffhanger, to be sure. But again this viewer saw in London a delightful "chase," but this one was laid in the city of Florence. And by the time the program was over the younger viewer not only was exposed to some history but also to representative samples of Florentine art. The masterpieces were woven into the narrative. Perhaps this was "sugarcoating," not forced education, but the fact remained it was both exciting and informative. Is it not worth a try?

There have been reports that the Random House "Landmark" books might come to television; so, too, the American Heritage Foundation series. One wonders why they have not come forth. There's talk of expense. But are not such works infinitely more promising and substantial than last week-end's indescribably crude "Eloise" or the tortured version of "Jack and the Beanstalk." The last two ventures must have cost veritable fortunes. Yet to what avail?

Every library is a vast untapped reservoir of priceless material for children's programming. But before it can be fruitfully employed a number of video producers and sponsors must outgrow their fear of childhood. Nothing is quite so exasperating as seeing classics for the young subjected to sterile adult embellishments. Modernize them if one wishes as many, including "Peter Pan" have been modernized, but do not tamper with their fundamental spirit and joyous simplicity.

Where such programming errs is in either writing down for children or writing up for weary adults. The state of executive mind that ballyhoos a show for youngsters and then puts it on until 11 o'clock at night is symptomatic of this elementary confusion in purpose.

Perhaps television's handicap is in thinking of children as children; there is a far happier and more accurate phrase, "young adults." Commercial television may always find it competitively awkward to try to address specific age groups; that task is one strong argument in favor of noncommercial educational broadcasting. But the whole range of so-called children's programming on advertiser-sponsored outlets could be enormously improved if broadcasters would raise their sights.

In their hearts the networks know that they have given child's programming only lip service; at no network is there an executive trained in the field with real and meaningful authority. The task is worthy of their best efforts.

Parent-Teacher Organization Issues Its First Appraisal of Programs

September 13, 1959

The National Congress of Parents and Teachers has decided to review television programs with an eye to their suitability for youngsters and teen-agers. In its initial sortie into video criticism the mother organization bestows its blessings on "Captain Kangaroo" and Dick Clark, among others, and tidily demolishes "Mighty Mouse" and "Howdy Doody."

The action of the parent-teacher organization in taking a sustained look at the outpourings of TV should be welcomed. For some years the matter of programming for children, especially the younger tots, has constituted one of the more glaring shortcomings of the video industry. While the networks employ eager executives to supervise the sale of one-minute commercials in Lower Slobbovia, they still have not thought it necessary to entrust anyone with the responsibility of devising imaginative and literate programming for the younger generation.

If The National Parent-Teacher monthly organ of the Congress can help persuade broadcasters that Tiny Tim's television horizon could extend beyond the returned box-top, then the national PTA will have rendered a helpful service. At least it's worth a try.

By way of inaugurating the new service of the Congress, Mrs. Eva H. Grant, editor of The National Parent-Teacher, has dashed off a lively polemic on the general state of TV vis-a-vis the child and come up with some tart observations that should send the newly formed Television Information Committee into executive session.

Mrs. Grant holds no brief for the argument that TV's plethora of gunplay siphons off the latent hostilities of the younger generation or that a diet of mediocrity must be passively accepted because of the ominous forces that influence the behavior of a mass medium.

"The National Congress, through its official magazine, seeks to convert the mounting protests against shoddy TV programming into intelligent discussion that can be helpful both to the TV industry and the viewing public," Mrs. Grant writes.

When the National Congress announced its TV viewing project, some of the resultant editorial comment and newspaper cartoons depicted the PTA as an incipient censor.

Mrs. Grant says—and altogether reasonably—that trying to apprise parents of what is attractive on TV and what is rubbish is a far cry from wielding a blue pencil or demanding that producers enter negotiations with a committee of self-appointed guardians of the school child's weal.

To review video programs, a start has been made by utilizing the services of a group of monitors—incidentally, a rather distasteful description that the PTA should abandon—who belong to the Illinois Congress of Parents and Teachers. The California Congress of Parents and Teachers is establishing a cooperating viewing group and other panels are to be organized in the East.

On the basis of the first example of its reviewing technique, contained in the current issue of The National Parent-Teacher, the Congress has made a generally encouraging start, albeit still not so adequate as it could be.

Over a space of two pages, the Congress reviews only a total of twelve programs, a pitiful portion of the video total that should be included in a helpful guide for parents.

As for the programs analyzed, the Congress probably will encounter the inevitable difference of opinion that in itself is the best assurance that it never will be an obnoxious censor. The chief laurels go to "Captain Kangaroo," a selection that every adult will heartily second. For kindergarten and early-grade levels this is a program of superb taste, quality and inventiveness.

The Congress also waxes ecstatic over "Miss Ding Dong," scheduled to be seen again on independent stations this season. Here a prayer or two would seem very much in order. Let us hope that Dr. Frances Horwich has abandoned the practice of cajoling very small tots to persuade their parents to purchase the products of her sponsors. And let her also abandon her artificially slow and whining method of speaking.

"Howdy Doody" is described as "monotonous or stupid," for which, quiet hurrahs. "Lassie" is justifiably praised. "Mighty Mouse" is recommended for mice and "Romper Room" is dismissed as "harmless." In the category of teen-age TV there are raves for "Father Knows Best," still the most delightful family show on the air, and for Mr. Clark, whose programs are described as reflecting wholesome and "disciplined zest." How Mr. Clark's "Bandstand" encourages a sense of participation, apparently one of the PTA goals for good children's TV, is not very convincingly detailed.

The Congress tackles three shows in the bracket of Westerns and thrillers—"Bold Venture," "Shock Theatre" and "Wanted—Dead or Alive." Understandably enough, it can't find a good word to say for any of the drab trio.

Apart from the dubious value of such a limited sampling, the Congress perhaps is overlooking the one area in which it not only could contribute significantly to better TV but also meet a long-felt need on the part of teachers and parents.

This need is the publication in advance of what promise to be major worth-while TV programs that could supplement school work in almost every grade. From all indications this season the most exciting and valuable TV will not be the regular series but rather the "specials," some of which, notably in the revival of classics, could be of great importance.

At present there is no organization with the nation-wide structure of the PTA movement that conveys such information sufficiently far in advance to enable teachers and parents to take advantage of superior programming.

Perhaps the deadline problems of The National Parent-Teacher preclude such a project. But at least the idea should be carefully explored and the networks should bend over backwards to cooperate.

The crying need with respect to children and television is not one more summary of shows that could be missed; these the children usually know more about than their parents. What is required is a larger audience for the newer quality programs that may be ignored in favor of hackneyed old favorites.

Chapter Eight

Tracking the Impact of Television

During the late 1940s and the early 1950s, my father often wrote about the new phenomenon of television for *The New York Times Magazine* as well as his regular and Sunday columns. The magazine's editor, Lester Markel, valued these periodic updates on the medium, and my father appreciated the $300 checks that he received. In these appraisals, he provided an overview of the medium and the industry as it captured the imagination of the American people. This chapter assembles several of these summary essays along with glimpses of his interest in how television was developing in Europe. He occasionally traveled across the Atlantic to get a sense of how the American product looked from overseas. He also wanted to explore the innovations and practices of European television as they might affect video in the United States.

These early overviews give a good sense of the excitement he felt about television in its infancy and the hopes he held for its impact as a force for good in the United States. As the industry developed along lines that emphasized commercialism and an appeal to a mass audience, he became more disillusioned with television.

The Paradoxical State of Television

The video art has made strides since the war, yet nobody seems to know where it is going

***The New York Times Magazine*, March 30, 1947**

Television finally has received the "green light" for which it has been waiting nearly three years. Ten days ago the Federal Communications Commission ruled that the burgeoning video art should proceed with the presentation of pictures in black and white and should not attempt at this time to offer images in full color. By removing the uncertainty over what the technical standards should be in the foreseeable future, the commission has cleared the way for stepped-up production of receivers and installation of transmitters.

The clarification of television's technical status comes after many notable strides in the field of electronic reportage. In recent weeks the video camera has brought the family hearthside pictures of the opening of Congress, an event which proved rather conclusively that the politico who is photogenic may have a decided edge in future campaigns. It has scooped the motion-picture newsreels on the coverage of the Harlem tenement explosion, leaving the Hollywood brethren a little aghast at the meaning of the advent of the electron. It has presented the video debut of Charlie McCarthy, who clicked anew in front of the cathode-ray tubes. It has won grudging concessions from the sports experts that a prizefight can be seen probably better on a television set than from a seat at ringside.

Yet for all these advances, television for the present at least, still is perhaps the foremost enigma on the post-war industrial scene. While in public pronouncements television broadcasters envision underwater-ballets of breathtaking beauty and panorama, on the air for the most part they are providing second-rate vaudeville and ancient "B" pictures. Video's spokesmen speak glowingly—and justifiably—of the industry's many superhuman technical achievements but in the same breath concede they are currently troubled by such elementary matters as the aerial for a set in an apartment house or one receiver causing interference with another. Manufacturers anticipate the sale of at least 350,000 receivers this year—the better brands are scooped up as quickly as they appear in the stores—but thoughtful retailers note that there are not enough programs telecast even to demonstrate sets properly in a store.

The fundamental cause of this abundance of paradoxes nowhere has been more directly explained than by James C. Petrillo, president of the American Federation of Musicians and the most succinct economist of the ethereal arts. More than a year ago he issued a rule—still in effect—that a musician could not work for television at any price.

Asked why, the indefatigable Jimmy had the $64 answer: "We want to find out first where television's going."

To which might be added: So does everyone else.

The problems of the video art fall largely into three different, if overlapping classifications: the technical, the programmatic and economic. Much to the embarrassment of those who as prematurely as ten or fifteen years ago proclaimed that television was "around the corner," their solution has proved singularly complex, time-consuming and, to those who have not had to foot the bill, fascinating. In retrospect, however, such difficulties hardly seem surprising since the potential of television truly represented an unprecedented challenge to the human imagination.

In resolving the major technical problem of the moment, the FCC's decision found that no proposed method of telecasting in color had been sufficiently field-tested to warrant commercial introduction, as had been asked by the Columbia Broadcasting System. Accordingly, it gave the nod to those proponents of black and white who held that the monochrome image would provide satisfactory service and would enable the new industry, already representing a total investment of perhaps $100,000,000, to get started.

But the lone fight by CBS against virtually all the rest of the industry did serve the useful purpose of proving beyond doubt that once they attain comparable steadiness and brightness the color pictures will be infinitely superior. And, under the spur of the CBS competition, the chief advocate of monochrome video—the Radio Corporation of America—did bring out an all-electronic color system which it predicted might be ready for commercial introduction in five years. Few in television anticipate that black-and-white video can be operating profitably on a national basis before that time, so it is still probably that television will undergo a major technical change before it enjoys long-range stability.

To come to the programming of television, one fact is obvious. The industry has not yet had a chance to show how it will capitalize in public on the technical ingenuity it has displayed in the privacy of the scientist's laboratory. What pictures will be shown in television and in what manner? Old showmen stay up nights trying to decide and visionary pamphleteers flood the book stalls with their conclusions on what is destined to prove the video art's most provocative and controversial operation.

Television's effectiveness in covering sports and special events already has been proved beyond serious doubt—the sense of being in two places at once is very real. However, in the programs originating in the studio, which ultimately will constitute the backbone of video fare, television has barely begun to assert itself.

The physical appearance of the image on the screen of the home receiver has a great deal to do with programming. The clearest and brightest picture today is to be had on a relatively small screen—6 by 4 inches—and the two qualities of definition and illumination tend to decrease as the size of the picture increases. Yet increased size is important in reducing eye fatigue. Instinctively, a televiewer tends to sit too close to a receiver in hopes of seeing a brighter and sharper picture. When he does so, the picture tends to look grainy and blurred. It takes time under present conditions to adjust one's self to television reception, and how far the public will be willing to cooperate in this regard is admittedly a moot point.

On the other end of television—at the video studio—this same problem, which essentially is one of camera scope and focus, necessarily dictates to some extent program form. Today it is difficult, if not impossible, for instance, to show more than six chorus girls without their becoming so minute as to appear dancing at the wrong end of a telescope. When Bill Robinson did a tap dance before the cameras, his feet generally were in focus though not always his hands.

In dramas, this confinement is disconcerting until one becomes accustomed to it. Productions of "Angel Street" and "Abe Lincoln in Illinois" lacked the dimension of even the Broadway theatre, let alone the Hollywood film. It was not unlike seeing a series of picture postcards with rather serious consequences to the play's fluidity and continuity. More skillful use of cameras is raising the standards of production, but it promises to be a while yet before there are Pulitzer Prizes in television.

Pending the day of artistic liberation, television is busy just now bringing back vaudeville. Magicians, puppeteers, ventriloquists and other oldtimers no longer reminisce about Keith and Loew's, but don their glad rags for the edification of NBC and CBS.

That the electron is reviving the two-a-day is not without considerable significance. For the "live" television show the actor of the theatre again will be on top. The player who can move about a stage and memorize that "you" comes after "I" and "love" will not lack for work. This painful fact is not lost on some of today's top radio stars, accustomed to work from a script, many of whom are discreetly trying to become familiar with the workings of the theatre. A revolution in show business such as accompanied the advent of talking pictures may come in television's wake, one major blessing certainly being that announcers will have to learn to shut up.

To consider the basic economic issue which television has to face, it is only necessary to decide whether the chicken or the egg comes first. The two parts of the issue are these: (1) Will the public invest in television before the good shows are there? (2) Will the advertiser invest in television before the audience is there?

It is the special nature of television which makes this problem particularly complex. Technically and artistically, television is something wholly different, yet unlike the car, radio or the motion picture, it is not something which is entirely new. It is a wedding of radio, films and theatre—the few experimental programs which have recognized this fact have been much the most imaginative and provocative—and economically, at least in the early stages, it is in competition for the present national audiences of the first two media.

Up to now the Hollywood film industry has carried on a cautious flirtation with television—trying to decide whether it should woo the girl and take her into the family or hit her on the head with the big financial rolling pin it possesses. The West Coast's present monopoly of the nation's most popular visual talent cannot be minimized; many studios insert restrictive television clauses in their contracts with stars and refuse to release to video broadcasters any film which retains a wisp of box office life. Indicative of Hollywood's advance thinking on video is one player's suggestion that a star should have a copyrighted interest in his own face, so that a film could not be used repeatedly for commercial purposes in television as phonograph records now are in radio. The lawyers in television should not go hungry.

But the question is, will the public accept and, if so, to what extent, either "live" or film television programs inferior in "name" and production values to what it now receives on the air and in the Hollywood picture? Only the mad visionaries, which television has never lacked in numbers, would attempt a definitive answer at this stage.

It is incontrovertible, however, that television will be enormously expensive. The need for production settings, longer rehearsal time, large studio equipment perhaps ultimately comparable to Hollywood's facilities, will make radio's costs seem more modest by comparison. And the bill is not going to be any smaller by reason of television's fantastically ebullient promotion campaign, which has prompted the labor unions to prepare for many bitter jurisdictional fights as a prelude to sharing the promised gold.

Necessarily, the clue to television's economics will lie in video's effectiveness as an advertising medium. Will the visual plugging of goods sell more merchandise than the purely aural presentation? The answer almost unanimously is in the affirmative but the art of huckstering carries an equally important concomitant. Will television sell enough more goods to justify its greatly added expense and far smaller circulation? The Park Avenue agency boys indicate that they will get their feet wet slowly and carefully.

But what is already apparent is that there will be no lack of effort to promote television's sales function. The ugly plug of radio is not going to disappear with the addition of sight; it may very possibly become uglier. On a telecast recently at dinner time there was shown a little girl going into the bathroom and, under mother's guidance, dutifully massaging her gums with a toothpaste. A manly gentleman on television also has adorned his upholstered chest with an appropriate salve for a cough. On another occasion, four actors sat down to dinner and discussed the patented features of the table glass-ware. Integration of advertising messages with the context of the entertainment is also being tried. Television, with all its educational possibilities, may take the country's cultural level down as well as up.

All in all, the hot-stove league of television is in continuous convention, yet of necessity it must always talk around the point. What's going to happen when pictures travel through the air and can be seen in the comfort of one's own living room by merely flicking a switch? Nobody knows for sure. It's never been done before.

Family Life, 1948 A.T. (After Television)

Privacy goes out the window when the video party enters through the door

***The New York Times Magazine*, August 1, 1948**

The American household is on the threshold of a revolution. The wife scarcely knows where the kitchen is, let alone her place in it. Junior scorns the late-afternoon sunlight for the glamour of the darkened living room. Father's briefcase lies unopened in the foyer.

The reason is television. If the art of video carries a boundless promise, it also has brought an upheaval in pantry and environs. Today's pioneer owner of a set is not only a looker and a listener. He also is a boniface. Yesterday it was the game of charades which intrigued the avant garde; now it is the television party.

Superficially, video may seem no more sinister than mah jongg or gin rummy, a trifling example, as it were, of paralysis in the parlor. Indeed television's host of experts have maintained a meaningful silence on the impending crisis. However, it is no longer possible to conceal that our way of life since Lincoln and Jackson is more than just in danger. It has gone.

The television party comes upon a family gradually, relentlessly. The first step leading to a cathode carnival comes when Mr. Jones, the one who is to be kept up with, puts foot inside the television store. Whether he favors a table model or a console has no bearing on his imminent fate. Once he makes a deposit on a screen of his own, he opens his home to the world.

The world is not long in coming in, three or four at a time. The first crew to arrive is the covey of specialists assigned to convoy a television set to its ultimate resting place in the unsuspecting domicile. Wire is strewn over roof and out of window. Favorite chairs are moved to one side, books and magazines are swept off the one strong table, lamps are shifted to new spots where there are no wall outlets.

Mrs. Jones of course can only sit grimly by, as the electron demands sacrifice of the hours spent in arrangement of the furniture. In a facile lingo of their own, having to do with weird matters of ohms, microfarads and millivolts, the service men explain it is necessary. Daddy's den must become an amphitheatre.

Before leaving the men make sure no Jones will have to live alone. Upon the rooftop they put an assortment of fishing poles, the social booby-trap of the atomic age, to let neighbors know that here is a house with wherewithal and video. The television party is on.

The television party runs in two shifts, starting in late afternoon and lasting through whatever bedtime is chosen by DuMont or NBC Electronic festivities in the home begin with the arrival of the younger set, eager for the movie marathon embodied in "Howdy Doody," "Small Fry Club," CBS "Scrapbook," and the offerings of the two-fisted if balding Tim McCoy.

Children's hours on television admittedly are an insidious narcotic for the parent. With the tots fanned out on the floor in front of the receiver, a strange and wonderful quiet seems at hand. The adolescent bedlam which customarily heralds the approach of the final meal of the day is sublimely absent. A cocktail can be had with nothing worse than a distant echo of video's Uncle Dons. The weary feet of the household's distaff division can be put up for a merciful few minutes before another bout with the dishpan. Marconi's cup truly runneth over.

The dream of years, alas, soon starts to walk. As word passes along the moppet grapevine, alien mamas decide there is no use in merely leaving off the offspring and then making a second trip later to pick them up. It is simpler to stay with the video hostess who soon finds that her cocktail shaker, once adequate for a tolerable amount of company, is no better than a thimble. Like radio and television, the hen party goes on a five-a-week basis. So does the supply of olives.

Thereafter the kinescope confusion mounts in the home. The head of the house makes an appearance to find dinner assuming an increasing likeness to a GI menu. Sliced Spam becomes a fixed staple, if only because it can be served without regard to an orthodox hour for the evening's vitamins. A simple salad, i.e., a few greens doused in chain-store dressing, is also offered as though it were substitute for something to eat. But hot coffee? In the video house it long since has boiled away.

The repast is served with all the eclat to be found in a one-arm cafeteria. Even if one would, one cannot dawdle over the Spam. In the three and one-half minutes between dinner and the start of the CBS schedule there are things to be done. The children must be sent to bed, bathless just this once, of course. The dishes must be washed. The living room must be tidied up. Company is coming for the second shift.

The requirements for the successful television party are many. The first essential is that the participants rid themselves of all the outworn notions for the informal get-together. Here, in brief, are the accepted rules of behavior for the video guest:

(1) Do not sit too close to the receiver; it makes the picture look fuzzy.

(2) Resign yourself to the fact that you will not grab one of the really comfortable chairs in any house.

(3) Don't fuss or squirm if you saw the motion picture ten years ago.

(4) When seeing a prizefight, keep cool when the host says he can make the picture clearer and brings in a jumpy black-and-white crazy quilt just as the announcer says Joe Louis knocked down Jersey Joe Walcott.

(5) Under no circumstances rub your eyes, clean your glasses or just go to sleep. You're seeing history in the making, man.

(6) Never suggest that you saw a better television receiver at somebody else's house.

(7) Don't ever fail to ask the host if there is not a better program on another station. Tuning the television receiver is the host's crowning glory, the Common Man's link with the atomic age.

(8) Don't talk. Ben Grauer is the Voice of Authority.

The rules for the host are no less stringent. Their text follows:

(1) Upon installation of the television receiver, the fireplace must be sealed off. The heart-warming glow of hickory logs can only prove distracting. One flicker in a home is enough.

(2) All deliveries of milk must be discontinued upon the first peep of light in the cathode tube. Even the refined refrigerator cannot accommodate both bovine juice and soda pop for the first shift and soda for the second.

(3) In the case of televised prizefights, the host will display patience and fortitude when a guest, who has not read a sports page since the days of Walter Camp, asserts categorically the fight will end by a technical k.o. in the fifth round.

(4) Greater patience yet will be shown when, upon the third roll-call of states at a political convention, the guest maintains, "Isn't it interesting?"

(5) The host will be on his guard against the neighbors who bring their own refreshments. It takes them longer to drink up.

(6) When your "guests" bring their guests, do not call the Homicide Bureau. The pioneer always was a sturdy chap.

(7) When longing for the good old days, sympathize with the laymen still pursuing a grand slam or an inside straight. The odds are against them, too.

(8) For all the tribulations of his present lot, the television set owner should appreciate his temporary role as a social arbiter. Once the

crystal set owner was important; today he is but a decimal point in a Hooper rating.

With both factions adhering to the platform of the television party, success is assured. The family's evening is not tainted with such an archaic pursuit as one person talking to another, a practice, it may be recalled, which once was known as conversation. The Kinsey report, the Berlin blockade, "Mister Roberts," the price of a Pontiac and the state of the weather no longer are allowed to heat the passions at the hearth.

Instead, a mute tranquillity has overtaken the American home. Who can argue the matter of the Lord & Taylor bill in the company of strangers? Who has the courage to read a book in a room full of wrestling fans? Not the proud owner of a new television set. He has a choice of programs and a new purpose in life: the off-and-on switch.

TV Daddy and Video Mama: A Dirge

What Hopalong and the rest do to children is nothing to what they are doing to parents

***The New York Times Magazine*, May 14, 1950**

For some reason there has been a lot of concern lately over what television is doing to children. The teen-ager and the tot in kindergarten are being studied to see if they fit into a new pattern which has significance and implications. The status of the youngster's I.Q. is no longer important. The urgent problem is to find out whether he prefers Channel 2 or Channel 13.

Such solicitude for the leaders of tomorrow may divert educators but it overlooks the real victim of television. The real victim is not the child at all but that epitome of suffering and the most unappreciated creature in American life today: the television parent.

The hardy adult who for several years has lived in the presence of both a set and a child is the forgotten man of the hour. With drooping eyelid and battered eardrum, he is now developing a cathode psychosis which desperately needs to be viewed with alarm. Public opinion can afford to pay less attention to the child; if television keeps up he is going to be an orphan anyway.

The veteran television parent has a hard time explaining the extent of his ordeal. People who live in the strange world apart from television have no idea what it is like to have CBS/NBC instead of 20/20 vision. Yet if we are to have a sound sociological understanding of what this country is coming to, we must heed the plight of the TV Daddy and the Video Mama.

Their troubles begin with the naive notion that television somehow unites the family. All along, the powers-that-be in television have insisted that their medium brings the kiddies into peaceable assembly before the hearth. Give TV a little more time, they keep saying, and the disruptive influence of the automobile will be a thing of the past.

Television's leaders, obviously, aren't family men. Just once in their lives they should experience tranquil moments of the kind that come a few minutes before the start of "Six-Gun Playhouse." Does the household's 4-year-old stand patiently by while the Old Man tunes in a perfect image? "Hey, wait till I get my holsters on," he cries sternly. And is his biggest brother sitting contentedly on the divan? Hardly. Master Gene Autry is perched on the arm of the one decent chair in the house, spurring his steed onward to the delight of nobody but the neighborhood upholsterer. In fact, there is nothing quite so peaceful and quiet as a last round-up in a dinette.

As school surveys have indicated, the three R's can now be discarded, thanks to TV. On this score, skeptics can find reassurance at every hand. Take the case of the tot touring a supermarket in a stroller. "What's your name, Sonny?" asked an amiable clerk. "Howdy Doody," piped up the tot. His mother tittered: "He can't say his own name yet." Or consider the little girl who, out for the walk with her parents, chanced to spot a saloon. "Ask the man for Ballantine's," said she.

Yes, they learn fast with TV, and this aptitude carries over into adolescence. Unhappily, homework sometimes interferes with the completion of a program. But such interference is taken philosophically. One junior high student has explained her attitude this way: Well, first, I do some Latin and then I look at television. Then I do some Latin and go back to the set. For some reason I kind of get mixed up." But getting mixed up is better than trying to split Gaul into three parts without the help of Kay Kyser.

Under such circumstances, however, it sometimes devolves upon the father to exercise cultural and educational leadership. If his family is not to be divided into warring camps, it is his responsibility to employ the critical acumen needed to decide whether an evening should be devoted to wrestling from Ridgewood Grove or to wrestling from Jamaica Arena. Only the father's conscience and personal sensitivity can guide him in accepting an impersonation of Humphrey Bogart on the Ed Sullivan show while rejecting an impersonation of Humphrey Bogart on the Milton Berle show. Children cannot be expected to make all the decisions.

In any case, television has impact. For the first time in history the child, regardless of his family's economic station in life, has every cultural advantage. If he can't commit a crime without botching the job it's only because the parent has not had the set turned on long enough. Eight-year-old Johnny, a progressive youngster, knew what he had to do when told he had to visit grandpa, an individual without a television set. Just like they do on "Suspense," he ran to the sink, mixed a deadly potion, warned his mother that unless the visit was called off somebody would suffer the consequences.

A major event for the television parent is the Sunday evening game: Who is going to get finished first, Hopalong Cassidy or You? This game often gets under way during the Sunday afternoon drive when the family is moving along bumper to bumper on an express parkway. Just as some idiot in the next lane threatens your front fender there comes the innocent voice from the back seat: "Is it Hopalong time yet?" (Drive carefully, the sign says.)

Mealtime is an event out of the ordinary for the television parent; for the child it may just be out. Only a true progressive can endorse the idea of little Buster's lapping up his cereal while watching Maggi McNellis conduct a quiz show. Hence, a delay of an hour or two in serving supper is often necessary. Such a delay never does lasting harm to a stomach, and by then it's bedtime anyway.

Even if members of a family should eat together, the event may turn into a variation on Russian roulette. It is not that conversation is impossible; it's just unlikely. Contrary to the dire predictions of several years ago, television does not altogether kill the art of two persons speaking to one another. All you have to do is learn a new language.

Possibly some persons may recall the winter when the ability to talk about loyalty tests, mercy killings and water shortages made one up-to-date. Unknown, unsung and uninvestigated were millions of adults bravely threading their way through mealtime bulletins on Dr. Pauli, Clarabell, Foudini, Beany and Kukla. For that matter, try carving a roast to the rhythm of the B.V.D. commercial.

At such times, just as the sociologists foresaw, the gregarious instinct in television parents may finally assert itself. With the children contentedly watching a homicide, the mother and father may begin to contemplate the possibility of an evening spent without permission of the Federal Communications Commission.

The first step toward a social life is the opening of negotiations with a baby sitter. In grandmother's day the sitter may have been investigated as to whether she was reliable, knew how to call the fire department and had a moderate appetite when raiding a strange refrigerator. But progress cannot be stopped.

Today it is the television parent who undergoes investigation. Even the apprentice baby sitter must receive reasonable assurances that there is at least a 12-inch image, a signal free from ghosts on all the high-band stations, a daylight screen, single-channel tuning and a 33 1/3 record player in the house. If there's no dipole on your roof, don't even call her.

Arranging for a sitter is not the only worry of a night out. Father wants to look sharp, feel sharp and be sharp. Mother wonders what Faye Emerson would think of her neckline. But, even if their eyes are not accustomed to the dark, they venture forth comforted by the knowledge that an occasional headlight is not different from a test pattern.

If the night out is given over to a party, the host and hostess usually sense everyone's need for a change. There are cocktails freshly mixed the same day. Dinner is served on a table. Several guests even confess that they have not yet canceled their memberships in the Book-of-the-Month Club. After dinner, as a matter of fact, there is only a little television, from 8 to 11:45.

The refreshing experience of having had supper without Perry Como may admittedly work a subsequent hardship on the children. For, without any real disloyalty to Como, to Marconi, or even to Arthur Godfrey, a parent might allow the idea to creep into his mind that the television set can be moved. For a night or two, say, try it in some place other than in the living room. If hearing the sound but not seeing the picture proves disconcerting, the set always can be taken upstairs.

Should it disturb the new baby upstairs, for heaven's sake stop screaming and yelling about the thing. Stick it in the attic if you have to. What d'ya want out of life in the 16-inch size?

What TV Is—and What It Might Be

Programs lack originality and variety, but news and education offer cues for the future

***The New York Times Magazine*, June 10, 1951**

The sprawling phenomenon of television, with all its implications for social good or ill, is under ever-widening scrutiny today—and not merely from the expanding audience, which now numbers 40,000,000 men, women and children. In just three years TV has become the colossus of the world of entertainment, information and education. Its dynamic growth has been underscored only recently by the $25,000,000 stock deal which saw a Hollywood motion-picture theatre chain enter network video and by the United States Supreme Court decision clearing the way for the latest electronic marvel—television in full color. But behind these spectacular developments there is a considerable amount of soul-searching going on in an effort to set directions and standards for television.

The Federal Communications Commission is considering a study of the basic standards governing television programs and the Senate Interstate Commerce Committee is weighing proposals that it put TV under the spotlight of investigation. Many educational organizations are critical of the industry and are campaigning for the right to operate their own stations. TV has been praised and damned with equal vigor. The National Association of Radio and Television Broadcasters has hurriedly set up a committee to consider a program code for the industry. How the debate will be resolved is a matter for the future, but there is no question that sufficient time has elapsed to permit an evaluation of what television is and is not doing, and to ask what, if anything, can be done about it.

This discussion, therefore, will deal, first of all, with the subject-matter of television and then offer certain conclusions. Broadly speaking, the many different types of TV presentations—from live studio shows to films and spontaneous broadcasts of news events—can be broken down into two major categories: (1) entertainment programs and (2) information and education programs.

ENTERTAINMENT

Comedy shows and revues. Comedy has enjoyed television's most concentrated attention this season. The early monopoly of Milton Berle and Arthur Godfrey in this field has been broken with the arrival of many of the top stars of Hollywood. The productions often have been extraordinarily lavish, comparable to the standards of Broadway, and may cost as high as $40,000 to $60,000.

The brightest spots have been the clowning of Jimmy Durante, the pantomime of Sid Caesar, the madcap antics of Jerry Lewis, the showmanship of Eddie Cantor, the hearty wit of Sam Levenson and the philosophical and relaxed humor of Dave Garroway. In contrast, some of the great names of radio, notably Fred Allen and Jack Benny, have found the TV sledding very difficult, chiefly because they have not understood that television requires a performance and not just a personal appearance.

But comedy on television is in serious trouble. TV's demand for something new every week is eating up material, routines and personalities so quickly that the dread plague of sameness already is a common blight. It is no reflection on the comedian that his sixth or fiftieth show lacks the freshness and sparkle of his premiere; both he and his audience grow weary of the same thing. Next year it may be commonplace for a number of top comedians to do only a few shows over the entire winter's season, which will place an added burden on television to keep the screens lighted by developing new acts and writers.

Informal variety shows. Besides the full-dress revue, there is another form of variety which is both plentiful and frequently incredible. On the informal show there is conversation to no particular point, a dance or a song, and a bit of this and that. It is a hangover from radio and thrives on the fellow who, before television, was known rather disdainfully as the life of the party, i.e., Jerry Lester, Bert Parks, Garry Moore, et al. Often this type of program is hung on the format of the contest or giveaway, but its chief claim to popularity is its low cost. It is the best evidence that television often does not know what to do with itself.

Drama. Many viewers are convinced that the most durable form of television program will prove to be the straight drama, and certainly some of the medium's greatest triumphs have been in this category. Such hour-long programs as "Pulitzer Prize Playhouse," "Studio One" and "Philco Television Playhouse" consistently represent imaginative and original use of the camera as an artistic tool in its own right. The acting, too, is often exceptionally fine.

Even more important, television drama, as it exhausts the supply of obvious revivals, is beginning to try an occasional work which has something to say and refutes the content of the mass-media experts that it is not "safe" to do the controversial or depart from the saga of boy meets girl. If the standards of television are elevated from within the industry, the leaders in drama may well set the pace and prove that culture and a Hooper rating are not necessarily incompatible.

At the other end of the scale, aged movies and live programs which ruthlessly condense a full-length work are only too prevalent, and there is a plethora of mystery stories which confuse violence and horror with characterization and suspense. The specialists in the macabre are having a holiday on TV and woe to the script writer who is not up to date on gruesome approach to a homicide. This is one of the real black marks against contemporary television. The soap opera, too, is being transplanted directly from radio to television in all its corniness.

Children's programs. If there is one type of program which runs to extremes in terms of desirable standards, it is the offering for children. Ever since television's earliest days, youngsters—ranging down to three and four years old—have been avid viewers, and the parent has been confronted with a whole new problem. The broadcasters have not always been particularly helpful.

There are many fine children's programs—the classic "Kukla, Fran and Ollie," which is an adult's delight too. "Magic Cottage," "Mr. I. Magination," "Big Top," the Sunday show of Gabby Hayes and a number of others. But quantitatively television puts its main emphasis on a veritable flood of Western pictures and futuristic serials. The accent is on violence, not on enhancing the child's artistic appreciation.

Chit-chat. Daytime programs are a comparatively recent addition to the television schedules and many of them must be seen to be believed. Several are nothing more than animated Sears, Roebuck catalogues. Pitchmen and pitchwomen stand in front of the camera and display merchandise by the hour. Cooking specialists give recipes and plug every ingredient that goes into the mixing bowl. The worst of the programs contain more advertising than anything ever heard on the radio.

Sports. As no doubt they always will, sports continue to rank high among TV's offerings. The athletic contest, where the outcome is in doubt, is the best ready-made spectacle of all. The Wednesday night boxing matches from the Midwest have stolen the play away from the Madison Square Garden bouts during the past winter, but there's still wrestling for those who have difficulty in getting to sleep. Baseball, which has enjoyed improved camera coverage of late, again is on the screen this summer.

Football, however, may be more scarce next fall because of the fear of many colleges that TV cuts down their "gates." The scandal over basketball didn't exactly stimulate the average viewer's interest in that sport. The last year has brought considerable improvement in the technique of announcers, who finally are beginning to talk less and let the picture tell the story. But if the television sports fan has one legitimate complaint, it is the uncanny knack of some stations for putting on a commercial at a climactic moment in a contest.

Information and Education

News. Television's straight news presentations are fewer in number than radio's, and there is a tendency to put pictorial values above news considerations. On an everyday basis there simply are not enough major stories which lend themselves to effective treatment through pictures, and TV is following the newsreel habit of glorifying the fashion show, bathing-beauty contest, etc.

When television goes out to cover a spot news event it has its greatest appeal. Then it deals in actuality and the viewer has a sense of being there when it happens. In giving the individual sitting at home the opportunity to witness his Government in operation, television's potentialities for good are almost breathtaking. The television of the crime hearings, the debate on sending troops to Europe, last summer's sessions of the U.N. and the return of Gen. Douglas MacArthur are but indications of how the magic of electronics can give new meaning to practical democracy.

Forums. Discussion programs on current affairs, notably "Meet the Press," may be very arresting and frequently produce news in themselves. Some, however, are too preoccupied with putting on "a show" and are apt to offer more emotion than information. The "American Forum of the Air" is a typical case. Curiously enough, "The Town Meeting," which logically would seem a made-to-order attraction for television, did not do too well on TV, primarily because it was poorly produced.

Education. Programs of a predominantly educational purpose are appallingly few on TV. While many regular programs undoubtedly have an incidental value in that they meet the broad test of having the individual increase his capacity for reasoned judgment, only a handful follow some semblance of a curriculum. The contrast between what television is capable of doing in visual education and what it is willing to do is likely to be a source of controversy for many years to come.

The most successful educational program, as a production, has been the United States Navy's series "Drill Call," which significantly employs a professional actor to play the part of the instructor. The runner-up is the Johns Hopkins "Science in Review," which translates the complexities of the scientific world into language readily comprehended by mass audiences.

But in the adult field most educational programs are very amateurish in execution. While budget limitations are perhaps a determining factor, several years of looking at educational experiments on TV suggest that it is a mistake to thrust the educator himself in front of the cameras. The obvious need is for the educator to provide the material and over-all direction for the educational program and then let the professional producers in television undertake its presentation. Until there is some such fusion of talents the educational program is not going to be very satisfactory either to the educator or the broadcaster—or to the audience.

Educational programs for children are offered on TV but with few exceptions are confined to the weekend and are not numerous. John Kiernan's visits to museums, the science demonstrations of Dr. Roy K. Marshall and "Mr. Wizard" and "Watch the World," the latter a current events program, are representative of the better types.

But depending on the whims of commercial sponsors, educational programs for children are shunted around here and there on the schedules and receive scant promotional support from the networks. On weekdays over the networks, there is only one straight educational program. In New York at least, the television broadcasters have made no genuine effort to arrange a working relationship with either the school systems or other educational institutions. In a number of other cities—Detroit, Baltimore, Washington and Philadelphia among them—the broadcasters have displayed much more initiative.

Religious presentations. On New York's seven stations these can be counted on the fingers of one hand. The leading producer in this field is the Rev. Patrick Peyton, a Catholic priest, of Hollywood, who has made a number of superb religious films with top-flight motion-picture stars. He, almost alone, has seemed to recognize that with mass media the mode of presentation is every bit as important as the message. On a less ambitious scale, "Morning Chapel" and "Lamp unto My Feet" are worthwhile.

Serious music. There is only one regularly scheduled program devoted predominantly to serious music, "The Voice of Firestone," and it does not always present artists in their best repertoire. In opera the possibilities are virtually limitless, and both the Columbia Broadcasting System and the National Broadcasting Company have done studio productions which for television were far better than direct pickups from the stage of the Metropolitan Opera.

But opera presentations have been distressingly few, and not even the Metropolitan is going to escape economic headaches merely by showing a willingness to go into TV. Operas are extremely expensive to produce and will not draw the same large audience as a vaudeville offering at comparable cost. Sponsors wanting a maximum return for their advertising dollar put Hoagy Carmichael before Verdi.

What conclusions can be drawn from this survey of the principal categories of programs? What clues are revealed as to why the programs should be subject to so much controversy?

As entertainment, television strikes the norm of show business. Its smash hits are few and far between; passable programs are reasonably plentiful; mediocre presentations are always available. Quantitatively, TV does so much more than any form of live theatre—and is watched by millions of people so much more often—that both its achievements and shortcomings stand out with special vividness. TV is a continuous first night—and at its worst, a continuous amateur night.

As a means of disseminating information and education, television does not yet have its heart in its work. Since programs in these classifications seldom produce revenue, they are regarded by the broadcasters as of secondary importance and often as a nuisance. In the general excitement over the Kefauver crime sessions scant attention was paid the fact that the most prosperous networks did the least comprehensive job of coverage and that the radio networks, where substantial commercial revenue was at stake, did nothing at all. Television looks to the advertiser, not the audience, for its most important cues as to what to do next.

The broadcaster's solicitude for the advertiser explains television's basic shortcoming in programming—the lack of balance in what it offers. During the peak listening periods there is not just a major emphasis, but almost an exclusive emphasis, on straight entertainment shows appealing to the popular mass taste. Listeners with minority preferences find their wants are met only at odd hours which may be no more convenient for them than for the majority of TV's audience.

Television may preach the gospel of vigorous competition, but in its studios it more often obeys the laws of imitation. The viewer finds that he has a choice between vaudeville shows, or between plays, or between boxing matches. This form of "block booking" effectively eliminates true diversity in programming. The problem is not so much what's on the air as what isn't.

What, then, can be done about the sameness in television, and what would constitute an ideal programming schedule? Necessarily, there will always be wide disagreement on these points, both among broadcasters and viewers; but there are several steps which should be taken to broaden the programming base of TV.

The first step involves the broadcaster's approach to his own industry and to what his role in contemporary culture is to be. As it has evolved in the last few years, television basically is not creative but a second or third run house for the products of stage and screen.

Its plays for the most part are not original, but "adaptations" of Broadway hits, books and movies. Its musicals, with one or two exceptions, are not indigenous to TV, but straight stage shows which are merely photographed. Many of its "filler" programs are borrowed directly from radio—and look it.

Television's desperate need is to realize that it no longer can go on exploiting existing cultural resources without a concerted and broad effort to do its part in replenishing these sources. Already it is showing signs of exhausting the possibilities of catering to what it thinks is the mass taste. Television has no alternative but to explore more thoroughly the limitless opportunities in the field of minority cultural preferences, if only to have something to put on the air.

As a second step, the ideal programming structure should be designed to meet the convenience more of the viewer than of the broadcaster. There must be diversity not just over a week's period, which is the industry's present criterion, but within the major divisions of the broadcast day—morning, afternoon and evening. In the morning let there be soap operas, shopping hints and cooking demonstrations. But also let there be programs which recognize that a housewife owns a mind in addition to a kitchen. In the afternoon, permit the puppets, the Westerns and visual comics to entertain the youngsters. But also offer with consistency throughout the week, programs which may instruct and acquaint the youngster with his cultural heritage.

In the evening, by all means continue the buffoonery of the clowns, the other forms of purely escapist diversion and the good drama with fine casts. But it is not too much to ask of a station or a network that it set aside half an hour an evening for discussions of current affairs, a course in art, literature or music appreciation, a series of experimental and classical dramas or a study of the social effects of television itself.

And for a third step, the commercial broadcasters should welcome and not, as at the moment, fear the prospect of educational institutions and other noncommercial interests entering TV. Whatever will expand the audience of the medium and, especially, reach those persons who are not now viewers can only mean added strength and security for all broadcasters and greater reward for all viewers.

In summary, television today is growing on a topsy-turvy basis with little sense of direction toward a specific goal. There is no flooring under the standards of the medium which utilizes the public airwaves, and there is being established the same set of conditions of expedience which so seriously thwarted the promise of radio.

To date there has been too much heat generated by, but not enough light cast on, the all-important question of what the television broadcasters can do and what they reasonably might be expected to do. The Federal Communications Commission, civic and educational groups and, above all, the broadcasters themselves all have a role to play in providing an answer. It is time that everyone took a careful look at the issue.

Television is moving too rapidly for no one to know where it is going.

TV at the Crossroads: A Critic's Survey

Here is a report on the good and the bad of TV's six years—and a look to the future

***The New York Times Magazine*, March 9, 1952**

How good is television? How bad? This season is a particularly opportune time to take a careful look at the medium which in six years has grown from a novelty to a habit for 50,000,000 people. Most of the big stars whom the public wanted to see have made their TV debuts. The types of programs which television can do, or is inclined to do, are known. The day-to-day schedules for the first time are comparatively stable and predictable. Television, in short, now can be judged fairly on its performance rather than its promise.

If the phenomenal expansion of television has proved one unarguable point, it is the futility of broad generalizations on its over-all quality. Television is too many things at the same time to be put into a convenient pigeonhole. It is theatre, motion-picture house, sight-seeing tour, sports arena, political convention, vaudeville stage, press conference, cooking school, concert hall, bank night, Congressional investigation, parlor charade, lecture platform and baby sitter. To pay for these pursuits it is of necessity also something else—America's foremost flea circus.

To attempt to digest all of contemporary television in one gulp is a manifest impossibility; the viewers who try it invariably suffer an advance case of cultural nausea. But, broken down into reasonably representative categories, the caliber of programming suggests that TV is basically much more human than electronic: it has hits and flops like everyone else. Each classification tells its own story.

Comedy

Last year the comedians were the smash hits of TV, chiefly because most of them were making their initial appearances and had the advantage of freshness. This year their success has been much less pronounced and they have not generated the same amount of viewing excitement. The reasons are not hard to find.

The public today is seeing more comedy—good, bad and indifferent—than ever before. Hardly an hour goes by on television without some energetic soul trying to make the set owner laugh. The sheer volume of clowning, all directed to essentially the same audience, inevitably has made the individual comedian's job much more difficult. In the jargon of show business, the competition is brutal.

In the first place, there is a limit to the distinctive talents and routines an artist can develop in a lifetime. With Jimmy Durante it is the infectious warmth of a one-man rebellion against society; with Jack Benny, the best sense of timing in the business; with Sid Caesar, a knack for homespun satire couched in adult pantomime; with Ed Wynn, an inspired appreciation of sheer foolishness; with Martin and Lewis, a knockabout clowning rooted in organized confusion, and with Arthur Godfrey, the relaxed ad libs of an observant humorist.

In television, the comedian has found, however, that whatever his individual style his manner of working becomes vividly familiar to millions overnight. He may be just as gifted on his twentieth or fortieth show as on his first or second but through sheer repetition the performance is not apt to have the same sparkle.

This problem of familiarity inevitably places an added premium on what always has been and will be the comedian's basic problem: material. If he is to survive he needs a constant supply of fresh gags, sketches and situations so that he has something to present besides himself. But with so many people in television going to the joke bin so often, the bottom of the barrel often is all that's left. The recent "Sound-off" time, with Fred Allen, Bob Hope and Jerry Lester as rotating stars, was one proof of this condition.

The net result of the hardships of the comedian's trade is that the overall quality of comedy undoubtedly has fallen off from what it was a year ago. Under the strain of successive performances the playing of many of the clowns has tended to become broader. Everybody has been forced to work harder. The effort often shows. By the same token, the material is more repetitive. Essentially the same sketch may show up several times within a few weeks. Producers cannot be too particular or they'd never get the shows on the air.

Among viewers to whom television seems less rewarding than formerly their own increased sophistication may be responsible in part. A few years ago it was only the critics of such trade papers as Variety and The Billboard who tried to catch every act in town; now millions all over the country do it without being especially conscious of the fact. The comedian often finds the more he tries the harder it is to please the more discriminating viewer.

But if the standards of television comedy have shown signs of decline as the medium settles down to a regular routine, there is no tangible evidence that the majority of viewers are especially concerned. Topping the popularity polls are Berle, Red Skelton and Godfrey, each of whom operates under the back-breaking grind of a weekly schedule.

The truth, of course, is that television comedy is not subject to the same exacting demands as apply in other fields. Each week's program is an unknown quantity and it doesn't cost anything to find out if it's going to be any good. A show may be an outrageous flop in a night club or theatre if it costs several dollars to see it; on television, where the expense and inconvenience are nil, the same show may not seem too bad as time-killing diversion in the home.

One dour forecast is that television in the long run is going to bring down the level of comedy merely because it must have something to do and that such is the hypnosis of TV that the public will accept it as the new norm. The only fallacy to this provocative thesis is that it presupposes the answer to an equally intriguing question: How high was the standard of American humor before television?

Drama

Studio plays, notably the full one-hour presentations, have enjoyed marked advances in production and for many viewers constitute the most satisfactory television to be offered on a regular basis. The best examples compare favorably with similar efforts on the Broadway stage; indeed, they may be superior, a point which received considerable substantiation with TV versions of "Anna Christie" and "Billy Budd."

The most effective video drama has proved to be the revival of past stage successes which have survived the trials of extended rehearsal and painstaking preparation. Original plays done for television, mostly in the form of adaptations of books and short stories, have not reflected anything like the same degree of craftsmanship in writing, though a number have been of interest from the standpoint of experimentation in production.

One serious black mark against TV drama has been the ruthless compression and distortion of several classics in order to fit them into preposterous time limitations: "Don Quixote" and "Twenty Thousand Leagues under the Sea" were almost unrecognizable after passing through the rewrite hopper. Some of television's more ambitious souls have a tendency to confuse artiness with art.

Going to the head of the class this season has been the Celanese Theatre, which obtained a corner on a number of works by Eugene O'Neill, Robert E. Sherwood, Maxwell Anderson, Elmer Rice, John Van Druten, Paul Osborne, among others. Sparing no expense in casting and production, it has been impeccable theatre directed with remarkable fluidity by Alex Segal.

"Studio One" continues to maintain excellent staging standards but, having been on the air several years longer, has had some script troubles this year. Worthington Miner, the producer, is of an adventurous turn theatre-wise but his adaptations are not always models of clarity. But "Studio One" does have the distinct merit of not shying away from adult or controversial material. It may not be realized but much of television is exceedingly grown-up.

Robert Montgomery's hour of drama is probably most representative of the application of movie-making technique to TV drama. The Schlitz Playhouse has established the precedent this season of recruiting its own company of stars and, while the quality of the scripts may be erratic, its production is generally first-class. On a relatively small budget, the hardy Kraft Theatre, which operates the year round, frequently does very well. The Pulitzer Prize Playhouse ranks with the leaders when not forced to contrived dramaturgy.

The half-hour drama programs come in two general types—situation items, either domestic or comedy, and the limitless mystery thrillers.

In the first category, Peggy Wood's vehicle, "Mama," is easily the delight of the air. Well written week in and week out, the saga of the Norwegian family is consistently warm and amusing. "My Friend Irma" and "I Love Lucy" meet the Hollywood concept of farce; "One Man's Family," "Young Mr. Bobbin" and "Claudia" are repetitious and trite. "Amos n' Andy" has its quota of laughs but nothing like the spontaneity and polish of its radio heyday.

The mysteries and adventures are noted for their quantity rather than their quality. Of the "live" presentations, "Danger" probably shows the most artistry. On film the nod goes to "Foreign Intrigue," which, interestingly enough, is produced in Sweden. For realism, "They Stand Accused," a simulated court trial, is the most authentic. Too many of the mysteries are woefully overproduced and top-heavy with effects, apparently to conceal the script inadequacies. But the sheer number of thrillers and horror pieces is not to television's credit; the medium is much too homicide-happy.

Quizzes and Variety

Television is long on the miscellany department, much of which will always defy very accurate classification. If George S. Kaufman on "This Is Show Business" and parts of "What's My Line?" are worth the viewing, most of the TV panels are pretty strained. They have produced an introverted television society all their own and badly need fresh personalities.

The give-aways offer everything from the spectacle of a wife pouring syrup on her husband's face, as on "Beat the Clock," to inexcusable exploitation of human misfortune, as on "Strike It Rich," to erstwhile announcers who have become the life of the party, as on "Stop the Music."

As for the plethora of pedestrian vaudeville used to bridge the gap between commercials, it's time somebody started thinking about bringing back television.

Children's Programs

Because youngsters always have ranged among the most avid of viewers, the presentation for preadolescents no doubt always will be among the most controversial items on video. The spectacle of tiny tots singing the praises of sponsors is not exactly an edifying sight and, if a parent does not elect to employ some method of rationing, there almost always is a Western or space opera to be found.

Actually, while the weekly programs for children admittedly are not too well-balanced or diversified, over the weekend there are numerous eminently worthwhile attractions. "Mr. I. Magination," Paul Tripp's delightful adventures in make-believe; "Mr. Wizard," a science series; "Zoo Parade" and "In the Park," a new puppet series, are just a few of the representative samples.

Complicating the problem of programming for children is one indispensable fact: they actually prefer many of the shows intended chiefly for adults.

News and Sports

The program which enables a viewer to be a witness to an event as it happens—and that embraces the whole realm of sports, the interviews with prominent figures and the spot news pick-up—constitutes television at its most absorbing. Then the viewer truly has a sense of sharing in the uncertainty of life itself; no studio production compares with it.

The sports contest always is going to rank among the best TV because the outcome is in doubt. Even if one contender is a prohibitive favorite the upset is always a possibility, as witness the Giants' pennant drive last fall. No producer can compete with the story-book home run or the desperation pass in the last quarter. The coverage of sports by television also has improved consistently. With football in particular, a viewer probably sees more of the game than the spectator in the stands.

In the realm of more serious news events, television unquestionably is a major stimulus to a better informed public opinion. The telecasts of Jacob Malik at the United Nations constituted a vivid primer in the deviousness of communism; for all its hippodroming overtones the Senate crime inquiry left an indelible impression of the scope of organized crime.

This year is going to see television bring the full weight of its influence on the Presidential campaign, with the probable result that the public as a whole is going to be more intimately acquainted with the candidates than ever before. But apart from such special occasions television is missing a bet in not doing more on-the-spot news pick-ups of important events and speeches and leaving its studio more frequently. The inelasticity of the commercial schedule all too often keeps off the air matters of major consequence and denies the medium the chance to exhibit its most basic power—that of enabling the individual at home to be his own reporter.

With the studio the press conference is the most interesting news program. "Meet the Press," on which reporters put the political celebrities through the mill, often produces front-page news in itself and gets to the heart of current issues. The "Chronoscope" is not nearly so lively and tends to repetition through use of the same questioners. "Keep Posted" has an excess of formal complications and often rambles away from the point.

The forums and panels vary sharply in quality, albeit each does achieve the end of stimulating discussion. The revised and improved "Town Meeting" has a high degree of spontaneity and, by not using too many speakers, a good deal of clarity. "America's Forum" and "The Editors Speak" get in difficulties when they have too many experts: there's apt to be more confusion than information. The recent "Author Meets the Critics," with Tex McCrary, George Sokolsky and Senator Robert A. Taft, was an example of that.

Of the regular news programs, the most comprehensive is Edward Murrow's "See It Now," a weekly summary that is less concerned with headlines than the background of events. If it is somewhat preoccupied with technical stunts, much of its documentary reporting on film is excellent. In an effort to see whether people will look at television at breakfast time, the National Broadcasting Company is experimenting under the title of "Today" with a form of newsreel, both "live" and film, every morning. Its premier was a pretentious flop, but since then it has begun to show signs of improvement.

After shamefully ignoring spot news for some time, all stations in New York now have a nightly summary at 11 o'clock. The process of getting films to the screen has been enormously speeded up, but a lot of these shows are still overly addicted to confusing charts and trick arrows flying through space.

Cultural

Programs appealing to minority tastes or intended to serve a reasonably specific educational function constitute one of the more debated problems in the development of television, chiefly because no one knows what the ideal standards for them should be.

Partly because of public pressure and the campaign for noncommercial television stations, the broadcasters have shown very substantial progress in the last year in offering presentations for more limited audiences. Sometimes it takes careful looking to find them, as they are not always put on at the most convenient hours.

"It's a Problem," seen four mornings a week, provides a thoroughly adult discussion of child psychology and family difficulties; "It's Worth Knowing" currently is exploring the subject of moral values in this county. Johns Hopkins University, Georgetown University and Columbia University participate in regular network programs. On local stations there are programming tie-ups with the Board of Education and parent-teacher groups.

Many of the finest cultural treats come on a highly irregular basis. The NBC Opera Theatre has acquitted itself very ably with experiments in opera in English, climaxed by its stunning Christmas Eve presentation of "Amahl and the Night Visitors." "Recital Hall," which makes periodic appearances, is a half-hour which presents instrumental soloists in a production noted for its superb simplicity.

The valid complaint against television on cultural programming is not that they do not know how to do fine things or lack the staff with the taste and sensibilities to do them well. Rather it is that they seem willing to do them only under pressure and without realizing that, if they can consciously and deliberately broaden public taste, they are making their own work that much easier and, in the long run, more profitable.

In evaluating the good and bad of contemporary television, the most obvious conclusion is that it reflects both the advantages and disadvantages of a mass medium. Its preoccupation with what will please most of the people most of the time indeed can be infuriating and frustrating to a discriminating viewer, but at the same time these efforts to do make possible financially the fine moments about which there can be no legitimate complaint. Inevitably, television is an artistic compromise; it can hardly afford to do anything else.

All in all, it is probably no exaggeration to state that the over-all standards of television today are substantially superior to those of the heyday of radio. Admittedly, television is not as basically creative as it should be or, if it is to survive economically, must be. But with television there are fundamental differences which never applied to radio; in these lies the medium's promise of tomorrow.

With radio the broadcasting industry lived pretty much in a world of its own, virtually isolated from the other arts, and set its own mores and codes of behavior. But with the addition of sight to sound broadcasting changed not only technically but organically.

Such is the appeal and power of television that it is recruiting many of the best minds in entertainment, education and information and they are bringing with them a wide variety of talent and background. For most of them the limited aural art of radio never had too much appeal. It is in the diversity of creative personnel, which as yet by no means has reached its peak, that television has its best security for the future.

By the same token, the television viewer is fundamentally different from the radio viewer. One of the great weaknesses of radio was that it was accepted passively by the public; this reaction is not being duplicated so far in television. Television has the inherent stimulus of theatre; it breeds a new batch of critics every time its curtain goes up. Where radio had the protective anonymity of the unseeing microphone, television operates in a goldfish bowl. It cannot hide either its shortcomings or accomplishments. Whatever it does in the future, it knows that it is going to be critically watched.

Europe's TV Picture—and Ours

Our programs stand out in pace and diversity, this critic finds. The contrast abroad is in quality and intellectual stimulus.

***The New York Times Magazine*, August 23, 1953**

LONDON—American television takes on a decidedly new and different look after a month of watching foreign television. In some ways our programming seems better than ever. Indeed a TV tourist on this side of the Atlantic sometimes can hardly help but wonder if the viewer in the United States knows how lucky he is—even if there will always be moments when he will want to hurl a brick at the screen at home. Yet in many ways television in Great Britain and Europe is so far ahead of our domestic TV that claims of American superiority sound completely foolish.

The fundamental distinction between television at home and abroad lies in the difference in the approach to the medium. Over here all TV is presented under Government auspices and on a noncommercial basis. One never hears either television or radio described as "an industry" as is commonplace in the United States. The concept in Britain and on the Continent is that broadcasting is an art, a form of theatre and an informational and educational medium. The needs of commerce or advertising do not enter the picture.

Comparing this noncommercial television with our sponsored video inevitably leads to only one conclusion: there are advantages and disadvantages to both methods and to argue that one is inherently finer than the other is the height of silliness. Where American video is the strongest and most spectacular, European and British TV is sadly wanting. And where our friends abroad shine, we are mere beginners.

To reappraise American television on the basis of a contrast with what other countries are doing—something that has not been done before—inevitably involves a number of handicaps which, in simple fairness, should be stated at the outset. First, looking at TV in a variety of lands raises a formidable language problem. Even with the help of interpreters and foreign TV officials, most of whom speak excellent English, one cannot fully detect all the defects and accomplishments of foreign video. This requires an idiomatic familiarity with all the tongues involved. That familiarity this writer certainly does not have.

Second, the whole scope of British and European television is, just as in the United States, too broad and too varied to permit of pat generalizations. In particular, one cannot be sure of whether he has seen a representative sampling of what a foreign country has to offer. In most cases the answer would be that he has not, if only because that would involve a stay of many weeks rather than days in each individual country.

But within these limitations, a visitor can absorb a surprising amount from the foreign screens themselves and at least come away with many varied impressions that put American video in a somewhat different focus than it was before. Herewith, then, a new balance sheet on TV in the United States as drawn up three thousand miles away from the hypnotic influence of the Empire State tower.

Variety of Programming

For the American visitor this undoubtedly is the most striking lack—and feature—of foreign video—a choice of what to tune in. The stultifying effect of having only one channel to watch with little likelihood of any more for several years to come, if then, must be experienced to be appreciated. Nowhere, not in Britain or on the Continent, is there anything like a fraction of the diversity of programming which we accept as a matter of course.

Television abroad is also largely television without stars. With the financing of TV for the most part limited to income from license fees on sets or direct governmental appropriations, there simply is not the means to put on television with any regularity the best that each country has to offer in entertainment. Complain as we may about the abuses of sponsorship, there is no denying that it has brought into the American home virtually all the headliners we have. Just try doing it without the top professionals in show business, particularly in the realm of popular entertainment, and our TV would wither away overnight.

In this connection our flourishing economy is in no small part responsible. The price of a television set is extremely prohibitive in terms of the purchasing power of British and foreign currencies. In Great Britain there are approximately 2,500,000 sets in use; in all the rest of Europe there are probably 200,000. The perennial riddle—which comes first, the better programs or the larger audience?—is much more acute under the post-war economic stringencies over here.

Commercials

What is television like with no commercials? At first it seems like heaven come true. The quieter and more leisurely presentation of programs made possible when there are no interruptions for station breaks, middle commercials and spot announcements, is something greatly to be desired. There is no question that, for the viewer's personal comfort and enjoyment, American video is much too commercial. The absence of the continuous boardwalk motif on TV is literally sublime.

But there comes a somewhat different reaction after sustained viewing. An American visitor almost wishes there would be a commercial to lend a bit of life to the evening. Let us be particularly thankful for a time limitation where most comedians are concerned. You cannot imagine the agony when an allegedly comic blighter goes on and on. Brother, it can be something! Bring on the spot announcement!

In drama, on the other hand, there can only be cheers and extremely robust ones for no commercials within the framework of the play. To see a play without having the mood rudely impaired by a pitchman is so completely sensible that American viewers are mad to put up with any other practice.

Quality of Pictures

Let no American viewer, broadcaster or engineer fool himself that we have the highest quality of images on the home screen. We don't. Our live studio quality of picture is easily matched in many parts of Europe, especially in Hamburg, Germany. In France, the picture is better technically, but we could not adopt their standards without disrupting our whole system. Besides, French insistence on their system may hamper European international video since all other countries on the Continent have agreed on a single standard.

But far and away the most significant and exciting technical development is what the British Broadcasting Corporation is doing with films made for television. Even though Britain uses lower standards of definition, their films are so much better than ours that American broadcasters should blush with shame. Both sponsors and viewers in the United States have been taken for one terrific sleigh-ride with the miserable reproduction of kinescopes and Hollywood pictures.

The British films are not only the equal of our "live" studio quality but far superior. The detail and definition are as good as what one sees in a movie house. The BBC system is an old familiar story: the English pursued quality where we pursued quantity. By comparison American video films are little atrocities that belong with the early "talkies." The irony is that the British modestly note that we have all the technical data on their system and they have never understood why we do not use it.

Documentaries and Newsreels

These programs on film represent one of the areas in which American television is most behind. The British in particular have developed the documentary art in TV to a very high degree and cover a fascinating range of subjects: juvenile delinquency, conditions in India, the role of the artist in modern society, the life of a chorus girl and, to be presented soon, a study of divorce. In short, the BBC is utilizing television for truly creative journalism and the only one coming close to their standard in the United States is Edward R. Murrow's "See It Now." That he should have so little competition where so much could be done is difficult to understand.

Similarly the nightly newscasts in most every foreign country—Britain, France, the Netherlands, Germany and Italy—are head and shoulders above our newscasts.

The European TV newsreels are put together in the same way as theatre newsreels. They are really visual magazines with items touching on all aspects of modern life. One never sees a fashion plate announcer reading from cue cards or a piece of paper—and what a relief that is! The commentator is kept in his proper place—off the screen—and pictures, not words, tell the story. And the foreign newsreels own a respectable period of time—at least fifteen minutes without interruption.

Spot news bulletins are handled separately and often are merely read with no picture at all. By contrast the American practice of trying to combine a newsreel with a radio news program seems extremely awkward and not quite one thing or the other. The British and European countries also do not try to disguise the fact that inevitably some newsreels may be a day or two old, as our network shows often do. When you have not seen the pictures before, they still are fresh and interesting.

One further point: foreign TV newsreels do not belabor their audiences with details of how they obtained their pictures or mention the trouble or expense entailed. They just show the pictures. American television's constant inclination to inject itself into the stories that it covers is very immature journalism by comparison.

Drama

Every video system over here is giving painstaking attention to drama. Unfortunately on this visitor's trip there was an opportunity to see very little, too little to form any firm opinions. But of what one did see, British drama was disappointing from the production standpoint. It was too much like photographing a stage show and had nothing like the camera mobility to be found in our TV plays.

From all accounts, French drama is sometimes extremely good on television and, judging from advance plans, the Italian video should be most interesting to watch next season. In both of these countries some of the striking composition to be found in their films is being translated into their television programming which, temperamentally, is often closer to the American norm than the British product.

Children's Programs

In perhaps television's most controversial branch of activity—programming for the younger generation—hardly enough can be said for the attitude of the British and European broadcasters. They simply do not believe that preparations for children can or should ever be compromised in purpose or goal. Either you put a program on for a child or you put it on to sell a sponsor's goods. You cannot do both, they say.

Certainly the ambition of all foreign systems to do a responsible job for young viewers is most commendable. Instead of the utter trash which for the most part litters our channels, there are special plays, newsreels, documentaries, talks and "television magazines" for boys and girls. Some countries perhaps stress culture a little too strongly—the Italians, however, do not believe a Western serial will do harm if there are other programs to go with it—but one cannot help but admire the sincerity and determination to use television to enrich a youngster's life. Particularly, in view of American television's infinitely greater resources, we have not begun to do the job we should.

The Dance

In practically every country ballet is receiving great attention on television. Even the Netherlands, operating its video on a virtual shoestring, has had several ambitious presentations. Here in London this viewer saw a ten-minute cameo of ballet that was lovely to watch. American TV is really missing something in not exploring ballet much more thoroughly and imaginatively than it has thus far.

Revues and Variety

American television's prominence in this field is not apt to be seriously challenged for a very long time. Quite apart from TV considerations the British and European standards in this area of make-believe often are so rudimentary and hackneyed as to seem of another age. Admittedly the financial problems of government-controlled television make it hard or impossible to acquire the better artists but there is also a decided prejudice against it in many countries.

Under monopolistic conditions and with no threat of competition, those in charge of television in many countries tend to see popular entertainment as consuming an enormous share of their budget and not really deserving of their time. They are more interested in the intellectual stimulus to be found in other branches of TV. This is understandable and not unusual among talented producers in the U.S. either.

But it becomes a horse of a different color when these same individuals—often it is just one individual—can decide what a whole country shall or shall not see in television. The competitive system in the United States does have its faults in this respect, to be sure, but the idea of one man or group of men having so much power over a TV system seems potentially a far greater danger. British and European officials seem to be convinced of the rightness of their position; few American video executives are so sure.

To sum up the relative merits of American and foreign video, this viewer would say that we excel in a variety of programming, and in the musical revue and comedy-type shows. The British and European systems have the advantage in documentaries and newsreels, in children's programs, in the dance and in quality of pictures.

As for commercials—after looking at the noncommercial foreign TV one comes away possibly a bit less hostile to the idea of commercials than formerly. For one realizes that it is not the commercial per se which disturbs the viewer. It is how, when and how often the commercial is put in a program. American sponsors, who have made tremendous contributions to television as an entertainment medium, should do some research in the rewards to be found in moderation of advertising. They could be fabulous.

But to list some of the points of contrast between American, British and European television is not sufficient; it omits perhaps the chief lesson to be learned by United States video. As at home, video abroad reflects not just a play, a show or a picture, but a country's whole culture and point of view. Here in London earnest if quiet attempts are being made to see to what extent programs can be exchanged for the common good of viewers in many lands. So far, distance and a preoccupation with our own programs have tended to keep America out of this cooperative effort.

It is time we played our part, because watching programs in many places—everything from the presentations of our allies to the drab propaganda of the Soviet-controlled stations in East Berlin—leaves one unforgettable memory. Television is no longer predominantly American; it is international. How will the world use it?

Chapter Nine

Television and Its Critic

Acting as a television critic for twenty-five years took my father in some unexpected directions. His technical knowledge of television and the workings of a set led him to attempt a brief stint as a repairman in Stamford, Connecticut. The result was his essay: "TV Tube Bites TV Critic." Though the venture lasted only a day, it did not curb his fascination with the innards of a television set. For years, whenever he went on the road for the *Times*, he toted a supply of tubes and wires with him just in case the set in his hotel went on the blink. Usually, he had more electronic equipment in his suitcase than fresh clothes.

During his periodic automobile trips through the South, either on business or to visit in-laws in Texas, he noted the changes in regional viewing habits, and once he recorded them, in "Tuning in on Dixie." Both articles, as well as his survey of the medium in 1956, give a good sense of his imagination and constant effort to connect with the experiences of the average viewer.

Sensitive to the television industry's disdain for critics and their opinions, my father wrote on occasion about the role he played and the standards he used to judge television programs. In May 1957 he laid out the objections often made to critics, and he answered the objections a week later. The last review in this chapter finds Dad appearing on television himself on David Susskind's *Open End* to discuss television. Never a pundit, my father was uncomfortable before the camera and remained dubious that reporters should become personalities and celebrities. On this occasion, the chemistry of the program did not work. Thus, the final review in the book conveys some of his self-deprecating wit, modesty, and lack of self-importance. The piece provides an appropriate place to leave the man I knew as a father, a journalist, and for a quarter-century the conscience of television.

TV Tube Bites TV Critic

He finds television is no "happy medium" as seen from the repairman's side

***The New York Times Magazine*, January 3, 1954**

At last there is an unquestioned authority on television. He is the man who shows up at the door in response to the plaintive cry, "Something's wrong with my television set!" Meet the television service man, one of the martyrs of modern society.

I know; I was one. For a day I traveled from house to house carting a box of spare tubes and tools and administering to receivers that inexplicably had gone blank, developed jittery lines or become mute. It was better than a college education.

Critics and broadcasters are wont to speak of TV as an art or a business. The poor fools! After you've spent a day comforting distraught viewers with broken sets you know better. Television is the twentieth-century narcotic. And a broken television set is not just a piece of inoperative equipment; it's a social and domestic crisis.

One man's induction into repair work can be laid to a youthful indiscretion. Finding out how radio sets work seemed—long ago—like a good idea and led to the building of some receivers. Then came television and there developed an elementary concern over picture circuits, tubes and adjustments. A few successful favors for neighbors added to the electronic fever. This was followed by a decision to find out how the other, or service, half lives.

Thus, at 9 o'clock one Monday morning, I reported in Stamford, Conn., at the appliance and television store of Alfred H. Barrett. My immediate fate was placed in the hands of John J. Ginter, head of TV repairs. First, there was the box of spare tubes to be filled before going out on the round of house calls. By conservative estimate, there must be something like sixty to a hundred different tubes that can be used in television sets. They all have identifications like 6SN7, 6J6, 5U4 or 1B3GT. After Mr. Ginter had contributed enough tools to build another Radio City, he gave his last instruction: "Use the green panel truck." I was on my own.

The first call of the morning was at a second-floor apartment. The set, I was told by an anxious husband, had not worked over the weekend, and his wife had missed it. He worked on a night shift so he didn't see much besides daytime TV. He was a viewer deserving of every consideration.

Alas, disaster was only around the corner. The set was turned on and worked beautifully. All seven channels were clear and the sound was fine. The only things wrong were the programs. The husband and wife who had done without their set for forty-eight hours looked at each other—and, it might be added, at the service man. For the first time in his life one newspaperman wished he had brought along a public relations expert.

The set obviously had an intermittent failure—the perennial nightmare of the TV technician—and there were three possible courses of action. Judging by the couples' description of their troubles, the probable cause (or causes) could be diagnosed and appropriate new tubes substituted. Tentatively, this approach was tried. "But if the set works," they wanted to know, "why do we need new tubes?"

Another tack was proposed. The set could be taken to the shop and run on the bench until the trouble showed up again, technically the most sensible if most expensive course. The couple just stared at their visitor. If a child looks and acts healthy, do you drag it off to the hospital? was the attitude.

A final alternative was advanced. Let the set run a while and call the store if it broke down again. Take a chance, in other words. (So you are not going to do anything, eh? Strange.)

Oh yes, there was a postscript. I was supposed to collect $4.95 for the house call. The housewife stiffened, looked at the set playing nicely and then at me. "I think we'll charge this one," she said.

The next stop was clear across town. This is always the case; two sets never break down in the same neighborhood. "Oh," said the kindly lady at the door, "you're the man from Electric Service," and related that something had gone "boom" in her set. What did it sound like? (An intern quickly learns to avoid that trap; examine the patient first.) She explained that her family really only looked at television a little bit, just a short time on Sunday evenings, really. The Sunday night play usually. Last night the picture and sound had just disappeared.

One tube manifestly had expired. A search through the box of spare tubes turned up every kind of part but the needed one. This led to a drive of forty-five minutes to and from the store for the tube. The picture instantly was restored to its former glory—you could see Art

Linkletter, somehow a strange reward for driving all over town. But the sound would not come back and in twenty minutes or so it was clear that some major mishap had occurred. The set would have to be taken to the shop.

The news was broken gently and the lady was most understanding, but the pained look on her face was very real. "Do you think," she asked hesitantly, "we could get the set back tonight? My husband enjoys it a great deal."

There was only one more call—on the other side of town, of course. It was just the thing to steady the nerves. While tracking down the trouble with the set, I enjoyed other diversions not to be found on any television channel. The grandmother who loved her TV explained that she had just been diagnosed as a heart case. She had been forced to give up coffee and smoking and could not go out driving alone. (Yes, the trouble was probably in the video strip; try a 6BA6.) The daughter came home crying. Another girl had pushed her and her knee was bleeding. (Let's look at the vertical oscillator, the 6SN7.) The knee is all better. (The vertical hold knob is beginning to function.) Supper time, supper time. (Amid the aroma of meat loaf, check through the sound I.F.) Now the second daughter is helpful. "Oh, you've got 'The First Show.'" (O.K., Mr. Service Man, hold the mirror with your left hand, adjust the linearity with your right and pay attention.) Now little sister must have her nightly piano practice.

The remedy—for me—was obvious. The truck was returned gratefully to the parking lot and upon arrival home a hot bath was drawn and neither woman nor child was allowed to raise a voice above a whisper for thirty minutes. Supper was served on a tray. The following morning a resignation was submitted to Mr. Ginter who had a comforting word. Wait till color TV, said he, and they'll call you at 10 in the evening to fix their reds and blues.

Clearly, spending a day in the homes of television viewers can play hob with what a critic thought was a reasoned perspective. Is a television set something merely to be bought and turned on? Apparently not. Evidently it is a box with a soul, an object of devotion and attention and even the owner is not fully aware of this until he must do without it.

Let the picture tube be bright and the loud speaker articulate and all is well. Viewers then may speak rationally of program preferences and favorite stars. But let the set give out and the viewer's personality undergoes an almost chemical change. Never mind then what's on the air. Just hurry. Fix the set so that it—and life—can go on again.

Television Today: A Critic's Appraisal

Now in its ninth year, the arts' fabulous infant shows commendable progress in some fields but is lagging badly in others. Here is a report card on the medium.

***The New York Times Magazine*, April 8, 1956**

Age is creeping up on television; it's in its ninth year. In 1947 the infant medium was tenderly carried from the laboratory to the public stage. At home a handful of hardy pioneers squinted at strange, illuminated windows cut in cumbersome boxes. Before their eyes cavorted an assortment of little figures, the dancing omens of a nation's new way of life.

Today the TV set ranks with the kitchen stove as a family essential. The youngsters who were introduced this year to the regimen of high school are members of the first TV generation, boys and girls who cannot be expected to remember what life was like without video. The thought is quite a numbing one.

As perhaps need not be suggested, the advancing years have not always been kind to the viewer; to think back alone on the total number of hours wasted on ancient movies is a little terrifying. But in fairness it must be conceded that the passing of time has been just as cruel, if not crueler, to the TV broadcaster. The video operator, after all, is the only man in the television age who is denied the most exhilarating of intellectual privileges, turning the TV off. In his executive suite he cannot merely sit in contemplation of the ulcer that lies beneath the gray flannel; he must constantly devise new ways to nourish a monster that grows more hungry with every meal.

How goes life, then, with this unenviable figure, the broadcaster? How well is he succeeding in his multiple role of impresario, educator, journalist, psychiatrist and nursemaid to the millions? Is TV getting better or worse?

TV has gone through two stages of development and now is in its third. The first stage was the medium's pure technical novelty, when almost anything could be put on the screen and the public would look at it. The second was the era of personality novelty; the sight of a new face periodically refreshed interest in the TV medium. Now, in the third stage, with almost everybody and his brother having had a TV debut, the industry is confronted with the realization that it must rely on itself. This is the key both to its progress in some areas of programming and to its stalemate in others.

Television's special events—the occasional programs which are entities unto themselves—probably represent the medium's most significant single asset; its capacity to be extraordinarily good. In this season alone the viewer has been afforded the chance to witness George Bernard Shaw's "The Devil's Disciple," with Maurice Evans; Robert Morley in "Edward, My Son"; a superb live version of "The Caine Mutiny Court Martial"; a tour of India with Chester Bowles; an examination of the farm problem that disturbed the Secretary of Agriculture; Noel Coward; Mozart's "Magic Flute"; Sir Laurence Olivier's new film, "Richard III"; Mary Martin in "Peter Pan," and the Sadler's Wells Ballet.

Granted that the cited attractions would not be immune to some critical reservations, none the less such efforts are not the output of untutored morons; they are thoroughly commendable and sometimes brilliant illustrations of the fact that, when they want to, the broadcasters are entitled to hold up their heads proudly. The boring snobs who have tried to concoct an intellectual superiority out of a noisy refusal to watch television will have to find a more persuasive dodge.

To be sure, not all special events, some of which have labored under the colossally inept title of "spectaculars," have been an unmixed blessing. Quite a number were pretentious cathode atrocities. If the Sadler's Wells Ballet chalked up an impressive total audience of some 30,000,000 viewers, let the record show that Art Linkletter's incredible "tour" of Beverly Hills allegedly garnered a bigger one. "Spectacular" is not a reliable synonym of "culture."

But in this respect television differs not a whit from theatre, movies or book publishing. For every Pulitzer Prize or Oscar winner, there are scores of wretched products in these fields, dismal outrages that constitute huckstering at its worst. A fairer test is the ratio of good to bad. By this criterion, TV's special endeavors stack up rather well.

To represent TV at its best there is also another type of special attraction—the actuality broadcast that takes place outside the studio. The national political conventions, the coronation of Queen Elizabeth, the Kefauver crime hearings, the world series, the Presidential press conference and the heavyweight championship are samples of life itself, conveyed into the home. With such broadcasts the world of reality unfolds upon the screen in all its spontaneity and unpredictability. This has been and always will be TV at its most exciting because it is something that only TV can do, which is to enable the viewer to be his own reporter, editor and critic. Why television does not venture more often out of the studio continues to be quite baffling; the medium hasn't really begun to explore the vast amount of fascinating programming that may lie between Madison Avenue and the Hollywood Freeway.

Television's regular events—the programs that turn up according to a fixed schedule—are quite another story. The passing years are taking their toll of both the ingenuity of producers and the durability of viewers. It could not be otherwise after so many hundreds of nights of continuous programming. The creative artist of TV and the set owner are, each in his own way, bound to feel the consequence of over-entertainment. The program producer has done too much and the viewer has seen too much to make their relationship easy.

Comedy on television is in dire difficulty. The frayed tempers of Arthur Godfrey and Jackie Gleason and the physical exhaustion of other clowns are symptomatic of the law of diminishing returns that goes with trying to fit humor on an assembly line. The routines, mannerisms and gestures that once seemed so amusing inevitably wear thin; they are too fragile to survive repetition. This season Phil Silvers has been a great hit and justly so. But how long can even Sergeant Bilko last?

No comedian in his right mind, before the coming of TV, would have dreamed of going to the same house once a week and being the life of the party; yet this is what he tries to do in video. It is madness and the toll on comedians is one of TV's great tragedies. The country needs its warm and funny men too much to burn them out. The comedians should restrict their appearances to a few performances a year. Failing that, the viewer can only institute his own rationing system.

The dramas on television, with changing casts and authors, are perhaps doing best of the regular TV attractions. Some of the plays are extraordinarily good and the sustained high quality of acting on TV is astonishing. But drama is also facing troubles. Whereas once there were four hour-long shows, now there are nine every week. There simply are not that many good plays around and many more are just soap-opera rubbish in pretentious settings. There is a need for more drawing-room comedy and satire and certainly more theatre of the bravura school. TV drama is topheavy with social discussions conducted in cubby-holes.

Television variety this season brings one name to the fore: Perry Como. Ironically, his show represents a full turn of the TV wheel; its appeal and charm are based on the qualities of relaxation and informality that made "Garroway at Large" one of the first video successes. Mr. Como's philosophy might well be a guiding motto of all TV: easy does it. Ed Sullivan's "Toast of the Town" continues to thrive perhaps because it also combines the virtues of professionalism and low pressure. Most of the other variety shows seldom sustain themselves for many weeks; they try too hard, including "Omnibus."

The films especially made for TV? A sorry lot, by and large. Certainly they cannot stand comparison with the live hour-long dramas and the special events; more than ever, they seem inadequate in characterization and narrative, following the old- fashioned radio way of telling a story. But also, with few exceptions, they are trite and artificial, certainly not a good advertisement of the capabilities of Hollywood.

Of the major studios, Twentieth Century-Fox has done much the best with its extended dramas, Warner Brothers has come up with a satisfactory Western series, but Metro-Goldwyn-Mayer hasn't put its heart into TV. Economics will always assure a place for filmed series on video, but artistically it is shocking how really unimportant they are.

TV quizzes have come in a few years to the point it took radio quizzes nearly twenty-five years to reach—buying their audiences. "The $64,000 Question" started it all, of course, and its appeal at once was undeniable: watching a person gamble his knowledge against the possible loss of a fortune. The human values were indubitably there. But the imitations have not been especially successful and now the question is where does the quiz go next?

The inexpensiveness of most quizzes is their prime asset and no doubt they will be with us forever. But it surely would be fun if some of those old familiar faces could be replaced. The current members of television's café society elite, the mainstays of panel attractions, are fading. Let's bring on the younger girls.

The regular news programs on TV are not what they should be; journalistically, video is something of a disappointment. The fault does not lie with the backstage laborers in the news vineyard; they are able. But on the policy-making level the TV high brass is not really overly interested in news because it does not have the same commercial sales value as, for instance, vaudeville.

The best that TV can do, after eight years, is a quick newsreel once-over of the day's events. There is no sustained coverage in depth, little helpful evaluation of the significance of the headline, and virtually no interpretive commentary to stimulate the viewer to do some thinking for himself. TV has all but wrecked night-time radio, where news opinion once flourished, and has failed to offer an adequate substitute in the realm of regular informational programming. This is one of TV's black marks.

The weekly interview shows in which newspaper men examine front-page personages are consistently interesting, though at times the panels seem inordinately eager either to pack their guests off to jail or to let them off the hook with dismaying gentleness.

Programs for small children—the older youngsters would not be caught dead looking at children's shows—are not what they should be. "Captain Kangaroo" is a civilized delight, unhesitatingly recommended. Dr. Frances Horwich, principal of "Ding Dong School," is still imploring tots to guide their mothers to the right commercial products, a not too seemly performance for one trained in child education. "Howdy Doody" is every bit as objectionable as ever.

Daytime programming has not had much really new for quite a while. "Home," with Arlene Francis, has a number of worthwhile features, however, and Garry Moore, with his innocuous high-jinks, is diverting and one of the most consistently pleasant gentlemen on the air. The "Matinee" series of hour-long dramas seems to be teetering perilously close to soap opera, which is a pity. And, of course, there are movies and menus at all times.

The final program classification with a legitimate claim to attention is that of the full-length theatre movies now being shown on TV. Some are uncommonly good, particularly the more recent English features. And it now appears that the motion picture industry's unspoken boycott of TV has been broken with the release of major backlogs of films to TV. The cutting of some of the films for TV purposes, however, has not always been especially judicious. The narrative can become entangled by the interruptions for those blankety-blank, if altogether necessary, commercials.

What of the future of television programming? Very likely the broad outlines of today's pattern will continue, but no one would be too surprised if TV came to the "special evening" as opposed to the present "special event." This would entail the planning of a night's several shows as part of an integrated whole. Instead of a mixed assortment of bits and pieces, there would be an over-all design and point of view intended to hold an audience, say, 8:30 to 11 o'clock.

In European television there is the custom of an attractive hostess who appears periodically and provides a thread of continuity throughout an entire night's viewing. American television, in contrast, almost invites a viewer to tune out and look elsewhere every half-hour or hour. With the "special evening," presumably also would come better balance in programming, not one quiz back to back with another quiz but perhaps a quiz from 8 to 8:30, then a two-hour play until 10:30, and finally an hour of song and dance before the news and bedtime.

On the other hand, television cannot afford to abandon its present bread-and-butter staples. To suggest that this or that format will be predominant in the days to come is to misunderstand video's requirements: it must have a little of everything. There are some indications already that the "spectacular" has perhaps become too commonplace. TV's everlasting problem is not to worry as much about what it is doing but what it is not.

Essentially, both the viewer and the broadcaster are showing their TV years in the same way; they are becoming restless. As a fixture in the living room, television can be accepted as a matter of course; as a social force, TV's effects cannot. The people of the nation now see more plays in a year than a professional Broadway drama critic. They are more knowledgeable about vaudeville than the Monday matinee audience at the old Paramount; certainly they have seen the same acts more often. They can identify on sight more celebrities than the traveled cosmopolite of a generation ago.

Quietly but steadily, television has wiped out "the sticks" and "the road" from show business. The erstwhile hayseed is looking at the same thing as the supposedly more sophisticated resident of Park Avenue. The economic and geographical barriers that once separated the mass from the arts have simply been taken down. If, under the circumstances, the television impresarios are a little bewildered by the full long-range meaning of what they've started, who isn't?

The world of TV has a cultural bear by the tail and finds it cannot let go. In inundating the American home with things to watch morning, noon and night, it has set off a gradual process of selectivity on both sides of the screen. It matters not that the majority of millions may prefer the shows with which they are familiar; millions of other persons are willing to track down the unusual. There is a growing body of undeclared set owners who, having absorbed so much TV, are becoming choosy. The impact of TV is proving a double-edged sword; the show that can quickly impress a viewer can also quickly exhaust him.

The despair of television today—finding enough things to do—in the long run is the hope of television tomorrow. Video's appetite for material is so huge that even the supply of mediocrity is not enough to go around. To borrow Gore Vidal's immortal line, there comes a time when in sheer desperation it is necessary to scrape the top of the barrel.

Economically and artistically, television has no real alternative to expanding its interest and lifting its sights; it's done everything else. Undoubtedly it will receive far too much advice about how it should proceed, and unquestionably it will pay much too little attention to most of it. With baffling rapidity it can be expected to be charming and stimulating one moment and completely infuriating and tiring the next. But this should not surprise either viewer or broadcaster unduly. After all, isn't television the lusty child of the arts?

Tuning in on Dixie: Mocking Birds Sing, but Who Listens? Everyone's Inside Looking at TV!

April 15, 1956

Herewith some random notes and observations on the subject of television and radio, made while motoring down to Atlanta last week-end.

On U.S. Route 29, about ten miles north of Athens, Ga., is the home of Roy Brown, a farmer, and his wife, Mrs. Vinnie Brown. Their house, made of weather-worn, unpainted pine and raised off the ground on brick pilings, is set back on a small rise. Discarded automobile tires serve as a border for an attractive garden. The TV antenna sits prominently on the roof.

Mrs. Brown, leisurely chewing tobacco, says the set goes about seven hours a day, seven days a week. With the grandchildren and relatives there may be eleven persons looking at one set. "You can hardly see the television set," she said. Mrs. Brown said she had no program preferences. "We just look at any of it," she explained.

Had TV changed older habits? Moviegoing, perhaps? For the first time Mrs. Brown noticeably cooled. With unwavering eyes she said firmly and indignantly:

Young man," she said, "I never been to a movie show or a theatre in my life."

Farther along Route 29, near Tucker, Ga., the Rev. Lester Buice, pastor of the Rehoboth Baptist Church, a most strikingly modern edifice, confirmed that TV was regarded in a somewhat different light than either movies or the theatre by many older fundamentalists.

Children, he said, were responsible for the change. They insisted on having TV, and the older folk succumbed to the electronic revolution. With a twinkle in his eye, Mr. Buice noted: "Some of them didn't find the entertainment quite as bad as they feared."

Entering Gaffney, S.C., at 7:45 in the evening can provide a shock. At an intersection of two main streets a motorist is apt to be impressed less by the traffic light than by the smiling countenance and measured phrases of John Cameron Swayze. It seems "outdoor television" is upon the nation. For the benefit of Gaffney taxi drivers waiting for fares there is a TV receiver in an open lot. Without leaving their cabs they can pass the time watching video. The next obvious step: "Drive-in television."

Below Anderson, S.C., there was a house with a spanking new television antenna equipped with a rotating device and separate arrays for very high frequency and ultra high frequency reception. In the front yard a woman was boiling her laundry in a huge pot over an open fire and pounding the clothes with a plunger.

One of the residents of Winder, Ga., is Mrs. Modine Thomas, who has five children. Her home is just over the railroad tracks of the Seaboard line, and her family cooks, sleeps, lives and watches TV in the same room.

She says the children usually look from 11 A.M. to 2:30 P.M., when she makes them turn the set off after her return from doing housework in the home of Senator Richard B. Russell, Democrat of Georgia, whose house is across the road. About 5 o'clock, she said, the set is turned on again and the family watches until about 9:30.

What of school for the youngsters? Mrs. Thomas said that while she and her husband, who does plumbing jobs in Winder, were off at work "somebody had to stay with the baby." Two of her children are over 10 and three are 6 or under. The eldest, William Henry, said he thought Roy Rogers was swell on TV.

Mrs. Thomas said that the house in which she lived was owned by Senator Russell and that she did not pay rent. She recalled that her TV set cost $110, and added with a smile: "We've got it paid for."

Radio Station WGGA in Gainesville, Ga., has a fascinating "Swap Shop" program at 8:45 A.M., week days. Listeners call in with specific articles they want to buy, sell or trade. Some of last week's specials were these:

*A load of chicken fertilizer, if you would clean out the listener's chicken house

*A strong mule

*An outdoor toilet

On a highway outside of Atlanta a man was tinkering with his car, which still bore the "A" card of the wartime gasoline rationing days. Two weeks ago he invested $300 in a new twenty-one-inch set. "Now I got a night job and don't ever see it," he said. But all the neighbors sure ain't lonely now.

There'll be no more chit-chat out of Arthur Godfrey and Dave Garroway about their arduous working schedules. Farmer Russ (Russell Osshaus), the pride of WLOS and WLOS-TV in Asheville, N.C., puts in thirty hours a week on the radio. Ten of these hours are also televised. Incidentally, Farmer Russ of Carolina used to be a disk jockey—in Boston.

Pay-as-you-see television, at least one form of it, is now thoroughly commonplace in many parts of the country. Many of the automobile "motels" have TV sets equipped with meters and the charge is 25 cents for an hour's viewing. Do people pay?

Outside of Charlotte, N.C., one motel operator said that if a family came off the road by about 6 o'clock he could count on at least 75 cents to $1 revenue a night from each set.

In Charlottesville, Va., however, another motel operator said he could not see splitting his TV income with a service company that installs the meters and takes the lion's share of the quarters. He just leaves off the electric cord that connects the set to the wall outlet. In a matter of minutes, he said, his overnight tenant returns to the registration office and asks where the cord is. He's only too glad to provide it—for $1 for the evening.

Memo to TV repairmen planning a cross-country trip: take along a screw driver and an outlet cord, which, ironically enough, always has been known in video service parlance as a "cheater cord." For the electronically trained, it's a cinch to "jump" many of the meters.

Where TV Critics Strike Out: Some Sweeping Charges about Their Manifold Deficiencies

May 19, 1957

One of the handicaps under which television labors is the professional television critic's immunity from criticism. In the world of video, as in the theatre and motion pictures, it is almost an unwritten rule not to argue with a reviewer.

To take exception to a critic's unfavorable notice may leave one open to the charge of being a poor loser. To approve a review may suggest that one is trying to curry favor. Because one's motives may be so easily misconstrued, few people in TV are willing to put their names to a bill of particulars against the critics.

Under such circumstances, it would seem incumbent on the critics to seek out and report the indictment of themselves; certainly they cannot pretend it does not exist. To be sure, this procedure is no substitute for a complainant speaking out for himself, but it may help to let in a little fresh air on one phase of TV.

The following lines, therefore, are a composite summation of talks with many different persons, all actively engaged in TV, on the subject of video criticism.

The basic flaw in TV criticism is the critic's presumption that he is equipped to review anything and everything. Be it classical or modern drama, the arts of acting, writing or directing, serious or contemporary music, dance or politics, news or education, religion or sports, he is right in there with his definitive judgment. The cultural conceit of the television critic is unparalleled in its fundamental arrogance. Even commercial TV recognizes the need for different specialists in different fields; the TV critics are the only ones not similarly troubled.

The TV critic is the lord and master of a vacuum. His profound judgments come after the fact. A program may be over and done with, never to be seen again, and the critic arises with all his solemn dicta about how it should have been put on. His is an exercise in frustration because he cannot fulfill the critic's true function of directing the public to the meritorious and steering it away from the mediocre. His beacon burns most brightly after 100,000,000 viewers already have made up their minds and gone to bed.

The New York TV critic tends to reflect—or hopes he does—his community's reputed sophistication. But television has a broader obligation to serve the entire country. Neither economically nor artistically can it afford to pander to the tyranny and intolerance of an intellectual minority. Programs go out across the country; critics don't.

Through their choice of what to review, the critics are stimulating mediocrity and putting a premium on cultural achievement. Run of the mill television programs—the half-hour film series, the quiz show, the panel game and the Western—receive only cursory examination when they first go on the air.

Consciously or not, the critics dispense the lion's share of their praise or damnation only on those programs that strike them as out of the ordinary. It is the new play for television, not the routine series, and the special or spectacular effort that are subjected to the critic's microscope. Let Ed Murrow falter in a documentary or Rodgers and Hammerstein disappoint and it is coast-to-coast news in the morning. But Joe Dope who is on the air at the same time with stereotyped trash is not held up to ridicule or scorn. The critic's own boredom with most of TV has played into the hands of those whom he professes to disapprove.

The application of this peculiar critical standard is a major deterrent to the improvement of television. The lofty criteria by which most critics live are indeed noble, and superficially may seem grounded in common sense. But in actual practice their blind application may do as much harm as good.

Television contains people of just as good taste, judgment and theatrical experience as the critics can boast. But the critic lives in an unreal world quite his own: he can say this or that without coping with the headaches of getting it done. The critics are great at lashing to the mast all the executives, vice presidents, research men et al. But, ironically, they're toughest of all on the eggheads in TV.

The person in TV who aspires to a higher artistic standard lives in a thankless jungle. On the one hand he operates under the dark shadow of the critics; on the other hand he must juggle the oppressive commercial pressures under which TV survives.

Over the last several seasons, all networks have tried a variety of special efforts. Many have drawn extremely severe criticism often without complete justification. For what is so hard to explain to critics is that those who put on a show often are altogether aware of its faults but that in the present state of TV many of these flaws are simply unavoidable.

Where creative people in TV must part company with the critics is in what constitutes progress. Take, for example, a play with even a slightly off-beat theme. Network executives may be apprehensive that it will not draw sufficiently well to offset another network's competition. The sponsor may be unhappy that the production staff is not doing the true and tried, that the program does not reflect its advertising philosophy, that it does not coincide with its merchandising or promotion plans. So there may be a succession of compromises, perhaps in the choice of cast, in script revisions or in the over-all approach of the program. These can entail brutal hours of telephoning and arguing.

The outcome is that the producer may be forced to settle for a small part of his original hope. In due course the critics may notice these shortcomings. But from the standpoint of those on the TV firing line, at least some sort of the off-beat quality has been retained. Is it not better to settle for a slice of bread if the whole loaf cannot be obtained? The alternative is no progress whatsoever. Better TV will come only through a process of compromise, building step by step until compromise becomes less and less necessary.

It is after an exhausting ordeal to achieve even very limited gain that a critic's pan can be especially heartbreaking. After weeks of nursing along reluctant sponsors, agency men and network officials—then the blade may fall. The critic, for all his idealistic concern for artistic integrity, has had the negative effect of discouraging the handful of sponsors or network officials who had just been persuaded to get their feet wet in programming of higher cultural content.

The obvious assumption of the critics is that with enough pounding the sponsors will see the light. This is childish nonsense. Sponsors are under no compulsion to do experimentation in TV; indeed, the normal tendency of advertisers is to move in the opposite direction. Let them get clobbered often enough and they will just give up and revert to the type of programming that the critics claim to deplore. It is enough to accept the lower rating that may go with financing a so-called cultural undertaking; it is too much to pick up a newspaper and also be upbraided for failure.

By the same token, many stars and directors of other media have decided to leave TV, in part or in whole, because of harsh criticism stemming from backstage business they were powerless to correct.

The weakness of the critics is their own uncertainty as to what should be their criteria. Do they judge a TV program within the context of the TV medium? The creative people in TV believed fundamentally that this is the only fair standard. The conscientious individual in television is working in TV, not in some other media. He is prepared to match his achievements against film and theatre producers, assuming the latter, too, are quite willing to dispense with their box offices and accept advertiser financing. If the ground rules for all media were similar then comparisons might be in order.

TV's creative people do not expect critics only to approve and never question. But in the light of TV's operating realities let them temper their judgment with discernment and compassion. If they do not fan the creative spark of TV, even if it does not always burst into the glorious blaze of cultural accomplishment they would like to see, then they, too, must bear their share of responsibility for thwarting television's future.

This writer hopes he has done reasonable justice to those who were kind enough to express their views; he does not presume to have conveyed their thoughts in their entirety. In any event, this corner's own opinions of the subject of TV criticism will appear in due course.

A Critical Reply: An Answer to Objections Raised in the TV Industry to the Role of Critics

May 26, 1957

Last week this space was devoted to a summation of some of the major arguments against the television critics. Today this writer asks leave to add his personal opinions to the discussion.

The principal counts in the indictment were these: 1. the TV critic is the supreme know-it-all in reviewing anything and everything; 2. He wallows in frustration because his appraisal appears only after a program is finished; 3. He ignores much of the TV trivia and directs most of his analytical barbs at the original efforts in programming; 4. He should show more understanding of the realities of the TV creative life or accept his share of responsibility for thwarting TV's future; and 5. He often discourages sponsors from financing better things by being too uncompromising.

Before the particulars of TV criticism can be fruitfully examined, a word would seem in order on the basic function of video criticism. A medium which daily pre-empts the attention of millions of adults and children surely cannot be ignored. Television is not a static or passive force. It can either elevate or lower national tastes and standards; it cannot operate and leave them entirely untouched.

The context in which television must be placed therefore determines itself. Television can not be judged only by the rules and mores of its own making; it also must be weighed in light of contemporary life as a whole, just as the theatre, movies and books are. Television quite properly should be hailed in many ways for widening the horizons of the public. But it also must be mindful of the reality of its narcotic ability to deaden the national awareness of important standards and serious issues. Whether the television industry moves up or down is not just the intramural concern of the people of television. With its enormous power television can take much of the country along with it, either way. That is everybody's concern.

Broadcasters and sponsors certainly do not lack for ways and means of making their views known and felt in TV; viewers are not so fortunate. Critics in a sense are the proxies of the viewers. This does not mean that viewers necessarily will agree with the reviewers. But it does mean that there is the common bond of an independent opinion independently reached. The set owner in deciding whether he likes a show or not invokes only his own standards and doesn't give a hoot about mass tastes, ratings or cost-per-thousand; he looks at the screen and makes up his own mind. The critic is his stand-in.

If the TV critic presumes to have opinions about everything and anything he sees on TV, he is not exactly alone; every viewer does and so, incidentally, does everyone in TV. If the critical specialists in other media want to take a turn at TV, the more the merrier. But if TV criticism is to be comprehensive and meaningful somebody must be responsible for looking at the whole.

The transitory nature of TV criticism—the fact that a review of a program appears only after a show has disappeared for all time—is manifestly true. But television must be accepted in the form that it comes; the alternative is no criticism. It is to be suggested that favorable review does have beneficial influence on those who presented and prepared the program; certainly, it is not exactly a discouragement. By the same token, it is of no long-range service to TV to let utter trash and rubbish go unnoticed.

Part of the function of criticism is straight reporting of what is going on in television. When "Requiem for a Heavyweight" bursts upon the scene and Ed Wynn launches a comeback, it is part of the record of the day. So, too, may be a coast-to-coast distortion of a long-loved fairy tale. A newspaper covers news when and how it occurs; it does not insist on a convenient or ideal format.

The charge that the TV critics encourage mediocrity by ignoring much of the established tripe and concentrating largely on new plays and special programming efforts has a measure of validity. New and fresh events automatically call for coverage. The doings of a prominent individual naturally attract more attention than the activities of a pedestrian figure. But perhaps critics could do more in rechecking some of the established routine fare and pointing up its dominant force. With the sheer volume of TV material, no critic can claim that he covers everything.

But the most important issue in the indictment recounted last week concerned the fundamental matter of a critic's criteria of judgment. In particular it was stressed the recognition must be offered for such artistic progress as is discernible, with allowances made for the compromises inevitable in a field where commerce and culture come together in an uneasy union.

It is this philosophy which frankly most worries this writer. It is symptomatic of a virus which slowly is affecting many of the creative people in TV. The achievement of higher standards is so difficult that many are coming to rationalize the compromises they are making. A critic must understand why they are made, but he cannot be sanguine about them and join in the merry-go-round.

For here are the beginnings of Pavlovism in television. After heart-rending hours of fighting so hard for an idea, the creative people are accepting a little less for fear that they might otherwise lose much more. Gradually the very little is becoming the big standard. The affluent custodians of TV ring the bell and even the sincere and eager agree they have been well fed.

Are the creative people thus affected truly asking for compassion and understanding or are they asking for a critic's surrender to the gospel of commercial opportunism? The size of a programming effort, the amount of money spent, the number of stars recruited are no substitutes in themselves for honesty of intent or skill of execution. Similarly, because a program's theme is avowedly cultural, it does not automatically follow that the program is. To each and every program must be applied the same acid tests: what is it trying to do and how well is it done? The play, not the hazards and hardships of a craft, is the main thing.

In this connection there is an additional point to be made. The regular laborers in the television vineyard are subject to fearful commercial pressures; there is a limit to what they can achieve. But it is a different matter with the great figures of other media who occasionally deign to toy with video. They have the prestige and stature to write their own tickets. And nothing is more shocking than to see them pawn off shabby wares which they would not think worth presenting in their own fields.

Many have simply not taken the trouble to learn about TV, but others are simply cheapening their names for a fast dollar. Often they ostentatiously lick their wounds and speak contemptuously of TV. In such instances the frank business candor of a sponsor is to be preferred; his package is honestly labeled.

Still remaining, of course, is the vital final count in the indictment: the fact that criticism may discourage sponsors from undertaking the type of better programming which the critics profess to want. If sponsors suffer bad reviews, will they not retreat to the safety of Westerns and situation comedies?

There is no gainsaying that this is a very real problem. For their part, critics from time to time have erred; if it were possible to rewrite his reviews, each critic can think of times when he might wish to temper either the harshness or the praise which he bestowed. But no critic can ponder all the conceivable consequences of a review and still retain vigor and independence. If he tries to accommodate all of the people all of the time, he will only be a forlorn satellite of Madison Avenue. Heaven help the critic who worries about his personal Trendex.

The solution to the problem of approved programming surely cannot lie with the critics alone; the most they can do is to urge and plead, encourage and reprove from the sidelines. It is a long range task of station owners and sponsors alike to ask themselves how long they can afford to confuse imitations with competition, to compete for each other's ratings and forget about their larger problem, which is the steady expansion of the base of their audience.

The fainthearted sponsor or a hesitant network chief need only ask himself where a policy of safety in sameness and mediocrity, if it is universally pursued, will lead. Appeasement by any name has never solved many of man's problems.

Critic Dissects the Anatomy of a Flop, Ruminates about His Role on "Open End"

January 27, 1959

The anatomy of a flop is not something to be written about; it can only be lived.

As a general rule, newspapers have displayed commendable thoroughness in welcoming the advent of a hit in show business. But it is now abundantly clear that they have been most negligent in reporting the evolution of the age. Going to Newark for three hours is not the most convenient way of correcting the oversight, but it sure works.

On Sunday evening certain circumstances arose that led to the presence on Channel 13 of Sylvester L. Weaver, former chairman of the National Broadcasting Company; David Susskind, producer and moderator of "Open End," and this writer. An outlet for the ham in all mankind may yet rank as Marconi's supreme contribution.

The witching hour for the afore-mentioned three persons came between 8:30 and 9 o'clock on Sunday evening. Silently and stealthily, a deluxe omnibus slipped through the city's streets, plucking its victims from the security of hearth or office. A coterie of sympathizers, including a team of Henry Luce's ever-optimistic observers, also were in attendance.

Through tunnel and down turnpike there was a rising shrillness to the assorted voices. As Mr. Carey's elaborate conveyance approached New Jersey's cold, electronic chamber pleasantries concealed apprehensions. One's thoughts wandered endlessly to the wisdom of Jack

Benny, who concedes there is no tranquilizer like a prepared script. In Newark another three ad-libbers dutifully filed into video's waiting maw.

The first stop was the beauty bar. With the kindly solicitude of one who has prepared many for their fatal run through the branding chute, a make-up artist applied the necessary camouflage. Pancake powder, eyebrow pencil, cleansing tissue. But no three-way relief for stomach distress.

With manner of the polished maitre d', Mr. Susskind positioned his marionettes. An understanding member of the International Alliance of Theatrical Stage Employees, a great union, rushed in with coffee, which was also hot. A distant voice, the chief surgeon in the amphitheatre, began the countdown.

The three furies on the stage chorused their miscellany of laments while the trade editor of Advertising Age, in a remote living room, yearned for a bit of the popular touch. The evening wore on and the studio atmosphere grew oppressive with the complex me-tooism. Even the announcer felt it politic to suggest that Channel 2 was next to Channel 13.

The remedy was obvious: change anything. But overhead the glaring spotlights broiled the eyelids to a crisp. The personal microphone around the neck was strong enough to chain a St. Bernard. The second hand of the studio clock revolved relentlessly. Let the armchair critics rearrange the format. To be "on" in TV is living death; just breathing is a feat.

But even "Open End" finally closed down. The studio crew gently lifted the participants from the camp chairs and steadied them to the studio's edge. They were a source of enormous comfort; they discussed next week's show and last week's show.

The studio visitors also rallied. They made small jokes about the late hour and how, after all, the program was seen only on a local station, not a network. The photographer and reporter who worked for Mr. Luce had the sad eyes peculiar to journalists who live in the hope that editors will become understanding about night assignments.

All in all, the dignified solemnity was rather touching, especially because the night was so still.

Index

Abbott, John, 105
ABC. *See* American Broadcasting Company
Abe Lincoln in Illinois, 184
Actors Equity, 6
Actors Equity-Philco Television Playhouse, 38
Adams, Val, 16
Adler, Larry, 55, 72–73
Adler, Luther, 105
African Americans, 135–138
Alcoholics Anonymous, 50
Alcott, Louisa May, 7
Aldrich Family, The, 53, 54–55, 57, 70, 72
All About Radio and Television, 11
Allen, Fred, 195, 203
Allen, Steve, 131
Allen-Stevenson School, 2
Allison, Fran, 163
Aluminum Company of America (ALCOA), 75, 82, 84
Amahl and the Night Visitors, 208
American Broadcasting Company (ABC), 58–59, 156; and blacklisting, 70–71; and Muir, Jean, 72; and United Nations, 101–104
American Business Consultants, 55
American Civil Liberties Union (ACLU), 57–58, 59
American Farm Bureau Federation, 89
American Federation of Musicians, 7–8, 182
American Federation of Radio Artists, 55
American Federation of Television and Radio Artists (AFTRA), 62–65, 106
American Heritage Foundation, 177
American Jewish League Against Communism, 55
American Medical Association, 113
American Society of Composers, Artists, and Publishers (ACAP), 7
American Tobacco Company, 96, 97–98
America's Forum, 207
Amos 'n' Andy, 123
Anderson, Judith, 105, 107, 108
Anderson, Maxwell, 121
Andrews, Charles McLean, 2
Angel in the Wings, 38
Angel Street, 184
Anna Christie, 204
Anouilh, Jean, 105
anti-Semitism, 19
army, U.S., 9
Archdiocese of New York, 73
Army-McCarthy hearings, 72, 75
Arnaz, Desi, 122–125
Arsenic and Old Lace, 7
Atkinson, Brooks, 5
Atterbury, Malcom, 50
At Your Beck and Call, 112–113
Author Meets the Critics, The, 207
Autrey, Robert L., 6
Aware, Inc., 53, 63, 65–66, 67, 69

Bad Men, The, 121–122
Ball, Lucille, 59–62, 115, 122–125
Bandstand, 180
Barrett, Alfred H., 218
Barrie, Sir James M., 125

BBC. *See* British Broadcasting Corporation
Beat the Clock, 206
Begley, Ed, 45
Benny, Jack, 8, 124, 195, 202, 237
Bergen, Louie, 6
Berle, Milton, 129, 131, 192, 195
Berlin blockade, 190
Bernstein, Leonard, 12, 133
Bianculli, David, 24
Bickford, Charles, 50
Big Surprise, The, 142
Billboard, The, 203
Billy Budd, 201
blacklisting, 10, 53–74. *See also* communism, in television
Blaik, Col. Earl "Red," 81
Boddy, William, 23
Bogart, Humphrey, 192
Bold Venture, 180
Bourneuf, Philip, 40
Bowles, Chester, 222
Boys from Boise, The, 9
Brinkley, David, 11, 115, 129–130, 137
British Broadcasting Corporation (BBC), 92, 122, 177, 212
Broadcast Music International (BMI), 7
Broadway Open House, 12
Brown, Mrs. Vinnie, 227
Brown, Roy, 227
Brown School of Tutoring, 4
Bryn Mawr College, 2
Buice, Lester, 228
Burning Bright, 105
Burton, Barton, Durstine & Osborn (BBD&O), 73

Caesar, Sid, 202
Caine Mutiny Court Martial, The, 222
California Congress of Parents and Teachers, 179
California State Central Committee, Communist Party, 60
Camera 3, 134
Camp, Walter, 189
Campanella, Roy, 80–81
Cantor, Eddie, 195
Capp, Al, 167
Captain Kangaroo, 21, 178, 179, 225
Carmichael, Hoagy, 199
"carry-over," in quiz shows, 139, 144–145
Carson, Johnny, 115, 127–128
Cassidy, Hopalong, 192
Catholic War Veterans, 55
Catledge, Turner, 16–17, 19–20
CBS. *See* Columbia Broadcasting System
CBS Reports, 88–89, 136
Celanese Theatre, 204
Chaplin, Charlie, 59
Chayefsky, Paddy, 33, 43–44
"Checkers speech," 115, 119
Cherry Orchard, The, 107
Chess, Stephen C., 55
children, television and, 161–180
Children's Newsreel, 177
Childs, Marquis, 137
Churchill, Randolph, 142
Churchill, Winston, 77
Clark, Dick, 156, 178
Coe, Fred, 33, 50, 126
Cogley, John, 65, 66, 67
Collingwood, Charles, 69
Collins, Russell, 122
color television, 183
Columbia Broadcasting System (CBS), 9, 16–17, 35, 72, 75–76, 90, 128, 132; and Ball, Lucille, 60; and blacklisting, 69, 71; and children, 173; and Gould, John Ludlow ("Jack"), 16–17; and Kaufman, George S., 96–97; loyalty oath

of, 73–74; and McCarthy, Joseph R., 84–85, 87, 91; and Murrow, Edward R., 78–79; and *Omnibus*, 121; and *See It Now*, 87–88; and United Nations, 101–104
Columbia University, 151, 208
Commonweal, The, 65
communism, in television, 53–74. *See also* blacklisting
Communist Party, California State Central Committee, 60
Como, Perry, 193, 224
Congress, U.S. *See* House Special Subcommittee on Legislative Oversight; House Un-American Activities Committee; Interstate Commerce Committee (Senate)
Consolidated Edison, 104
Cook, Fielder, 45, 46
Cooke, Alistair, 122
Cooke, Jay, 2
Copeland, Katherine, 174
Counsellor-at-Law, 38
Counterattack, 57
Cousins, Norman, 167
Coward, Noel, 222
Cox, Wally, 44
critics, role of, 233–237; weaknesses of, 230–233
Crosby, John, 11, 17
Crouse, Russell, 6

Daily News, New York, 102
Daily Worker, 73
Daly, John, 141
Danger, 205
Dann, Michael, 18
Davis, Elmer, 135
Days of Wine and Roses, The, 50–51
Democratic National Convention (1956), 129
Democratic Party, 14
Derby, Joseph, 13
Devil's Disciple, The, 222
Dewey, Thomas E., 164
Diary of Anne Frank, The, 87
Ding Dong School, 21, 161, 174, 175, 176. *See also* Horwich, Frances
Dinner at Eight, 38
Dirksen, Everett M., 78
Don Quixote, 204
Dorsey, Tommy, 5
Dotto, 139, 143, 145
Draper, Paul, 55, 73
Dulles, John Foster, 103
DuMont Network, 35, 59, 187
Durante, Jimmy, 195, 202

Eden, Anthony, 77
Editors Speak, The, 207
Edward, My Son, 222
Egypt, 102
Eisenhower, Dwight D., 14, 103, 119
Eloise, 177
Engel, Lehman, 122
Engelking, Lessing L. ("Engel"), 4–5
Enright, Dan, 144
Ervine, St. John, 34–36
Europe, television in, 181, 209–215, 226
Evans, Clifford, 115
Evans, Maurice, 222
Executive Suite, 45

Falkenburg, Jinx, 19
Father Knows Best, 180
Faulk, John Henry, 68–69
Federal Communications Commission (FCC), 15, 57–58, 110, 111, 148, 153, 181–182, 193, 194, 201
Federal Theater Project, 5, 14
Feminine Mystique, The, 9
Ferguson, James E., 6
Fifth Amendment, 62–65

Fisk, Harvey, 1
Fisk, Pliny, 2
Fisk and Hatch, 2
Flanagan, Hallie, 5
Fleming, Jim, 117, 118
Ford Foundation, 121, 122
Foreign Intrigue, 205
France, 102, 212, 213
Francis, Arlene, 225
Francis, Clarence, 70, 72
Frank, Reuven, 22, 23
Frankenheimer, John, 50
Frawley, William, 124–125
Freedom Riders, 135
Freethinkers of America, 112
Friedan, Betty, 9
Friendly, Fred, 22, 75, 77, 79, 84, 85, 86, 88, 91. *See also* Murrow, Edward R.; *See It Now*
Fund for the Republic, 65, 66, 67
Furness, Betty, 19, 112

Garroway, Dave, 117, 118, 195, 224, 229
Garroway at Large, 224
General Foods, 53, 54–56, 70, 71
Georgetown University, 208
Germany, West, 86–87, 213
Gilbert, William, 119
Ginter, John J., 218, 220
Girl Talk, 70–71
Gleason, Jackie, 223
Glett, Charles, 109, 110
Gobel, George, 127, 128
Godfrey, Arthur, 165, 193, 195, 203, 229
Golden Age of Television, 33–51
Goldenson, Leonard, 13, 102
Goodman, Benny, 5
Goodman, Julian, 22
Goodson, Mark, 69
Gould, Carmen Lewis (wife), 6
Gould, Evelyn (sister), 2
Gould, Evelyn Louisa Fisk (mother), 2, 3
Gould, James, 1
Gould, John Ludlow ("Jack"), career of, 1–24
Gould, John Warren Dubois, (father), 1
Gould, Lewis L., 7, 161
Gould, Richard, 3, 7, 161
Gould, Robert, 7
Grafton, Samuel, 8
Graham, Billy, 98
Graham, Virginia, 70
Grant, Eva H., 179
Grauer, Ben, 189
Great Britain, 102, 210, 211, 212
Green, Martyn, 122
Greene, Graham, 105
Greenwich Time, 18
Griffith, Hugh, 105
Gunther, John, 11

Hagen, Uta, 105
Hagerty, James, 13
Hamel, Lisa, 16
Hammerstein, Oscar, 12, 231
Hands of Murder, 168
Harrison, Rex, 121
Hart, Lorenz, 12
Hartman, Paul, 38
Hartnett, Vincent, 65, 69, 71–72, 73. *See also* blacklisting
Harvest of Shame, 88–89
Hayes, Gabby, 196
Hayes, Helen, 107
Hear It Now, 75
Helbrun, Theresa, 34
Heller, Franklin, 4
Herald Tribune, New York, 1, 4–5
Herzberg, Joseph, 19
Highway Patrol, 108

Hitler, Adolf, 7, 87
Hoffman, Paul, 66
Hofheinz, Roy, 5
Hogan, Frank S., 144, 152, 156
Hollenbeck, Don, 72
Hollywood. *See* motion picture industry
Home, 225
Hoover, Herbert, 2
Hoover, J. Edgar, 72
Hope, Bob, 203
Horwich, Frances, 161, 174, 180, 225
House Special Subcommittee on Legislative Oversight, 147, 156
House Un-American Activities Committee, 55, 60
Houston Astrodome, 6
Howdy Doody, 161, 164–166, 180, 187, 225
Huntley, Chet, 129, 130, 137
Hutchens, John K., 8

Iceman Cometh, The, 110
Illinois Congress of Parents and Teachers, 179
I Love Lucy, 122–125
Internal Revenue Service (IRS), 157
International Alliance of Stage and Theatrical Employees, 238
International Ladies Garment Workers Union, 5
Interstate Commerce Committee (Senate), 194
In the Park, 206
It's a Problem, 208
It's Worth Knowing, 208

Jack and the Beanstalk, 177
Jackson, Andrew, 187
Jackson, Donald L., 60
Jaffe, Henry, 55, 72
James, Edwin L., 8
John Ferguson, 33, 34–36
Johns Hopkins University, 208
Johnson, Laurence, 65, 69, 72, 73
Johnson, Lyndon B., 20–21, 74
Johnston, Dennis, 34, 35
Joint Committee Against Communism, 55
Journal-American, New York
journalism, corrupt practices in, 149–151
Judges and the Judged, The, 57
Julius Caesar, 39–41
Just One Break, Inc., 112

Kammen, Michael, 24
Kaufman, George S., 95, 96–97, 205
Keep Posted, 207
Kefauver, Estes, 199, 223
Keith, Robert, 41
Kennedy, John F., 76
Kent School, 2–3
Kiernan, John, 192
Kiley, Richard, 45, 46
Kinsey Report, 190
Kintner, Robert, 20–21, 74
Kirkpatrick, Theodore, 55
Knickerbocker Greys, 2
Knickerbocker Holiday, 7
Kohlberg, Alfred, 55
Korean War, 78–79
Kraft Theatre, 45, 46, 48, 205
Kreitzer, Catherine, 141
Krock, Arthur, 137
KRUX (Phoenix), 104
Kukla, Fran, and Ollie, 161, 162–164, 168
Kyser, Kay, 191

Lamp Unto My Feet, 199
Landau, Ely, 105–106, 107, 108
Langer, Lawrence, 34
Lanning, John, 112, 113

Lassie, 180
Laurie, Piper, 50–51
Lawrence, David, 137
Lea Law (1946), 8
Lee, Pinky, 21, 161, 172–174
Lescoulie, Jack, 117
Lester, Jerry, 12, 195, 203
Let's Take a Trip, 176
Levenson, Sam, 195
Lewis, Jerry, 195, 202–203
Lewis, Joseph, 19, 112–114
Lewis, Richard R., 6
Lights Out, 168
Lincoln, Abraham, 187
Lindsay, Howard, 6
Linkletter, Art, 219–220, 222
Lippmann, Walter, 137
Litchfield Law School, 2
Loeb, Louis, 95
Lombardo, Guy, 103
Lone Ranger, The, 103
Loomis Institute, 3–4
Loomis Post, 3
Louis, Joe, 188
Lowe, David, 88, 89
loyalty oath, at CBS, 73–74
Luce, Clare Boothe, 7
Luce, Henry, 237, 238

MacArthur, Douglas, 196
Maceo crime family, 6
McCarthy, Joseph R., 13, 53, 71, 72, 75, 84–85
McCoy, Tim, 187
McCrary, "Tex," 19, 207
McCullough, Hester, 55, 56
McNellis, Maggie, 192
Magic Flute, The, 222
Malik, Jacob, 207
Mama, 205
Mamoulian, Rouben, 36, 38
Mann, Delbert, 44
Marchand, Nancy, 43, 44
Marconi, Guglielmo, 3, 193
Markel, Lester, 10, 23, 181
Marshall, Roy K., 198
Martin, Dean, 202–203
Martin, Mary, 115, 125
Marty, 43–44
Maverick, 153
Medea, 105, 107, 108, 110
Meet the Press, 207
Metro-Goldwyn-Mayer, 221
Mickey Mouse Theatre, 176
Middlecoff, Cary, 133
Mighty Mouse, 178, 180
Miller, J. P., 33, 50
Miller, Merle, 57
Million Dollar Movie, 108
Miner, Worthington, 33, 39–41, 110, 204–205
Minow, Newton, 15
Miss Ding Dong, 179–180
Mr. I. Magination, 168, 206
Mr. Peepers, 44
Mister Roberts, 190
Mr. Wizard, 176, 206
Mitchell, James P., 88, 89
Mitchell, Thomas, 35
Montgomery, Robert, 205
Month in the Country, A, 105
Moore, Garry, 195, 225
Morgan, J. Pierpont, 2
Morley, Robert, 222
Morning Chapel, 193
Mortimer, John, 105
motion picture industry, 37, 42–43, 150, 156, 157, 185, 195, 223, 224
Muir, Jean, 14, 53, 54–57, 70–71, 72. *See also* blacklisting
Munich crisis, 7
Murray, Thomas D., 69

Murrow, Edward R., 13, 69, 72, 118, 130, 231; career of, 75–93. *See also* Friendly, Fred; *See It Now*
Music Corporation of America (MCA), 106
Mussolini, Benito, 8
My Brother's Keeper, 44
My Friend Irma, 205

National Association of Radio and Television Broadcasters, 194
National Broadcasting Company (NBC), 35, 91, 151, 187, 207; and blacklisting, 55; and *Omnibus*, 133–135; and *Today*, 115–118; and United Nations, 101–104
National Congress of Parents and Teachers, 178
National Education Television and Radio Center, 109
National Parent-Teacher, The, 178, 179
National Telefilm Associates, 109
Natwick, Mildred, 105
navy, U.S., 198
NBC. *See* National Broadcasting Company
NBC Opera Theatre, 208
NBC Playhouse, 43–44
Nelson, Frank, 63
Netherlands, 214
News Caravan, 130
News in Perspective, 20
New York City, as television center, 11
New York Times, The, 22, 53–54, 104, 164
New York Times Magazine, The, 10–11
New York University, 4
Nichols, Lewis, 5
Nixon, Richard M., 21, 115, 119–121
Nizer, Louis, 69

O'Brian, Jack, 72
Office of War Information (OWI), 8
O'Hanlon, Redmond, 141
Oklahoma, 12
Old Greenwich, Connecticut, 10
Olivier, Laurence, 222
Omnibus, 12, 42, 115, 121–122, 133–135
O'Neill, Eugene, 204
One Man's Family, 205
On the Carousel, 176
Open End, 237–238
opera, on television, 199, 208
Osborne, Paul, 204
O'Shea, Danny, 73
Osshaus, Russell, 229

Palance, Jack, 49, 50
Paley, William S., 13, 23, 76, 102
Palmer, Lilli, 121
Parks, Bert, 195
Patterns, 45–46
payola, 155
Peabody Awards (George Foster Peabody Awards for Radio and Television), 17
Penn, Arthur, 24
Person to Person, 13, 76, 80, 91
Peter Gunn, 153
Peter Pan, 125, 177
Petrillo, James C., 7–8, 35, 182
Peyton, Patrick, 198
Phillip Morris Co., 62
Pins and Needles, 5
Playhouse 90, 49, 50–51
Playmakers, 9
Play of the Week, The, 33, 95, 104, 111
politics, and television, 119–121
Pope, John, 54, 73
Post, William, Jr., 41
Power and the Glory, The, 105
Prato, Gino, 141

Presley, Elvis, 12, 24, 115, 128–129, 131–133
Pulitzer Prize, 16, 17
Pulitzer Prize Playhouse, 205

Queen Elizabeth II, 223
quiz show scandals, 139–158

Radio and Television Directors Association, 76
Radio Corporation of America (RCA), 183
Radulovich, Milo, 75, 82–84
Random House, 177
Ray, Johnnie, 129
Recital Hall, 208
Red Channels, 14, 53, 54–55, 56, 57, 58, 59, 70. *See also* blacklisting; Muir, Jean
Redman, Joyce, 35
Requiem for a Heavyweight, 49–50, 235
Reston, James, 137
Rice, Elmer, 204
Rice University, 6
Richard III, 222
Ritchard, Cyril, 125, 126
Robin Hood, 176
Robbins, Jerome, 126
Roberts, Oral, 14, 95, 98–101
Robertson, Cliff, 50
Robinson, Bill, 184
Rochemont, Richard de, 42
Rockefeller, John D. III, 110
Rodgers, Richard, 231
Roginsky, Dr. David, 112, 113
Romper Room, 180
Roos, Joanna, 46
Roosevelt, Franklin D., 5, 14
Roosevelt, Theodore, 1
Rosenbloom, Maxie, 49–50
Rosenthal, Abraham M. ("Abe"), 1, 22, 24
Rosenthal, Phil, 24
Russell, Richard, 228–229
Rychtarik, Richard, 40

Sadler's Wells Ballet, 222
St. Bartholomew's Church, 7
Salomon, Henry, Jr., 42
Sarnoff, David, 13, 102, 116
Saroyan, William, 121–122
Saudek, Robert, 122, 133. *See also Omnibus*
Schlitz Playhouse, 205
Schultz, Benjamin, 55
Scott, Hazel, 59
Scourby, Alexander, 105
Scrapbook, 187
Search, The, 135
See It Now, 13, 77, 135, 207, 213. *See also* Friendly, Fred; Murrow, Edward R.
Segal, Alex, 122, 204
Seldes, Gilbert, 24
Sergeant Preston of the Yukon, 103
Serling, Rod, 33, 45–46, 49–50
Sevareid, Eric, 130
Seven Lively Arts, The, 135
Shanley, John P., 16
Shariland, 176
Shaw, George Bernard, 222
Shepard, Richard F., 16, 22
Sherwood, Robert E., 204
Shock Theatre, 180
Shore, Dinah, 72, 103
Shuman, Charles B., 89
Sinatra, Frank, 129
Six-Gun Playhouse, 191
$64,000 Question, The, 224
Skelton, Red, 203
Skolsky, George, 207
Sloane, Allen, 73
Sloane, Everett, 45
Small Fry Club, 187

Small World, 87
Smith, Bob ("Buffalo Bob"), 161, 164–166. *See also Howdy Doody*
Smith, Howard K., 11, 77–78, 115, 135–137
Snead, Sam, 133
Society of the Cincinnati, 1
Southern Select Brewing Company, 6
Spier, William, 122
Stamford, Connecticut, 9–10
Standard Oil of New Jersey, 18
Stanislavsky, Konstantin, 34
Stanton, Frank, 9, 16, 75, 76
Steiger, Rod, 43–44
Steinbeck, John, 105
Stempel, Herbert, 144
Stevenson, Adlai, 85, 104
Stoetzel, George, 40
Stokowski, Gloria Vanderbilt, 80–81
Stokowski, Leopold, 80–81
Stone, Joseph, 139
Stop the Music, 206
Stork Club, 17
Straight, Beatrice, 105
Strike It Rich, 206
Studio One, 195, 204–205
Suez crisis (1956), 13–14, 102
Sullivan, Arthur, 119
Sullivan, Ed, 131–133, 192, 224
Sulzberger, Arthur Hays, 14, 15–16
Supreme Court, U.S., 135, 194
Surgeon General, U.S., 21
Suspense, 193
Susskind, David, 69, 106, 110, 237, 238
Swayze, John Cameron, 228

Taft, Robert A., 78, 207
Taft-Hartley Act, 64
Talkaround, 175
Taylor, Vaughn, 41
Television Playhouse, 43–44
Theatre Guild, 33, 34–36
They Stand Accused, 205
This Is Korea, 78–79
This Is Show Business, 96–97, 205
Thomas, Mrs. Modine, 228
Thomas, William Henry, 228
Tiger at the Gates, 110
Tillstrom, Burr, 162–164
Times Talk, 18
Toast of the Town, 224
Today, 115, 116–118, 207
Toscanini, Arturo, 12, 38
Town Meeting, 36
Trial of Anne Boleyn, 121
Trial without Jury: A Study of Blacklisting in Broadcasting, 54. *See also* Pope, John
Tripp, Paul, 206
Truman, Harry S., 164
Turgenev, Ivan, 105
TV Guide, 15
Twentieth Century Fox, 224
Twenty-One, 139, 143
Twenty Thousand Leagues under the Sea, 204

Union of Soviet Socialist Republics (USSR), 102
United Nations Security Council, 13–14, 101–104
United Press, 130
U.S. Food Administration, 2
U.S. Information Agency (USIA), 76, 89–90

Valentina, 81
Valentine, James, 105
Vance, Vivian, 124–125
Vanderbilt, Sanderson ("Sandy"), 4
Van Doren, Charles, 139, 151–153
Van Druten, John, 204
Van Horne, Harriet, 164
Variety, 203

Veit, Ivan, 20
Verdi, Giuseppe, 199
Victor Emmanuel, 8
Victory at Sea, 42
Vidal, Gore, 227
Viscardi, Henry, Jr., 112–113
Voice of America, 89–90
Voice of Firestone, 1999

Walcott, Jersey Joe, 188
Walker, Stanley, 4
Wallace, Henry, 164
Waltz of the Toreadors, The, 105
Wanted—Dead or Alive, 180
Warner Brothers, 224
Warren, Susan Ludlow, 2
Watch on the Ruhr, 87
Watch the World, 192
WCCO (Minneapolis), 102
WCBS-TV (New York), 173
Weaver, Sylvester ("Pat"), 24, 115, 116, 118, 237. *See also Today*
Welch, Joseph N., 133
Welles, Orson, 39
WGGA (Gainesville, Georgia), 229
What's My Line?, 205
Wide Wide World, 135
Wilson, Lois, 54
Winder, Georgia, 228
Witch Doctor, The, 122
WLOS (Asheville, N.C.), 229
WNTA-TV (New York City), 18, 105, 107, 108, 109
WNYC (New York City), 101, 104
Wood, Peggy, 205
World-Telegram, The, New York, 164
WOR-TV (New York), 104, 108
WPIX (New York), 59, 101, 102
WQXR (New York), 104
Wynn, Ed, 49, 202, 235
Wynn, Keenan, 49

Yale University, 2
Young & Rubicam, 55

Zolotow, Sam, 5
Zoo Parade, 206
Zwicker, Ralph, 85